Alastair Sawday's

SPECIAL
PLACES TO STAY

SPAIN
AND
PORTUGAL

Typesetting	Avonset, 1 Palace Yard Mews, Bath
Maps	HarperCollins Cartographic,
Printing	Stige, Italy
Distribution	Portfolio in the UK, St Martin's Press in the US

First published in 1997 by Alastair Sawday Publishing Co. Ltd
44 Ambra Vale East, Bristol BS8 4RE, UK.

SPECIAL PLACES TO STAY

SPAIN
AND
PORTUGAL

*"Spain is but Spain, and belongs nowhere but where it is.
It is neither Catholic nor European but has a
structure all of its own, forged from an
African-Iberian past which exists in its own austere
reality and rejects all short-cuts to a smoother life."*

LAURIE LEE – A Rose for Winter: Travels in Andalusia

ASP
Alastair Sawday Publishing

ACKNOWLEDGEMENTS

I heard a story about Peter Mayle, who had offended many local people – and also many expatriates – in his best-seller about Provence. Someone placed an ad. in an English paper with a map of how to get to his house!

Should I do the same to Guy Hunter-Watts, on the assumption that you will want to drop in and tell him how you love his book? Well, I will tell you, anyway, that he lives in a little village in Andalusia, in a white-washed cottage with sublime views beyond the village to the National Park. He drives an old 2CV, is in his 30s, commands a rare range of Spanish, loves his *fino* and his *manchego* as I do, and has many devoted Spanish friends. The villagers have taken him to their communal bosom and he is in no danger of returning to the UK.

When he wanted to settle permanently in Spain Guy asked if he could produce this book and, as he had done much of the work on our other books and we share a vast array of tastes, I was enthusiastic. I trusted him totally, and the result was the first edition, a huge success. 95% of the letters we receive are full of praise. The rest are critical only in the most sympathetic way.

This new book, combining Spain and Portugal, is – again – Guy's. I can claim credit only, perhaps, for inspiring him and then backing him up. He does most of the writing; I offer advice and judgment. I salute him; he brings a deep love of Spain, and now Portugal, to this book. You are benefitting from his years of sensitive exploring and his real gift with people.

But not even Guy can function entirely alone. His Dutch neighbour, Lies Wajer, has been a magnificent one-woman support system. Not only has she helped with administration but she also did almost half of the initial inspecting in Portugal. Thank you, Lies.

Julia Morriss is the person who has eliminated errors, organised and gently harassed Guy and me, organised this book and generally made it as close to perfect as it might be. She has taken us from the Stone Age to the Age of Enlightenment ... or so I like to think.

Series Editor	Alastair Sawday
Editor	Guy Hunter-Watts
Production Manager	Julia Morriss
Administrative Support	Annie Shillito, Eliza Meredith, Dave Kelly, Sarah O'Mahoney, Anne Woodford and John Fullard.
Accounts	Sheila Clifton, Irene Musgrove and Maureen Humphries
Cover illustration	Liz Graham-Yooll
Symbols	Celia Witchard
Design	Springboard Design, Bristol and John Fullard
Back up photography	Lies Wajer
Advice and help	Ann Cooke-Yarborough
Additional help	Cristina Guerreiro in Lisbon for help with translations; Tony and Shirley Taylor-Dawes of Finca Río Miño for help in Northern Portugal; Maria de Ceu de Lima of Turihab; Maggie Redway for help with the mail-out; David JJ Evans and the Cadogan guide for ideas in Portugal; William Pullman for second opinions on many of the hotels included here; and to numerous readers who have taken time to write and let us know what YOU think ...

Finally, we must thank Isabel and Carlota of Rusticae for recommending the following hotels to us : La Posada del Balneario, Can Boix, Palacio de la Rambla, El Milano Real, Aultre Naray, Atalaya, El Esparragal, El Convento, El Molino del Río Viejo.

And from Guy a million thanks to Alastair for the fun, trust and friendship. Work should be like this ... ¡Eres único!

INTRODUCTION

Have you ever been to Salamanca? It has two cathedrals but its glory is the Plaza Mayor, one of the greatest squares in Europe. As Michelin would say, it 'merits the detour'.

Once in my youth I found myself paying a pittance for a simple, wooden-floored room in a 'fonda', late one tired night after a nightmarish journey across Spain. It was in Salamanca and I didn't know – or care – where I slept.

In the morning I awoke, pottered to my window and was delighted to find a balcony. It took me a long moment to understand that I was gazing in stupefied rapture over the magnificent Plaza Mayor. I treasure the memory, and have returned. But I cannot for the life of me find that room. Let me know if you do; it would probably slip straight into this book.

I am irredeemably romantic, and I make no excuse with such memories to guide me. When I travel, I chase them. In Catalonia that might be a log fire, flagstone floors, a pig roasting on the spit under dark wooden beams with a view over a Romanesque church in the valley below.

Andalusia has provided its own memories for me to chase: a delicate Moorish arch, colourful tiles, spotless simplicity... see the cover of this book. There may not be a wide-brimmed hat on a horse at every turn, yet these things can happen.

Guy Hunter-Watts, the compiler and editor of this book, shares these pictures; within these pages you will find dozens of them. They are made real by imaginative Spaniards (and some happy immigrants) who know that there are thousands upon thousands of us seeking an escape from the harsh 'reality' that is the 1990s, from the hysterical conformity of mass tourism.

I first loved Spain when, as a child, I witnessed a spontaneous eruption of flamenco in Sitges. In those days it was a fishing village and the combination of Spain and flamenco was intoxicating. That memory haunted me so effectively that I retired from teaching Spanish, aged 24, to take up with the gypsies in the caves of Granada. I never got there... but that is another story. And I still can't play flamenco.

A later inspiration was a book by H.V. Morton, *'A Stranger in Spain'*, without which I dare not go to Spain. In fact, I have been so captivated by his prose and the depth of his cultivated interest in Spain that in the late 60s I sought out one of his old characters in Toledo cathedral, unaware that it was in the 1930s that Morton had described her. She was, of course, long dead. Now that was vivid writing. I urge you to seek Morton in a second-hand bookshop and take him with you. Maybe you, too, will find yourself following in his footsteps around Spain, for the pure pleasure of his company.

Sadly, Morton never, I think, travelled around Portugal. He would have loved its history and the gentle ways of its people, so different from their Spanish neighbours. He would have talked of Wellington and Braganza, of tired Empire and intricate Manueline architecture. He would have gloried in the great country houses, called *quintas*, that populate this new edition of our Iberian book.

Guy, too, gloried in them and I thought it would be hard to extricate him from Portugal, a new love that inspired some passionate inspections and crazed drives up long tracks in pursuit of yet more human and architectural discoveries.

So the inclusion of Portugal in this edition is, we think, a huge success. Please let us know if we are right.

THE HOTELS OF SPAIN AND PORTUGAL

If you are used to travelling in France and Italy, for example, you may occasionally be surprised by the hotels of Spain and Portugal. Often, they seem to lack the character and personal touch so welcome elsewhere. It is easy to fall into a concrete monster if you don't plan ahead, or spend a ghastly evening clutching your ears in a TV-dominated bar or restaurant. So USE THIS BOOK!

The Spanish Paradors and Portuguese Pousadas are as magnificent as ever but they still, largely, lack warmth and personality. Run by the state, they show it, however glorious the building. But more and more managers are imposing their own style and sense of proper welcome, so there is hope.

Yet our policy is still to encourage owner-operated hotels because we think they are the best value and, often, simply the best. Our own selection also offers you interesting and handsome buildings; and equally interesting people.

HOW DO WE CHOOSE OUR SPECIAL PLACES?

Each one has to be special, in some way or another. If it is modern, it will be run by good people, or have wonderful views, or be in the best part of town, or even be a really successful modern building. If it is kitsch in places then redeeming features might be the best food in town plus vast beds. Or it may be the only place to sleep in glorious countryside.

We ignore the chain hotels (with a few exceptions), the noisy ones, those that are over-priced or bad value, the ugly, the dreary and those with awful taste. Even more assiduously do we seek to exclude the ones run by awful people. And we hold dear our right to be utterly subjective on these matters. (Tell us, please, when you think we've got it wrong.)

So in the countryside we look for lovingly-converted farms, barns, abbeys, monasteries, inns and manor-houses. We look for quiet country, long views and nature at its best. We find places that set us alight, rekindle our faith in humanity's capacity for creating beauty. Flashes of originality, exotic taste, plain honesty of style... all these things help.

In the cities and towns, we have found quiet places to hide in, hotels of panache and style, places run by devoted family members, and old monastery buildings steeped in atmosphere.

Non-Iberian owners

We do not deliberately seek out immigrants from more northerly climes who have chosen to run B&Bs or small hotels in the Peninsula but, in Spain particularly, there are a lot of British, Dutch and German folk, for example, running some of the nicest hostelries, often leading the way in agro-tourism and also doing remarkable renovation work on fine but neglected old buildings. The number of such places in the south of Spain reflects the size of the ex-pat community there.

Andalusia

Again, the large proportion of hotels in this guide in Andalusia reflects an undeniable fact: this is by far the most visited part of Spain.

SUBSCRIPTIONS

You should, I think, know that we charge owners a small sum to appear in this book; without it the book would not exist. But we do NOT include hotels and houses because they can pay; we select them and then invite subscription. Clearly, some then drop away, but mercifully few. The book now has a reputation and people ask us if they can come in. The only ones to get in are the ones we LIKE.

HUNTING AND FISHING

We only mention these activities to enable you to avoid, if you wish, such dinner-time conversations as :

a.   I saw a red-legged snipe this evening.
b.   Did you manage to get a good photo?
a.   No, I shot it.

HOW TO USE THIS BOOK

Abbreviations: c/   calle = street
                   s/n   sin número = unnumbered
                   Pts   Pesetas (Spanish currency)
                   Esc   Escudos (Portuguese currency)

Spelling of proper names in Spain

In regions where there are two official languages – Castilian and one of Spain's other languages (Catalan, Gallego,...) – the names of people and places will often have two spellings. We have endeavoured to use the ones you, the traveller, are most likely to SEE in each instance and this may mean one version in the address, another in the directions to get there. For example, village is *puebla* in Castilian, *pobla* in Catalan, *poboa* in Gallego (cf No 14); *baños* in Castilian becomes *banhs* in Catalan (cf No 57).

Coding and prices

D = Double, Tw = Twin, S = Single (or single use of D/Tw), Tr = Triple, Q = Quadruple, Ste – Suite, Apt = Apartment.
M = set menu; C = à la carte.

Prices are given for the room unless otherwise specified, i.e. p.p. for per person.

All prices exclude VAT unless otherwise stated. Some prices quoted may, despite our best efforts, be for 1997; so they may be increased slightly for 1998.

MEALS

Times of

The Spanish eat much later than we do: breakfast sometimes doesn't get underway until 8.30/9am, lunch from about 1.30/2pm and dinner from 8pm onwards – some restaurants don't start serving before 9.30pm...

Portuguese habits are closer to ours. Lunch is between 12.30pm and 2pm, dinner between 7.30pm and 10pm, NOT later. If you have picked up Spanish habits, beware of expecting to dine at an hour when they are closing.

Breakfast etc.

The universal 'continental' offering tends to be uninspired in both Portugal and Spain: coffee, toast (perhaps cakes), butter and jam. Seville oranges may grow here but don't expect marmalade. Freshly-squeezed orange juice is widely available but not often with breakfast. Few places will object should you add your own fruit to their breakfast.

Tea (especially in Spain) can be poor (a very basic tea bag) so if you really need it take you own brand and ask for hot water. *Té* in Spain and *chá* in Portugal usually comes plain. Ask for *con leche/com leite* for 'with milk' and *con limón/com limão* for a slice of lemon. In Portugal, much tea is drunk in elegant *casas de chá*. In Spain, bars and restaurants serve camomile tea – *manzanilla* – if you prefer.

Portuguese coffee comes in three sizes: small black espresso – *uma bica* or *um café*; small white – *um garoto*; large white – *um galão*. This last is all milk with a dash of coffee so for a normal-strength white coffee ask for *um café duplo com um pouco de leite* (double [black] coffee with a little milk).

Lunch and dinner
SPAIN
The daily set meal – *el menú* – is normally available at lunch and dinner though you are not always told so. Ask for it – it is often much cheaper than dining à la carte.

Cocina de autor – the chef's (often elaborate) personal creations – is more common in the North of Spain.

Tapas and Raciones are an essential part of eating out in Spain and great fun. A *tapa* is a small plate of hot or cold food served with an aperitif before lunch or dinner. It could be a small portion of olives, anchovies, cheese, spicy chorizo sausage, fried fish, a small kebab, Russian salad... portions vary as does the choice. But it is a delicious way to try out local specialities and if your Spanish is poor, don't worry – *tapas* are often laid out along the bar for you to gesticulate at. The size of the *tapa* varies from bar to bar.

Sometimes a choice of four or five will be a meal in itself and a very cheap meal at that – between 100 Pts and 200 Pts per *tapa* is the going rate. If you'd like a whole plateful of any particular *tapa*, ask for *una racion de* (e.g) *queso*. Most bars will happily give you a half portion – *media ración*.

Tipping is still the norm here – 5% to 10% – but you would rarely be made to feel mean if you didn't. Similarly, your taxi driver does not automatically expect a tip.

PORTUGAL
It is remarkably inexpensive to eat out in Portugal. The set meal – *ementa turística* – may offer a small choice, while à la carte – *à lista* – is a full choice. The dish of the day – *prato do día* – is usually a local speciality and helpings can be enormous. It is perfectly normal for adults to ask for a *media dose* – half portion – or for *uma dose* to share between two.

When you sit down, you may be given some bits to nibble while you wait – olives, *chouriço* (spicy sausage), sardine spread – and *you will be charged for what you eat* . *Bacalao* – salt cod – is the national dish; there are said to be 365 ways of preparing it and the variety can indeed be astounding. Pork is also much used but we would advise fish rather than meat on the whole, and above all, don't despise the humble sardine – it is usually the cheapest item on the menu and invariably very good. Puddings are very sweet. The basic salad mix for *salada mista* is tomatoes, onions and olives. You can ask for it *sem ólio* – without oil.

In general, a cover charge is added to the bill and there is no need to tip. In some very smart places, a 10% service charge may be added or you are expected to leave a little something.

The Iberians are not yet very vegetarian-conscious. Indeed, vegetables rarely appear and, when they do, are often boiled beyond recognition. So get yourself a bunch of carrots at one of the colourful street markets.

SPANISH AND PORTUGUESE HOTELS – THINGS TO KNOW
Seasons and public holidays
When we give a price range, the lower is the Low Season, the higher the High Season. There may be a Mid Season price in between! In MOST of Spain, High Season includes Easter, Christmas, public holidays and the summer. In skiing resorts, High will include the snowy months. Some hotels classify weekends as High and weekdays as Low. If in doubt, ring or fax to check prices.

Public Holidays
In both countries, everything closes down for –
January 1st, Good Friday, May 1st, Corpus Christi (early June), August 15th, November 1st, December 8th, December 25th.

In addition, Spain feasts on January 6th, Easter Monday, June 24th, July 25th, October 12th, December 6th;

Portugal on April 25th, *Día de Camões e das Comunidades* (June 10th), October 5th, December 1st.

PAYING

The most commonly accepted credit cards are Visa, Mastercard and Eurocard. Many hotels take Eurocheques though they sometimes charge extra for this. Larger establishments will probably take Amex or Diner's Club. You will often find a cash dispenser close at hand; again, Visa, Mastercard and Eurocard are the most useful.

BOOKING

You should book ahead and most certainly well ahead if you are planning to be in Spain or Portugal in the summer or at Easter. August tends to be overcrowded and is best avoided. We include bilingual booking forms for sending or faxing your reservation. Readers have found them very useful, though hotels are often inefficient about replying.

BATHROOMS

Note that baths in both countries vary from half to full length but in our drought-stricken times you will probably prefer to shower. There are nearly always bidets. Just occasionally, simpler establishments do not provide soap; have a bar of your own just in case.

REGISTRATION

It remains law that you should register on arrival in a hotel. Hotels have no right, once you have done this, to keep your passport!

ALL THOSE NAMES

These pages reveal a plethora of different terms to describe the various hostelries. We include no star ratings in our guides; we feel they are limiting, rigid and often misleading. Also, as different types of places to stay (hotels, B&Bs, etc) are classified according to a variety of criteria, it would be confusing. Our description, and the prices, should guide you. This list serves as a rough guide to what you might expect to find behind each name; many of the terms describe similar places.

Can	A fairly isolated farm-house (*can* means *chez* followed by family name).
Casona	A grand old house in Asturias.
Cortijo	A free-standing Spanish farm-house, usually in the south.
Finca	A farm; most of those included here are working farms.
Fonda	A simple inn that may or may not serve food.
Hacienda	A large estate with rooms in the main farm building.
Hostal	Another type of simple inn where food may or may not be served.
Hostería	A simple inn where food is available.
Mas	A Catalan farm-house, usually quite isolated – and handsome.
Mesón	First and foremost a restaurant; rooms often come later.
Posada	A coaching inn.
Pousada	In Galicia, a coaching inn.
Pousada	In Portugal, same origin but now a grand place to stay, similar to a Spanish state-run *Parador*.
Parador	A village inn; the one included here in NOT part of the state chain.
Pazo	A grand country or village manor house in Galicia or Portugal.
Venta	A simple restaurant with rooms.

HINTS AND TIPS FOR TRAVELLERS IN SPAIN AND PORTUGAL
Passport
The British Visitor's passport is no longer accepted; a full EC/British passport is now required. Keep it with you at all times; many museums offer EC citizens free entry but you will need to show proof.

Security
A degree of caution is necessary in larger cities and especially in narrow side streets. Best not to carry ostentatious bags or cameras.

Telephoning
From Spain 07 then country code then area code without first 0
    e.g. ASP in Bristol, UK No. 0117 929 9921 = 07 44 117 929 9921

From Portugal: 00 then country code then area code without first 0
    e.g. ASP in Bristol, UK No. 0117 9299921 = 00 44 117 9299921

Within Spain to another province: Provincial dialling codes have either two or three digits and the full number always has nine digits, e.g.
    95   is Málaga   so to Málaga from elsewhere in Spain = 95 2180404
    956 is Cádiz   so to Cádiz from elsewhere in Spain = 956 132020

No provincial code is needed when dialling within a province so a number has six or seven digits when called within its home province.

From outside Spain or Portugal:
The country code for Spain is   34
The country code for Portugal is 351

In Spain, a 908 or 989 code means a mobile phone number: more expensive to call; accessible from outside Spain.

Phone cards
In Spain a *tarjeta telefónica* is worth buying at the beginning of the holiday at a tobacconist's (*estanco*). Cost 1000 Pts or 2000 Pts. Remember that telephoning from a hotel room can be almost twice as expensive as from a public telephone box – *una cabina*.

Worth buying in Portugal, too, at 875 Esc or 2100 Esc (1997). Some phone boxes in larger cities now also take Visa or Mastercards.

Driving
"... the road signs are still bad enough to fuddle even a Spaniard. They don't point the way, like proper signs, at unequivocal 90-degree angles; they just gesture, reluctant to offer one possibility at the expense of another. The result is an existential decision at every intersection..." (JARED LUBARSKY – Lost and Found in Spain).

It is best to avoid driving if you possibly can on public holidays – enormous numbers of cars are already out there. The same goes for the beginning of August when many emigrant workers rush to and from France/Germany/Switzerland, etc.

Motorway driving is expensive in northern Spain but you may well think it is worth the extra cost of the *peaje* (toll). In southern Spain, there is only one very short paying section of motorway between Seville and Cádiz.

In both countries, it is compulsory to have in the car: a spare set of light bulbs, a warning triangle and, in Portugal, a fire extinguisher and a basic first aid kit.

DON'T FORGET YOUR DRIVING LICENCE – it is an offence to drive without it.

Car hire is generally cheaper than in other European countries.

Remember that foreign number plates attract attention; don't leave your car unattended on the streets of larger cities. Some city hotels in this book have their own car park; all the others have a public car park nearby where 24-hour parking costs from £8-£12.

Maps

Driving in northern Portugal, especially, requires patience as does finding some rural hotels in Galicia. The maps in the front of this book should give you an approximate idea of where places are but do take a good detailed road map with you, e.g. Michelin (1/400000 series – 1cm to 4 km – Nos 440-446) or Hildebrandts, available in the UK by phone from Stanfords – 0171 836 1321; in the USA from, for example, The Complete Traveller Bookstore – 212 685-9007.

Ferries to Spain from the UK

P&O sail to Bilbao twice a week from Portsmouth. Two nights on the boat going out, one on the return journey. Tel: 0990 980980.

Brittany Ferries sail to Santander twice a week from Plymouth. One night on the boat both ways. Tel: 01752 221321.

Train

Train travel in both countries is cheap compared to UK prices. Ask for details from the respective National Tourist Offices.

Spanish Tourist Offices

UK   57/58 St. James's Street, London SW1A 1LD.
      Tel: 0171 499 0901   Fax: 0171 629 4257
USA   665 Fifth Avenue, New York 10022
      Tel: 212 759 8822

Portuguese Tourist Offices

UK   PNTO, 22/25 Sackville Street, London W1X 1DE
      Tel: 0171 494 1441
USA   PNTO, 590 Fifth Avenue, New York 10036-4704
      Tel: 212 354 4403/4/5/6/7/8

Winter in Spain and Portugal

There can be very marked variations in temperature; marble and terracotta floors that keep things cool in summer can be numbing to the feet in winter. You may be glad you packed a pair of slippers.

Plugs (electrical and auricular)

Virtually all sockets are now 220/240 AC voltage and are nearly always two-pin. Secondly, don't feel silly taking ear plugs – the Spaniards, especially, are natural nightbirds and great talkers and will often exercise their skills below your bedroom window into the early hours.

YOUR COMMENTS

We need your comments about those places we have included in this guide and welcome your suggestions for places we haven't included. At the back of the book you will find report forms; please use them with abandon! There will be a free copy of next year's guide book for any recommendation leading to an inclusion in it (you may have to put in a claim!) and a bottle of 'Cava' for the most interesting/wittiest report from a reader. We hope you will remember that a place does not have to be grand or luxurious to qualify for inclusion. We are particularly keen to find more family-run B&Bs, especially those where fresh farm produce is available, and small, charming town 'pensiones'.

We hope to cover the Canary and Balearic Islands in the next edition; any recommendations will be most welcome, be they from readers or hoteliers.

Do remember that if you think a hotel in NOT up to scratch, the first person to tell is the owner/manager. Give him or her the chance to put things right while you are still there. We do of course need to know about it too, so please write to us afterwards. Your feedback is hugely helpful in keeping us up to date and accurate. Many thanks once again to all readers who have taken the time and trouble to write – often long and detailed – letters telling us what YOU thought of individual hotels. This has been an enormous help to us.

Explanations of symbols

Your hosts may speak any form of English, from pidgin to perfect.

Pets are welcome although at times would be housed not in your rooms but in an outbuilding. Check when booking if restrictions/small supplement apply.

Garden with shady area for sitting out and where meals can normally be taken.

Hotel has its own swimming pool though not necessarily in use all year round.

Good **country** walks close by the hotel.

At least a part of the building is more than a hundred years old.

Some or all of the buildings have air-conditioning.

Credit cards accepted; most commonly Visa and Mastercard.

Vegetarians catered for with advance warning.

You can garage your own bike here or hire one locally.

DISCLAIMER

We make no claims to pure objectivity in judging hotels. They are here because we LIKE them. Our opinions and tastes are ours alone and this book is a statement of them; we cross our fingers and hope that you will share them.

We have done our utmost to get our facts right but apologise unreservedly for any mistakes that may have crept in. Sometimes, too, prices shift, usually upwards, and 'things' change. We would be grateful to be told of any errors or changes, however small.

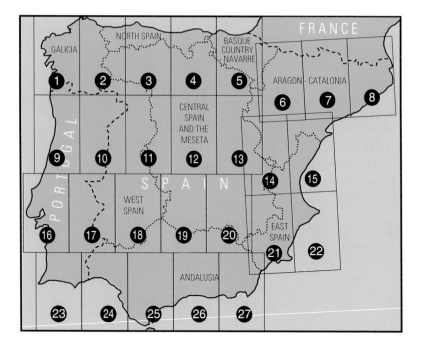

Spain and Portugal
General Map

CONTENTS

MAP

West Spain
Entry numbers 101 – 110
- Badajoz ⓱
- Cáceres ⑩ ⓱ ⑱
- Salamanca ⑩ ⑪

Central Spain
Entry numbers 111 – 142
- Avila ⑩
- Burgos ❹
- Cuenca ⑬
- Ciudad Real ⑲
- La Rioja ❺
- León ❸
- Madrid ⑫
- Palencia ❹
- Segovia ⑫
- Toledo ⑫ ⑱

Andalusia
Entry numbers 143 – 200
- Almería ㉗
- Cádiz ㉔ ㉕
- Córdoba ㉕
- Granada ㉖
- Huelva ⓱
- Jaén ⑲ ㉔
- Málaga ㉕ ㉖
- Sevilla ⑱ ㉔ ㉕

PORTUGAL
Northern Portugal
Entry numbers 201 – 224
- Minho ❶ ❾
- Trás-os-Montes ⑩
- Douro ❾ ⑩

Central Portugal
Entry numbers 225 – 253
- Beira ❾ ⑩ ⑯
- Estremadura ⑯
- Ribatejo ⑯

Central Portugal
Entry numbers 254 – 283
- Alentejo ⑯ ⓱ ㉓
- Algarve ㉓

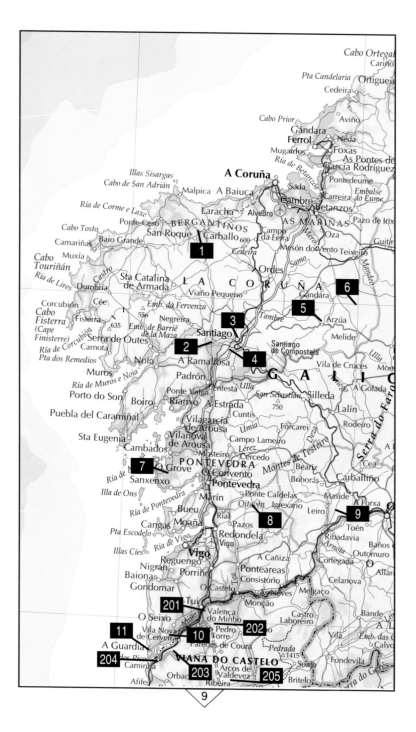

1

Map scale 1cm : 13km

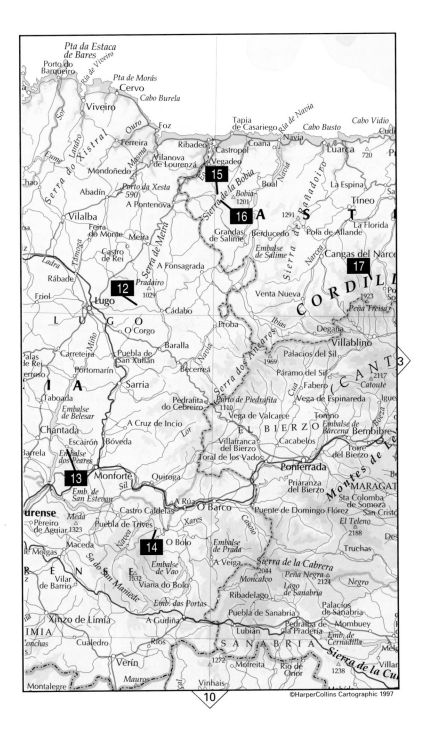

Pta da Estaca
de Bares
Porto do
Barqueiro
Pta de Morás
Cervo
Cabo Burela
Viveiro

Ría de Viveiro

Foz
Ferreira
Vilanova
de Lourenzá
Ribadeo
Castropol
Vegadeo
Tapia
de Casariego
Coana
Navia
Cabo Busto
Cabo Vidio
Cudi
Luarca
720
P

Mondoñedo
Porto da Xesta
590
Abadín
A Pontenova
Sierra de la Bobia
Bobia
1201
Boal
La Espina
Tineo

Vilalba
Feira
do Monte
Meira
Grandas
de Salime
Berducedo
Pola de Allande
1291
La Florida
Sa

Castro
de Rei
A Fonsagrada
Embalse
de Salime
Cangas del Narce

17

Rábade
Ladra
Támoga
Pradairo
1029
Venta Nueva
1923
Peña Freisa
Po
So

Friol
12
Lugo
Cádabo
Proba
Ibias
Degaña
Villablino

L U G O
O'Corgo
Baralla
Palacios del Sil
2117
Catoute

Carretera
Puebla de
San Xulián
Becerreá
1969
Páramo del Sil
Fabero
Vega de Espinareda
Igue

I   A
Portomarín
Sarria
Pedrafita
do Cebreiro
Porto de Piedrafita
1110
Cua
Toreno
Embalse de
Bárcena
Bembibre

Taboada
Embalse
de Belesar
A Cruz de Incio
Vega de Valcarce
EL BIERZO
Cacabelos
Torre
del Bierzo

Chantada
Escairón
Bóveda
Villafranca
del Bierzo
Toral de los Vados
Ponferrada

Barrela
Embalse
dos Peares
13
Monforte
Quiroga
Priaranza
del Bierzo
Sta Colomba
de Somoza
MARAGAT
San Cristó

urense
Emb. de
San Esteban
Castro Caldelas
A Rúa
O Barco
Puente de Domingo Flórez
El Teleno
2188
Des

Pereiro
de Aguiar
Méda
1323
Puebla de Trives
Xares
14
O Bolo
Embalse
de Prada
A Veiga
Truchas

le Molgas
Maceda
Sa do San Mamede
Embalse
de Vao
1532
Viana do Bolo
Sierra de la Cabrera
2044
Moncalvo
Peña Negra
2124
Negro

R E N
Vilar
de Barrio
Emb. das Portas
Ribadelago
Lago
de Sanabria
Palacios
de Sanabria
Mombuey

IMIA
Xinzo de Limia
A Gudiña
Puebla de Sanabria
Pedralba de
la Pradería
Emb. de
Cernadilla
Mel

Conchas
s
Cualedro
Ríos
Lubián
S A N A B R I A

Verín
1272
Mofreita
Río de
Onor
1238
Villar

Montalegre
Mauros
Vinhais

15
16 A
CORDILI
Sierra dos Ancares
Montes de Le
Sierra de la Cu
Narcea

10

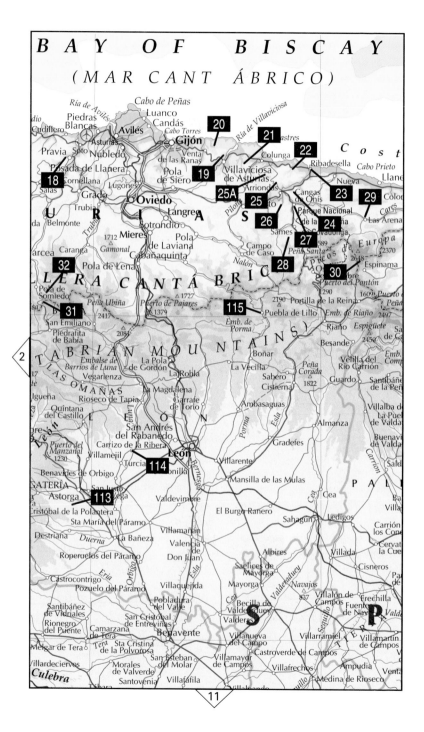

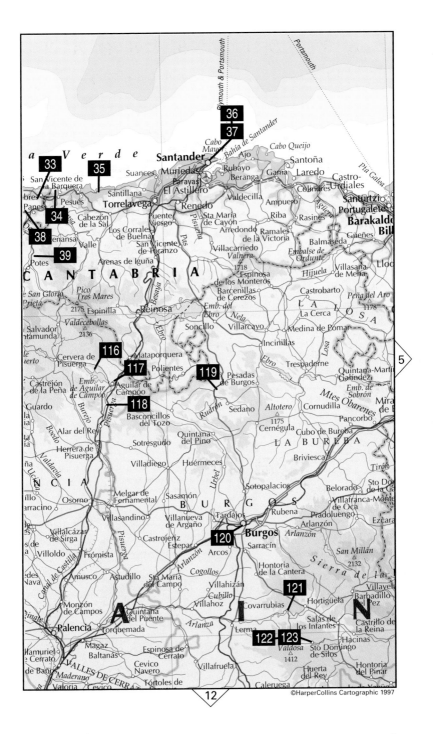

©HarperCollins Cartographic 1997

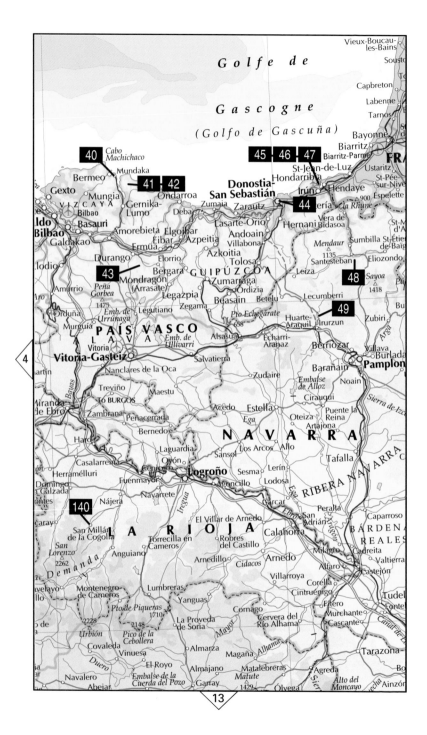

Golfe de

Gascogne

(Golfo de Gascuña)

Vieux-Boucau-
les-Bains
Sousto

Capbreton

Labenne

Tarnos

Bayonne

Biarritz
Biarritz-Parme

40 Cabo Machichaco
Mundaka

45 **46** **47**
St-Jean-de-Luz
Hondarribia

Bermeo

41 **42**
Ondarroa

**Donostia-
San Sebastián**

Iñún Hendaye
44 ería la Rhune

Gexto
Mungia
Gernika-
Lumo
Zumaia
Zarautz

Vera de
Bidasoa

St-Pée-
sur-Nive
Espelete

Ido
Bilbao
Basauri
Amorebieta
Elgoibar
Eibar
Azpeitia
Lasarte-Orio
Andoain
Villabona

Hernani
Mendaur
1135
Santesteban
Sumbilla St-Étie
de-Baïg

Galdakao
Ermua

Azkoitia

Eliozondo

lodio
Durango
Elorrio
Bergara
Tolosa

43
Mondragón
(Arrasate)
Zumarraga
Ordizia

GUIPÚZCOA
Leiza

Amurrio
Peña
Gorbea
1475
Legazpia
Beasain
Betelu
Lecumberri

Sayoa
1418

48

Orduña
Emb. de
Urrúnaga
Legutiano
Zegama
Pto Echegárate
658

Huarte-
Araquil
Irurzun

Zubiri

49

Murguía
PAÍS VASCO

Alsasua

Echarri-
Aranaz

Berriozar

Villava
Burlada

Pamplon

Vitoria
Emb. de
Ullívarri

4
Vitoria-Gasteiz

Salvatierra

Barañain

Noain

Nanclares de la Oca

Zudaire

Ciraúqui

rtín
Treviño
Maestu
Acedo
Estella

Puente la
Reina
Sierra de Iza

Miranda
de Ebro
Zambrana
Peñacerrada
Ega
Oteiza
Artajona

Haro
Bernedo

NAVARRA

ón
Herraméluri
Laguardia
Oyón
Los Arcos
Allo
Tafalla

Domingo
Calzada
ntes
Casalarrema
Fuenmayor
Sansol
Sesma
Lerín
Lodosa

RIBERA NAVARRA

Logroño
Agoncillo

Peralta

Caparroso

140
Nájera
Navarrete
Cárcar
San
Adrián
BÁRDENA

caray
San Millán
de la Cogolla
El Villar de Arnedo
Calahorra
Milagro
Cadreita

REALES

San
Lorenzo
2262
Torrecilla en
Cameros
Robres
del Castillo
Arnedo
Alfaro
Castejón

Anguiano
Arnedillo
Cidacos
Villarroya
Corella

A RIOJA

Demanda

velayo
llo
Montenegro
de Cameros
Lumbreras
Yanguas
Cornago
Cintruénigo
Entero
Murchante

Tudel
Fonte

Pto de Piqueras
1710
La Proveda
de Soria
Cervera del
Río Alhama
Cascante

Urbión
2228
Pico de la
Cebollera
2148
Magaña
Alhama

de
Covaleda
Vinuesa
Almarza
Mataleblas
Matute
1429

Tarazona

Navalero
Abejar
El Royo
Embalse de la
Cuerda del Pozo
Garray
Almajano
Ólvega
Agreda
Alto del
Moncayo
Ainzón

ia
Duero

13

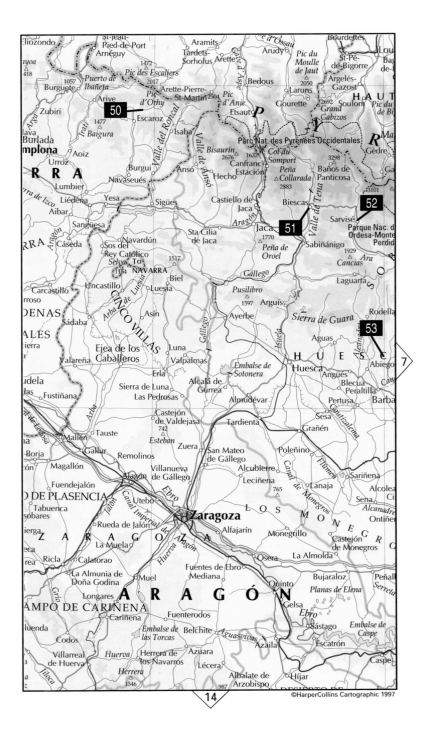

Tiozondo
St-Jean-Pied-de-Port
Arnéguy
Aramits
Tardets-Sorholus
Arette
Gave d'Aspe
Arudy
Bourdettes
Pic du Moulle de Jaut
St-Pé-de-Bigorre

anyoa
418
Pic des Escaliers
2017
Bedous
Laruns
2050
Argelès-Gazost
Lou
Bag-de-B

Burguete
1057
Puerto de Ibañeta
1472
Arette-Pierre-St-Martin
2504
Pic d'Anie
Etsaut
Gourette
2692
Grand Gabizos
Soulom
HAUT
Pic du de Bi

Zubiri
Arive
Pic d'Orhy
2017
Isaba
Valle del Roncal
Valle de Ansó
Bisaurín
2676
Parc Nat. des Pyrénées Occidentales
Col du Somport
3298
Baños de Panticosa
Gèdre
Ga

lava
Burlada
mplona
1477
Baigura
Escaroz
Ansó
Hecho
Canfranc Estación
1632
Peña Collarada
2883
R
Ma

Aoiz
Urroz
Lumbier
Liédena
Burgui
Navascués
Sigües
Castiello de Jaca
Biescas
Valle de Tena
43101
52

R R A
Yesa
Aibar
Sangüesa
Cáseda
Sta Cilia de Jaca
Aragón
Jaca
1770
51
Sabiñánigo
Sarvisé
Parque Nac. de Ordesa-Monte Perdid
1929
Cancias
Ara

rra de Izco
Aragón
Navardún
Sos del Rey Católico
Selva To
1154
NAVARRA
1517
Peña de Oroel
Gállego
Laguarta
SO

Carcastillo
rroso
DENAS
Uncastillo
Asín
Luesia
Biel
Pusilibro
1597
Arguís
Sierra de Guara
Rodella
Abiego
53

ALES
ierra
Sádaba
CINCO VILLAS
Arba de Luesia
Ayerbe
Isuela
Aguas
7

dela
Valareña
Ejea de los Caballeros
Luna
Valpalmas
Embalse de Sotonera
Huesca
Angüés
Blecua
Peraltilla
Barba

las
Fustiñana
Sierra de Luna
Erla
Las Pedrosas
Alcalá de Gurrea
Almudévar
Pertusa
Sesa
Cantizalema
Barba

Mallén
Tauste
Gállego
Castejón de Valdejasa
742
Esteban
Tardienta
Grañén
Alcolea
Ci

Borja
Gallur
Remolinos
Zuera
San Mateo de Gállego
Alcubierre
765
Poleñino
Flumen
Sariñena
Sena
Alcanadre

ón
Magallón
Fuendejalón
Utebo
Alagón
Ebro
Villanueva de Gállego
Leciñena
Canal de Monegros
Lanaja
Ontine

O DE PLASENCIA
Tabuenca
sobares
Rueda de Jalón
ZARAGOZA
Alfajarín
LOS
MONEGRO
Castejón de Monegros

ierga
Z A R A G O
La Muela
Jalón
Canal Imperial de Aragón
Huerva
Monegrillo
La Almolda
Peñal
Serreta

rea
Ricla
Calatorao
La Almunia de Doña Godina
Muel
Fuentes de Ebro
Mediana
Osera
Quinto
Bujaraloz
Planas de Elena
Ebro

luenda
Longares
A R A G Ó N
Cariñena
Fuenterodos
Gelsa
Sástago
Embalse de Caspe

Codos
AMPO DE CARIÑENA
Belchite
Aguasvivas
Azaila
Escatrón
Caspe

Villarreal de Huerva
Huerva
Herrera de los Navarros
Azuara
Lécera
Híjar
a

Jiloca
Hérrera
1346
987
Albalate de Arzobispo

50

14

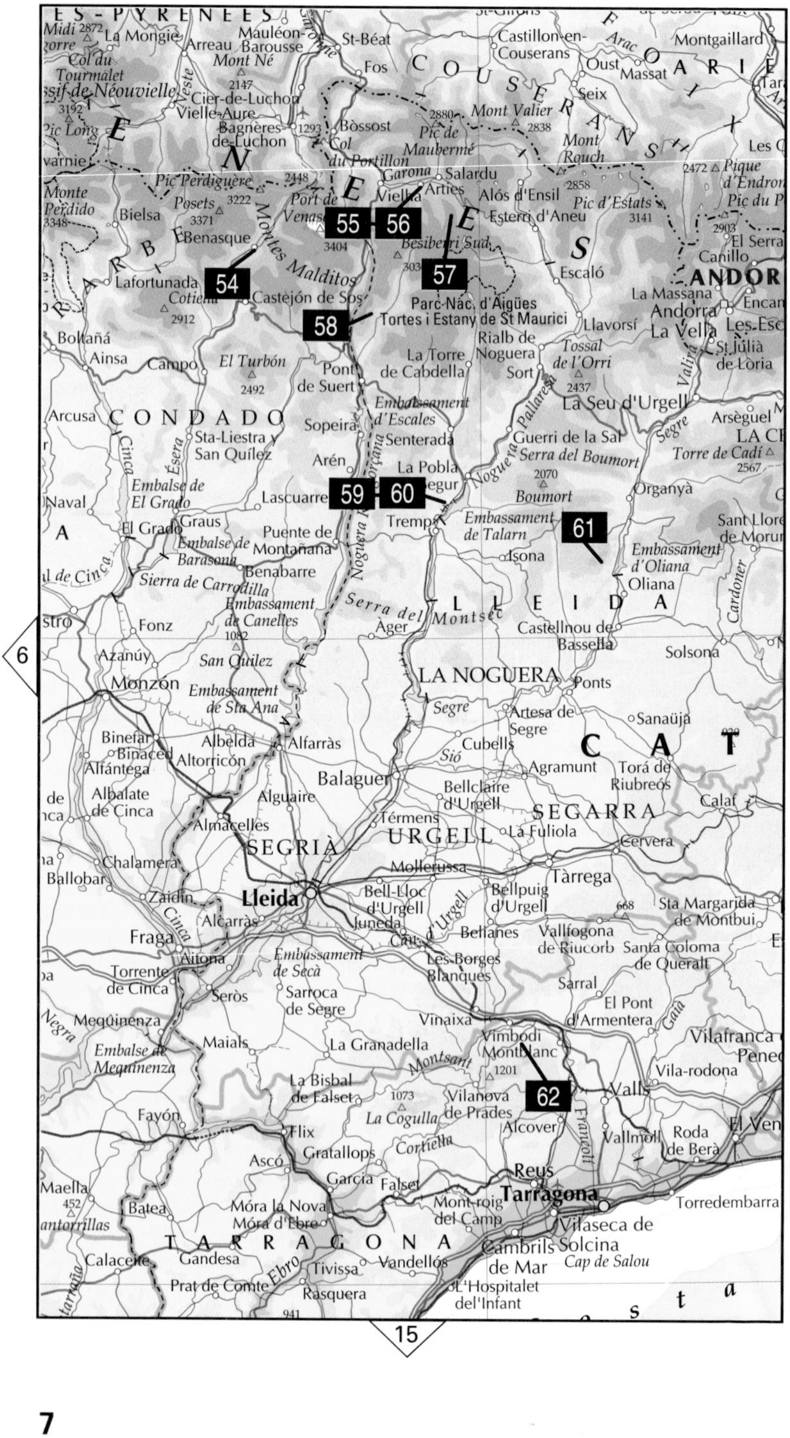

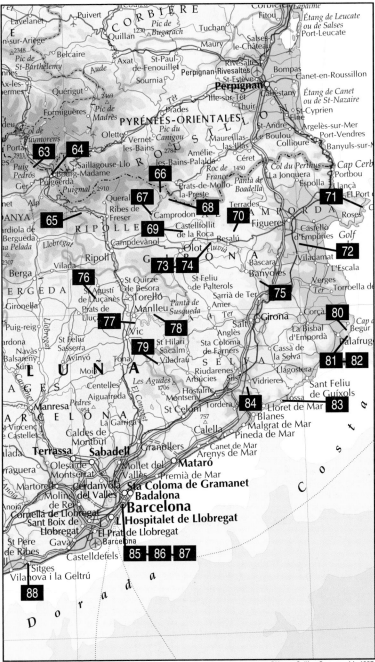

©HarperCollins Cartographic 1997

8

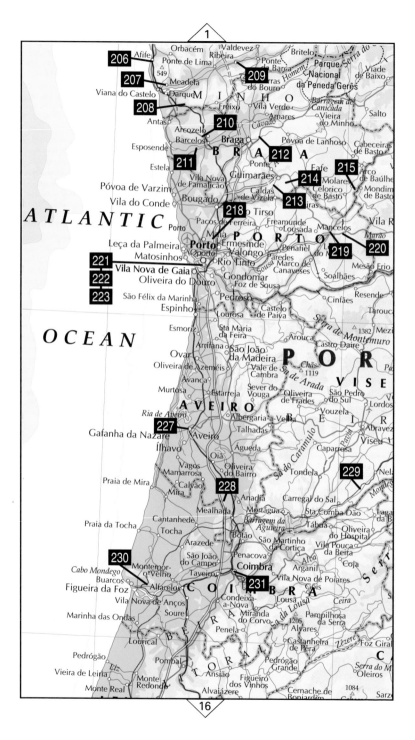

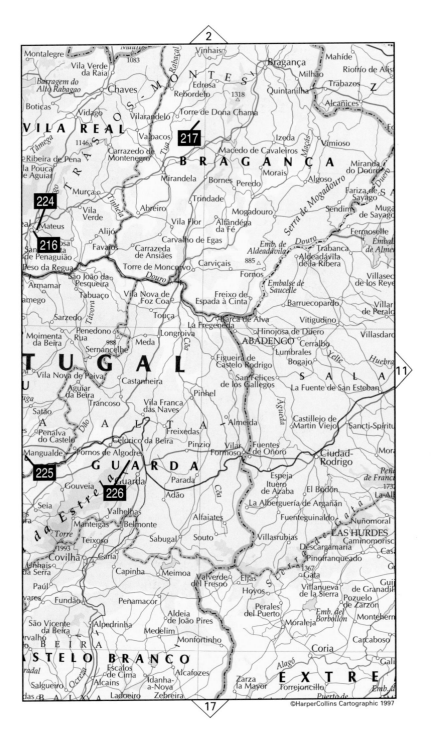

Montalegre
Vila Verde
da Raia
1083
Vinhais
Bragança
Mahíde
Riofrío de Alís
Barragem do
Alto Rabagão
Chaves
Edrosa
Rebordelo
1318
Quintanilha
Milhão
Trabazos
Z
Boticas
Vidago
Vilarandelo
Torre de Dona Chama
Quintanilha
Alcañices
VILA REAL
Valpaços
1146
217
BRAGANÇA
Izeda
Vimioso
Ribeira de Pena
la Pouca
e Aguiar
Carrazedo de
Montenegro
Mirandela
Bornes
Peredo
Macedo de Cavaleiros
Morais
Algoso
Miranda
do Douro
224
Murça
Trindade
Mogadouro
Fariza de
Sayago
Sendim
Muga
de Sayago
216
Vila
Verde
Abreiro
Vila Flor
Alfândega
da Fé
Serra de Mogadouro
Douro
Trabanca
Fermoselle
Embal
de Almei
Mateus
Favaios
Carrazeda
de Ansiães
Carvalho de Egas
Emb. de
Aldeadávila
885
Aldeadávila
de la Ribera
Villaseo
de los Reye
Sa
de Penaguião
Torre de Moncorvo
Carviçais
Fornos
Embalse de
Saucelle
eso da Regua
São João da
Pesqueira
Douro
Freixo de
Espada à Cinta
Barruecopardo
Villar
de Peralo
Armamar
amego
Tabuaço
Vila Nova de
Foz Coa
Barca de Alva
Vitigudino
Villar
Sarzedo
Touça
La Fregeneda
Hinojosa de Duero
Villasdar
Moimenta
da Beira
Penedono
Rua
Meda
Longroiva
ABADENGO
Cerralbo
Velle
Huebra
TUGAL
Sernancelhe
988
Figueira de
Castelo Rodrigo
Lumbrales
Bogajo
SALA
11
Vila Nova de Paiva
Castanheira
San Felices
de los Gallegos
La Fuente de San Esteban
U
Aguiar
da Beira
Trancoso
Vila Franca
das Naves
Pinhel
Agueda
Castillejo de
Martín Viejo
Sancti-Spíritu
uga
Satão
ALTA
Freixedas
Almeida
Mora
Penalva
do Castelo
Celorico da Beira
Pinzio
Vilar
Fuentes
de Oñoro
Ciudad-
Rodrigo
Peña
de Franci
173
Mangualde
Fornos de Algodres
GUARDA
Formoso
Espeja
Ituero
de Azaba
El Bodón
La-Alb
225
Gouveia
Guarda
Parada
La Alberguería de Argañán
Nuñomoral
Seia
Adão
Côa
Fuenteguinaldo
LAS HURDES
es
ra
da Estre
226
Valhelhas
Alfaiates
Villasrubias
Sierra-de-Gata
Descargamaría
Caminomorisc
Cas
Torre
1993
Manteigas
Belmonte
Souto
Pinofranqueado
G
Teixoso
Sabugal
1367
Gata
Covilhã
Caria
Meimoa
Villanueva
de la Sierra
Gui
de Granadil
nhaes
Paúl
Capinha
Valverde
del Fresno
Eljas
Hoyos
Pozuelo
de Zarzón
ares
Fundão
Penamacor
Perales
del Puerto
Emb. del
Borbollón
Montehern
São Vicente
da Beira
Alpedrinha
Aldeia
de João Pires
Medelim
Moraleja
Carcaboso
Carvalho
BEIRA
Monfortinho
Coria
Gali
ASTELO BRANCO
Escalos
de Cima
Alcafozes
Alagó
EXTRE
radal
Salgueiro
Alcains
Idanha-
a-Nova
Zebreira
Zarza
la Mayor
Torrejoncillo
Emb.
das
B
Ladoeiro
Puerto de

©HarperCollins Cartographic 1997

10

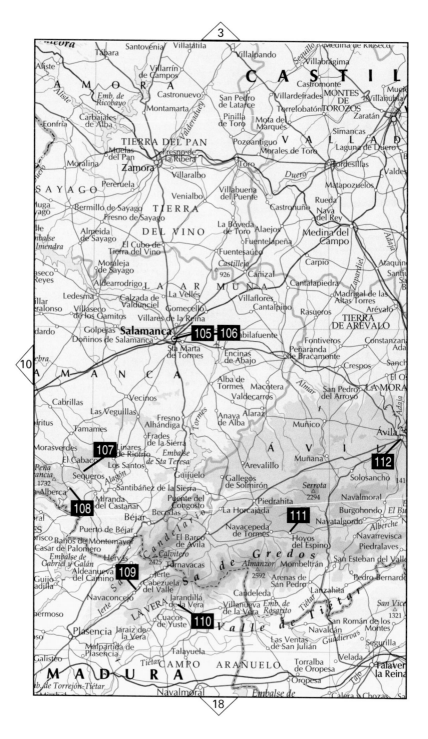

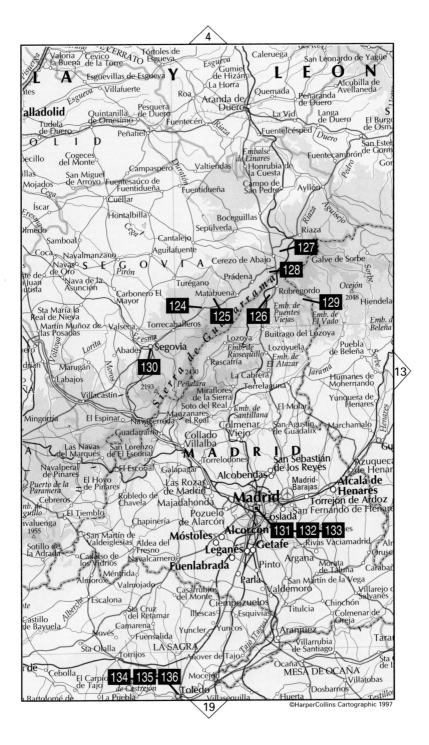

CASTILLA Y LEÓN

Valoria la Buena · Cevico de la Torre · Tórtoles de Esgueva · Esgueva · Caleruega · San Leonardo de Yagüe

Esguevillas de Esgueva · Gumiel de Hizán · Alcubilla de Avellaneda

Villafuerte · Roa · La Horra · Quemada · Peñaranda de Duero

Valladolid · Pesquera de Duero · Aranda de Duero · La Vid · Langa de Duero · El Burgo

Quintanilla de Onésimo · Fuentecén · Riaza · Duero · Fuentelcésped · Fuentecambrón · de Osma · San Esteban de Gormaz

Tudela de Duero · Peñafiel

Vecilla · Cogeces del Monte · Campaspero · Valtiendas · Embalse de Linares · Honrubia de la Cuesta · Gor

Navas del Monte · San Miguel de Arroyo · Fuentesaúco de Fuentidueña · Fuentidueña · Campo de San Pedro · Ayllón

Mojados · Cuéllar · Boceguillas · Cega

Íscar · Hontalbilla · Sepúlveda · Riaza

Olmedo · Cantalejo · Aguilafuente · 127

Samboal · Navalmanzano · Cerezo de Abajo · Galve de Sorbe · 128

Coca · Navas de Oro · SEGOVIA · Prádena · Ocejón · 2048 · Hiendelaencina

Nava de la Asunción · Turégano · Matabuena · Robregordo · 129

Carbonero El Mayor · 124 · Emb. de Puentes Viejas · Emb. de El Vado · Emb. de Beleña

Sta María la Real de Nieva · Valseca · Torrecaballeros · 125 · 126 · Sierra de Guadarrama

Martín Muñoz de las Posadas · Abades · Segovia · Lozoya · Emb. de Riosequillo · Lozoyuela · Emb. de El Atazar · Puebla de Beleña

Marugán · 130 · Rascafría · La Cabrera · Jarama · Humanes de Mohernando · 13

Labajos · 2430 · Peñalara · Miraflores de la Sierra · Torrelaguna · Yunquera de Henares

Villacastín · 2193 · Soto del Real · Emb. de Santillana · El Molar · Marchamalo

Mingorría · El Espinar · Navacerrada · Manzanares el Real · Colmenar Viejo · San Agustín de Guadalix

Guadarrama · Collado Villalba · Torrelodones · San Sebastián de los Reyes · Azuqueca de Henares

Las Navas del Marqués · San Lorenzo de El Escorial · MADRID · Alcobendas · Alcalá de Henares

Navalperal de Pinares · El Escorial · Galapagar · Madrid-Barajas · Torrejón de Ardoz

El Hoyo de Pinares · Las Rozas de Madrid · Madrid · San Fernando de Henares

Cebreros · Robledo de Chavela · Majadahonda · Coslada

El Tiemblo · Chapinería · Pozuelo de Alarcón · Alcorcón · 131 · 132 · 133

San Martín de Valdeiglesias · Móstoles · Getafe · Rivas Vaciamadrid

Sotillo de la Adrada · Aldea del Fresno · Leganés · Argana · Morata de Tajuña

Cadalso de los Vidrios · Navalcarnero · Pinto · San Martín de la Vega · Carabaña

Almorox · Méntrida · Fuenlabrada · Parla · Valdemoro · Villarejo de Salvanés

Escalona · Valmojado · Casarrubios del Monte · Ciempozuelos · Chinchón · Colmenar de Oreja

Castillo de Bayuela · Sta Cruz del Retamar · Illescas · Esquivias · Titulcia

Novés · Camarena · Yuncler · Yuncos · Aranjuez · Villarrubia de Santiago

Sta Olalla · Fuensalida · LA SAGRA · Ocaña · MESA DE OCAÑA · Villatobas

Torrijos · Añover de Tajo · Mocejón · Dosbarrios

Cebolla · El Carpio de Tajo · 134 · 135 · 136 · Toledo · Villasequilla · Huerta

San Bartolomé · La Puebla de Castrejón · Villaluenga

©HarperCollins Cartographic 1997

12

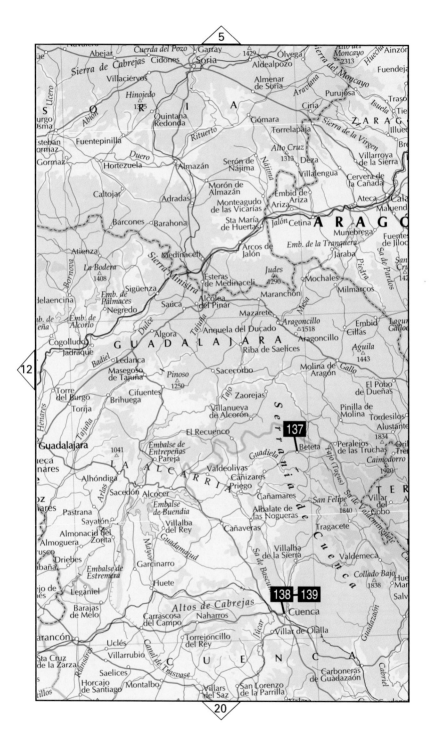

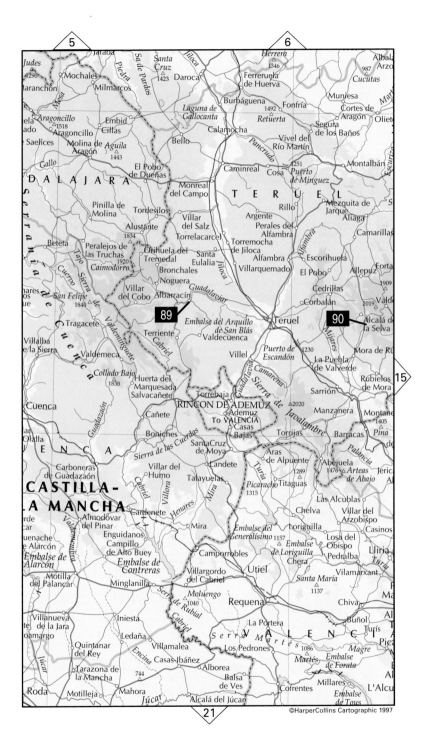

Judes
1290
Mochales
Maranchón
Milmarcos
Jaraba
Sa. de Pardos
Piedra
Santa Cruz
1423
Daroca
Herrera
1346
Ferreruela de Huerva
Cucutas
Albal
Arzo
Muniesa
987

la
ado
Aragoncillo
1518
Aragoncillo
Embid
Cillas
Laguna de Gallocanta
Burbáguena
1492
Fonfría
Retuerta
Cortes de
Aragón
Oliet
Saelices
Molina de Aragón
Aguila
1443
Bello
Calamocha
Vivel del
Río Martín
Segura de los Baños
Gallo
El Pobo de Dueñas
Caminreal
Cosa
Puerto de Minguez
Montalbán

D A L A J A R A
Pinilla de Molina
Tordesilos
Monreal del Campo
T E R U E L
Rillo
Mezquita de Jarque
Aliaga
Camarillas

Serrania de
Beteta
Peralejos de las Truchas
Alustante
1834
Orihuela del Tremedal
1920
Villar del Salz
Torrelacarcel
Argente
Perales del Alfambra
Torremocha de Jiloca
Escorihuela
Allepuz
Forta

Cuerco
Tajo
Sierra de
Caimodorro
Santa Eulalia
Alfambra
Villarquemado
El Pobo
Cedrillas
1909

ares
os
ue
San Felipe
1840
Villar del Cobo
Albarracín
Noguera
Bronchales
Guadalaviar

Corbalán
2019
Valde

Tragacete
Terriente
Embalse del Arquillo de San Blás
Valdecuenca
Teruel
Alcalá de la Selva

Villalba
e la Sierra
Valdemeca
Valdemingueta
Villel
Puerto de Escandón
1230
La Puebla de Valverde
Mora de Ru
Rubielos de Mora

Cuenca
Collado Bajo
1838
Huerta del Marquesado
Salvacañete
Torrebaja
RINCON DE ADEMUZ
Ademuz
To VALENCIA
Casas Bajas
Sarrión
2020
Manzanera
Montane
1405
Pina

Carboneras de Guadazaón
Cañete
Boniches
SantaCruz de Moya
Torrijas
Aras de Alpuente
Abejuela
1476
Arteas de Abajo
Jeric

CASTILLA-
LA MANCHA
Villar del Humo
Landete
Talayuelas
1289
Picaracho
1315
Titaguas
Las Alcublas
Chelva
Villar del Arzobispo
Casinos

Almodóvar del Pinar
Cardenete
Mira
Embalse del Generalísimo
1157
Embalse de Loriguilla
Loriguilla
Losa del Obispo
Pedralba
Lliria

Enguidanos
Campillo de Alto Buey
Embalse de Contreras
Camporrobles
Chera
Vilamarxant
Turi
Ma

Motilla del Palancar
Minglanilla
Villargordo del Cabriel
Utiel
Santa María
1137
Chiva

Villanueva
tel de la Jara
oamargo
Iniesta
Ledaña
Moluengo
1040
Requena
La Portera
Buñol
Turís
Al
Pic
Magre

Quintanar del Rey
Villamalea
Casas-Ibáñez
Los Pedrones
Serra
Martés
1086
Martés
Embalse de Forata
Al
L'Alcu

Roda
Motilleja
Mahora
744
Alborea
Balsa de Ves
Alcalá del Júcar
Cofrentes
Millares
Embalse de Tous

©HarperCollins Cartographic 1997

Balate de Arzobispo

Híjar

DESIERTO DE

Maella 452

Batea

Ascó

García Falset

Mor del

CALANDA

Ariño

Alcañiz

Calaceite

Prat de Comte

Móra la Nova
Móra d'Ebre

T A R R A G O N A

Castelseras

Calanda

Valjunquera

Gandesa

Tivissa

Vandellós

Oliete

Andorra

Alcorisa

Arnes
L'Espina 1182

Xerta

941

La Creu de Santos

Rasquera

Cap d

L'Ametll

Mas de las Matas

Aguaviva

Monroyo

Valderrobes
Fuentespalda

Roquetas

El Perelló

Golf

92

93

Ejulve

Sierra de la Garrucha

Guadalope

Zorita del Maestrazgo

Encanadé 1393

Ports de Beseit

B A I X
E B R E

Tortosa
L'Hostal

Sant

illas

91

Mirambel

Forcall

Morella

Castell de Cabres

Servol

Stá Bárbara

Amposta

del Als

La Dreta
La Cava

Puerto de Cabrillas

Cinctorres

94

La Sènia

Ulldecona

Ebre

de l'Ebre

St Carles de la Ràp

ortanete 1909

La Iglesuela del Cid

Villafranca del Cid

Muella de Ares 1318

Ares del Maestre

St Mateu

La Jana

Seco

Traiguera

Alcanar

San Jorge

Costa de Fora

C
o
s
t
a

d
e
l

A
z
a
h
a
r

aldelinares

Linares de Mora

Montleón

Benasal

Albocácer

Salsadella

Vinaròs

Benicarló

lá de lva

e Rubielos

C A S T E L L Ó N

D E   L A   P L A N A

Adzaneta

Cuevas de Vinromá

Vilanova d'Alcolea

Vall d'Alba

Sta Magdalena de Pulpís

Alcalá de Chivert

Alcossebre

ora

Embalse de Arenos

Zucaina

Figueroles

Cabanes

Villamalés

Torreblanca

Pta de Capicorp

anejos 505

Alcora

Argelita

Ribesalbes

Embalse de María Cristina

Oropesa

Cabo de Oropesa

na

Fuentes de Ayódar

Caudiel

Onda

Tales

Millárs

Benicasim

Castelló de la Plana

érica

Altura

Segorbe

1089

Nules

Almassora

Vila-real de los Infantes

Burriana

Algimia de Alfara

Vall de Uxó

Almenara

nos

Sagunto

Puçol

Golfo

d
e

ria

Bétera

Massamagrell

Paterna
Manises

Burjassot

Alaquás

Valencia

V
a
l
e
n
c
i
a

Torrent

Alfafar

A

Catarroja

Picassent

Silla

Montroy

L'Albufera

Benifaió

El Perelló

Alginet

lcudia

Suèca

V a l e n c i a

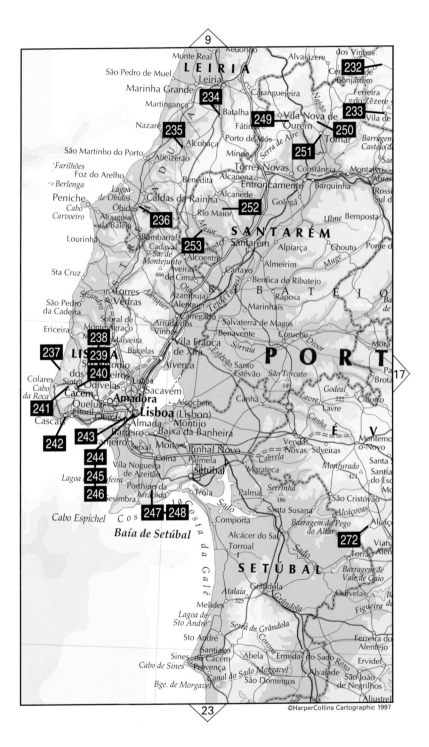

LEIRIA

Monte Real
Alvaiázere
dos Vinhos
São Pedro de Muel
232
Leiria
Caranguejeira
Cer
Bonjardim
Marinha Grande
234
Ferreira
do Tâzere
Martingança
Batalha
249
Vila Nova de
Ourém
233
Vila de
Nazaré
235
Fátima
250
Alcobaça
Porto de Mós
Tomar
251
São Martinho do Porto
Minde
Serra de Aire
Barragem
Castelo do
Aljeizerão
Montalvo
Farilhões
Torres Novas
Constância
San
Foz do Arelho
Benedita
Alcanena
Entroncamento
Barquinha
Rossi
Berlenga
Lagoa
de Óbidos
Alcanede
Golegã
Sul d
Peniche
Caldas da Rainha
Abras
Cabo
Carvoeiro
Óbidos
236
Rio Maior
252
Ulme
Bemposta
Atouguia
da Baleia
Maior
SANTARÉM
Ponte d
Lourinhã
Bombarral
Cadaval
253
Santarém
Alpiarça
Chouto
Sta Cruz
Sa. de
Montejunto
Alcoentre
Almeirim
Muge
Ponte d
666 de Cima
Aveiras
Cartaxo
Benfica do Ribatejo
R
B
A
T
É
J
O
Torres
Vedras
Azambuja
Alenquer
Raposa
Ba
São Pedro
da Cadeira
Alenquer
Marinhais
de
Ericeira
Sobral de
Carregado
Salvaterra de Magos
Mora
Monte Agraço
Arruda dos
Vinhos
Benavente
Coruche
Brota
Colares
237
LISBOA
238
239
Malveira
Bucelas
Vila Franca
de Xira
Sorraia
Estôrão
Santo
Estêvão
Divor
São Torcato
Godeal
Ciborro
P
O
R
T
Pa
Cabo
da Roca
Sintra
240
Odivelas
Alverca
Canha
Lavre
222
Cacém
Queluz
Lisboa
Sacavém
149
Lavre
Canha
É
V
241
Estoril
Amadora
Alcochete
Montemo
o-Novo
Cascais
Lisboa
(Lisbon)
Montijo
Vendas
Novas
Santa
242
243
Almada
Bajxa da Banheira
Moita
Pinhal Novo
Silveiras
Santia
do Esc
244
Barreiro
anjeiro
Seixal
Cabrela
Monfurado
424
Mo
245
Vila Nogueira
de Azeitão
Coina
Palmela
Marateca
246
247
248
Porinho da
Arrábida
Setúbal
Serrinha
186
São Cristóvão
Alcáçovas
272
Cabo Espichel
Cos
Comporta
Barragem do Pego
do Altar
Alcác
Baía de Setúbal
Sado
Alcácer do Sal
Torroal
Santa Susana
Setúbal
SETÚBAL
Barragem de
Vale de Gaio
Torrão
Atalaia
Grândola
Odivelas
B
Melides
325
Figueira
Grândola
Lagoa de
Sto André
Serra de Grândola
Ferreira do
Alentejo
Sto André
Corona
Ervidel
Sines
Santiago
do Cacém
Abela
Ermidas do Sado
São João
Cabo de Sines
Provença
Alvalade
de Negrilhos
Bge. de Morgavel
Canal do Sado
São Domingos
Aljustrel

17

©HarperCollins Cartographic 1997

16

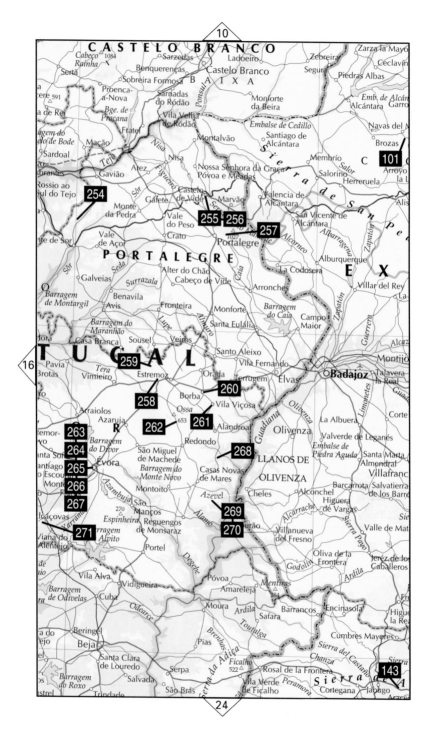

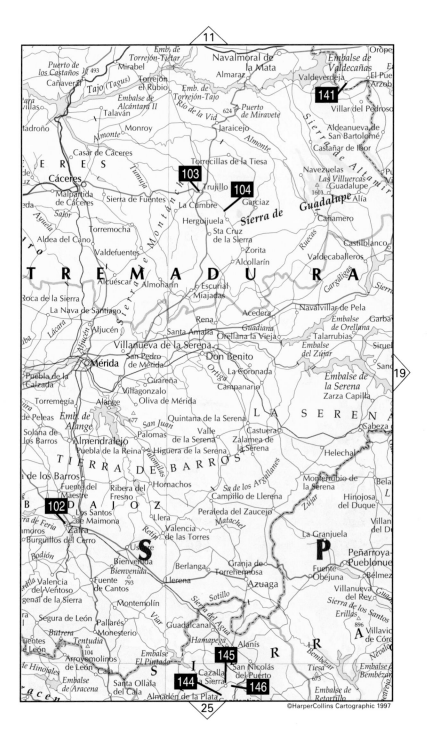

Orobe
Embalse de
Valdecañas
Navalmoral de
la Mata
Almaraz
Valdeverdeja
El Pue
Arzob
Puerto de
los Castaños
493
Cañaveral
Mirabel
Torrejón
el Rubio
Tajo (Tagus)
Emb. de
Torrejón-Tiétar
Emb. de
Torrejón-Tajo
141
Villar del Pedroso
Embalse de
Alcántara II
Talaván
Río de la Vid
624
Puerto
de Miravete
Villas
adroño
Monroy
Almonte
Jaraicejo
Almonte
Aldeanueva de
San Bartolomé
Castañar de Ibor
E R E S
Casar de Cáceres
Torrecillas de la Tiesa
Navezuelas
Las Villuercas
Guadalupe
1601
Sierra de Altamir
Pu
Cáceres
Tumuja
103
Trujillo
104
Garciaz
Alía
de
uz
Malpartida
de Cáceres
Sierra de Fuentes
La Cumbre
Hergüijuela
Sierra de
Guadalupe
Cañamero
Salor
eda
Torremocha
Sta Cruz
de la Sierra
Castilblanco
Ayuela
Aldea del Cano
Valdefuentes
Zorita
Alcollarín
Ruecas
Valdecaballeros
ro
E X T R E M A D U R A
Alcuéscar
Almoharín
Escurial
Miajadas
Navalvillar de Pela
Gargáligas
Sierra
Roca de la Sierra
La Nava de Santiago
Lácara
Aljucén
Rena
Santa Amalia
Guadiana
Orellana la Vieja
Acedera
Embalse
de Orellana
Garba
Alijucén
Villanueva de la Serena
Embalse
del Zújar
Siruel
iba
Mérida
San Pedro
de Mérida
Don Benito
La Coronada
Embalse de
la Serena
Zarza Capilla
19
Puebla de la
Calzada
Guareña
Ortiga
Campanario
Torremegía
Villagonzalo
Oliva de Mérida
L A   S E R E N A
ra
de Peleas
Emb. de
Alange
Alange
677
San Juan
Quintana de la Serena
Castuera
Cabeza
Solana de
los Barros
Almendralejo
Palomas
Valle
de la Serena
Zalamea de
la Serena
Palomillas
Puebla de la Reina
Higuera de la Serena
Helechal
T I E R R A   D E   B A R R O S
de los Barros
102
Fuente del
Maestre
Ribera del
Fresno
Hornachos
Su de los Argallanes
Monterrubio de
la Serena
Bela
B
A
J
O
Z
Llera
Zújar
Hinojosa
del Duque
L
ra de Feria
imoros
Burguillos del Cerro
Los Santos
de Maimona
Zafra
Peraleda del Zaucejo
Matachel
Villan
del D
Bodión
Usa
Valencia
de las Torres
Retin
La Granjuela
P
Bienvenida
Bienvenida
Berlanga
Granja de
Torrehermosa
Azuaga
Fuente
Obejuna
Peñarroya-
Pueblonue
Bélmez
Valencia
del Ventoso
genal de la Sierra
Fuente
de Cantos
793
Llerena
Sotillo
Villanueva
del Rey
Guad
ra
Segura de León
Montemolín
Viar
Guadalcanal
Sierra del Agua
Sierra de los Santos
Erillas
Butrera
Pallarés
Monesterio
Hamapega
Alanís
896
Villavic
de Cór
uentes
e León
Tentudia
1019
1104
Arroyomolinos
de León
Cala
Embalse
El Pintado
145
San Nicolás
del Puerto
R
Bembézar
de Hinojales
Embalse
de Aracena
S
Santa Ollala
del Cala
I
144
Cazalla
de la Sierra
146
Tiesa
673
Embalse de
Bembézar
racen
Almadén de la Plata

©HarperCollins Cartographic 1997

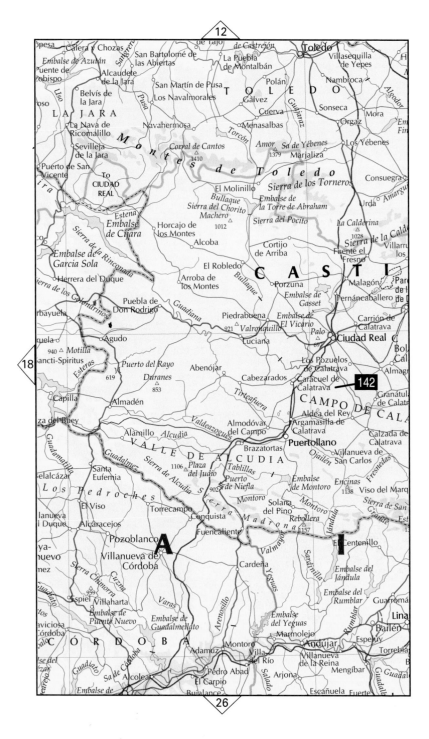

opesa · Calera y Chozas · de Tajo · de Castrejón · Toledo · Villasequilla
de Yepes

Embalse de Azután · San Bartolomé de
las Abiertas · La Puebla
de Montalbán · Nambroca

uente de
obispo · Alcaudete
de la Jara · San Martín de Pusa · Polán

Belvís de
la Jara · Los Navalmorales · Gálvez · Sonseca

oso · LA JARA · La Nava de
Ricomalillo · Cuerva · Orgaz · Mora

Navahermosa · Menasalbas · Torcón

Montes · Corral de Cantos · Amor · Sa de Yébenes · Los Yébenes
Sevilleja
de la Jara · 1410 · 1379 · Marjaliza

Puerto de San
Vicente · *de* · *Toledo* · Consuegra

To
CIUDAD
REAL · El Molinillo · Sierra de los Torneros · Urda · Amargu

Bullaque · Embalse de
la Torre de Abraham

Estena · Sierra del Chorito
Macbero · Sierra del Pocito · La Calderina
1028 · Sierra de la Calde
*Embalse
de Cijara* · Horcajo de
los Montes · 1012 · Villarru
los

Cortijo
de Arriba · Fuente el
Fresno

Alcoba · El Robledo · C A S T I

*Embalse
García Sola* · Arroba de
los Montes · Porzuna · Malagón · Par
de l
Fernáncaballero · de l

Herrera del Duque · Embalse de
Gasset

Puebla de
Don Rodrigo · Guadiana · Piedrabuena · Embalse de
El Vicario · Carrión de
Calatrava

921 · Valronquillo · Palo

rbayuela · Luciana · Ciudad Real · Bol

ruela · 940 · Motilla · Los Pozuelos
de Calatrava · Cal

Sancti-Spíritus · Puerto del Rayo · Abenójar · Cabezarados · Caracuel de
Calatrava · Almagr

619 · *Duranes*
853 · 142 · Granátul
de Calat

Capilla · Almadén · Tirteafuera · CAMPO DE CALA

za del Buey · Aldea del Rey · Calzada de
Calatrava

Alamillo · *Alcudia* · Almodóvar
del Campo · Argamasilla de
Calatrava · Puertollano · Villanueva de
San Carlos

elalcázar · Santa
Eufemia · Guadalmez · 1106 · Plaza
del Judío · Tablillas · Embalse
de Montoro · Encinas
1138 · Viso del Marq
Sierra de San

lanueva
Duque · El Viso · Torrecampo · Puerto
de Niefla · Montoro · Solana
del Pino · Rebollera · El Centenillo

Alcaracejos · Conquista · 1157

ya-
uevo
ez · Pozoblanco · Fuencaliente · Valmayor · Cardeña · Embalse del
Jándula

Villanueva de
Córdoba · Embalse del
Rumblar · Guaromá

Sierra Chiquorra · Varas · Lina

spiel · 959 · Villaharta · Arenosillo · Embalse
del Yeguas · Bailén

aviciosa
órdoba · *Embalse de
Puente Nuevo* · *Embalse de
Guadalmellato* · Marmolejo · Andújar · Espeluy · Torrebla

C Ó R D O B A · Montoro · Villanueva
de la Reina

se del
zar · Adamuz · Villa
del Río · Arjona · Mengíbar

Alcolea · Pedro Abad · Escañuela · Fuerte

El Carpio

Embalse de · Bañance

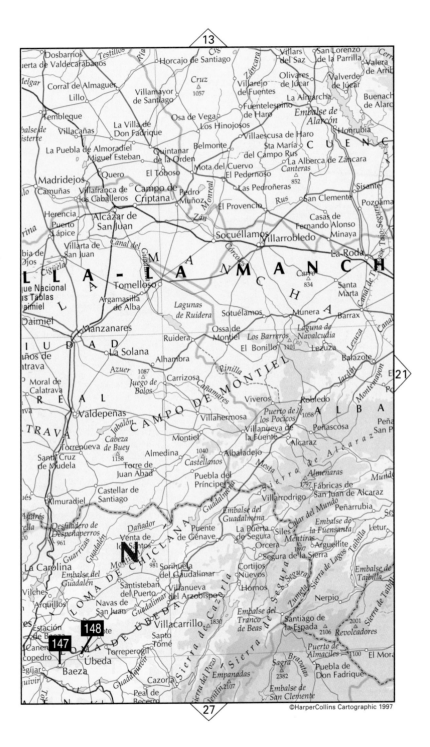

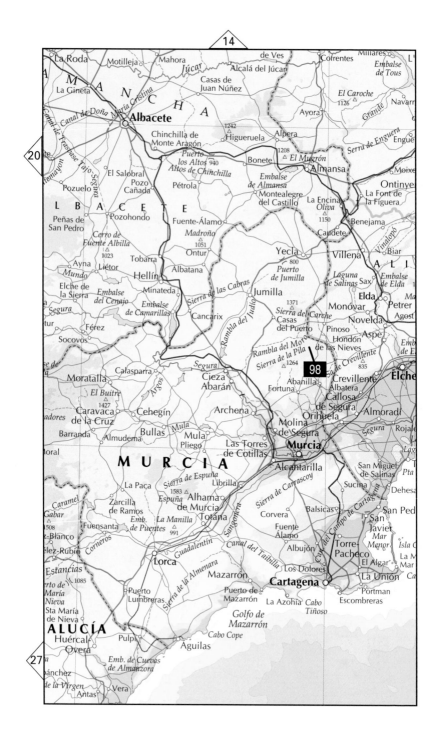

La Roda
Motilleja
Mahora
Júcar
de Ves
Alcalá del Júcar
Cofrentes
Millares
Embalse
de Tous
L'
La Gineta
M
A
N
C
H
A
Casas de
Juan Núñez
El Caroche
1126
Navarr
Canal de Doña María Cristina
Albacete
Chinchilla de
Monte Aragón
1242
Higueruela
Alpera
Ayora
te
Canal de Trasvase Tajo-Segura
El Salobral
Pozo
Cañada
Puerto
los Altos
Altos de Chinchilla
940
Bonete
1208
El Mugrón
Almansa
Moixe
Sierra de Enguera
Engue
Pozuelo
Embalse
de Almansa
Ontinye
L
B
A
C
E
T
E
Peñas de
San Pedro
Pozohondo
Pétrola
Montealegre
del Castillo
La Encina
Oliva
1150
La Font de
la Fíguera
Benejama
Biar
ALI
Cerro de
Fuente Albilla
Fuente-Álamo
Madroño
1051
Candete
Vinalopó
Villena
Ayna
1023
Tobarra
Ontur
Yecla
800
Sax
Embalse
de Elda
Mundo
Liétor
Albatana
Puerto
de Jumilla
Laguna
de Salinas
Elda
Petrer
Elche de
la Sierra
Embalse
del Cenajo
Minateda
Sierra de las Cabras
Jumilla
1371
Monóvar
Novelda
Agost
Ma
Segura
Embalse
de Camarillas
Cancarix
Sierra del Carche
Casas
del Puerto
Pinoso
Hondón
Aspe
Emb
de E
tur
Férez
Rambla del Judío
Sierra de la Pila
Rambla del Moro
de las Nieves
98
de Crevillente
835
Elche
Socovos
Segura
Argos
Cieza
Abarán
Abanilla
Fortuna
Crevillente
Albatera
Callosa
de Segura
de
a
Moratalla
El Buitre
1427
Cehegín
Archena
Orihuela
Almoradí
Rojale
adores
Caravaca
de la Cruz
Barranda
Almudema
Bullas
Mula
Pliego
Molina
de Segura
Seg
Segura
Lag
oral
M U R C I A
La Paca
Sierra de Espuña
1583
Librilla
Las Torres
de Cotillas
Murcia
Alcantarilla
San Miguel
de Salinas
Sucina
Pta
Dehesa
Caramel
Gabar
1508
Zarcilla
de Ramos
Espuña
Alhama
de Murcia
Emb.
de Puentes
La Manilla
991
Totana
Sangonera
Corvera
Sierra de Carrascoy
Balsicas
Campo de Cartagena
San
San Ped
z-Blanco
Fuensanta
Fuente
Álamo
San
Javier
Mar
Menor
Isla G
elez-Rubio
Corneros
Guadalentín
Canal del Taibilla
Albujón
Los Dolores
Torre-
Pacheco
El Algar
La M
Mar
Estancias
Lorca
Mazarrón
Cartagena
La Unión
Ca
1085
to de
María
Nieva
Puerto
Lumbreras
Mazarrón
Sierra de la Almenara
Puerto de
Mazarrón
La Azohía
Cabo
Tiñoso
Portman
Escombreras
Sta María
de Nieva
A L U C Í A
Huércal
Overa
Pulpí
Golfo de
Mazarrón
Cabo Cope
ánchez
de la Virgen
Antas
Emb. de Cuevas
de Almanzora
Vera
Águilas

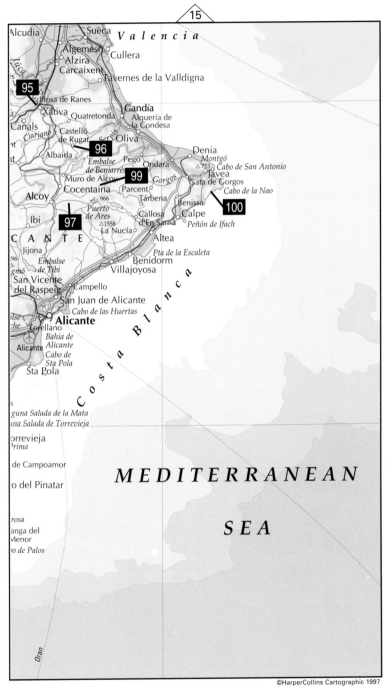

Alcudia Sueca *V a l e n c i a*
Algemesí Cullera
Alzira
Carcaixent
Tavernes de la Valldigna
95
llosa de Ranes
Xàtiva Quatretonda Gandía
Canals Alquería de
Castelló la Condesa
Clariano de Rugat Oliva
Albaida 96
Embalse Pego Denia
de Beniarrés Ondara Montgó
Muro de Alcoy 99 △753 Cabo de San Antonio
Cocentaina Parcent Gorgos Jávea
Alcoy Gata de Gorgos
Tárbena Cabo de la Nao
966 Benissa
Puerto Calpe 100
Ibi 97 de Ares Callosa
△1558 d'En Sarrià Peñón de Ifach
La Nucía
C A N T E Altea
Jijona Pta de la Escaleta
'96 Embalse Benidorm
gin⁰ de Tibi Villajoyosa
San Vicente
del Raspeig Campello
San Juan de Alicante
Cabo de las Huertas
Lorellano
Alicante
Bahia de
Alicante Alicante
Cabo de
Sta Pola
Sta Pola

C o s t a B l a n c a

guna Salada de la Mata
ina Salada de Torrevieja
orrevieja
Prima
de Campoamor
o del Pinatar
rosa
anga del
Menor
o de Palos

M E D I T E R R A N E A N

S E A

Oran

©HarperCollins Cartographic 1997

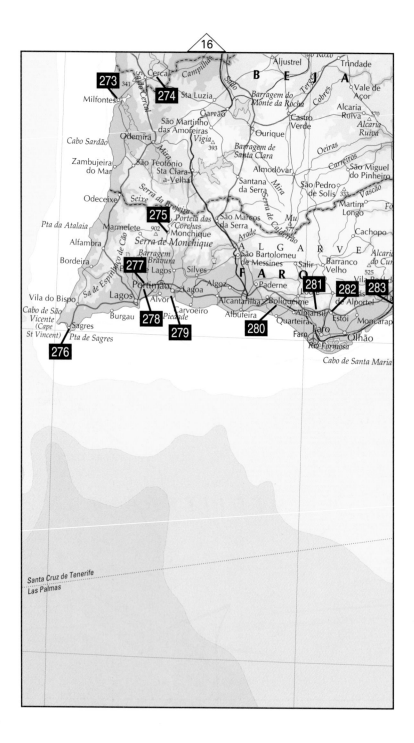

Aljustrel
Roxo
Trindade

B E J A

Cercal
Campilhas
Sado

273 341
Milfontes
274 Sta Luzia

Barragem do
Monte da Rocha
Cobres
Vale do
Açor

Garvão

Castro
Verde
Alcaria
Ruiva 370
Alcaria
Ruiva

São Martinho
das Amoreiras
Vigia
393
Ourique

Cabo Sardão
Odemira
Mira

Oeiras
Carreiros
São Miguel
do Pinheiro

Zambujeira
do Mar
São Teotónio
Sta Clara-
a-Velha
Barragem de
Santa Clara
Almodôvar

Santana
da Serra
São Pedro
de Solis 333
Mira
Vascão

Odeceixe
Seixe
Serra da Brejeira

Martim
Longo
Fo

Pta da Atalaia
Marmelete
Portela das
Corchas
275
São Marcos
da Serra
Mu
571
Serra de Caldeirão
Cachopo

Alfambra
Serra de Monchique
902
Monchique
Arade
Alcaria
do Cur

Bordeira
Barragem
Bravura
277
São Bartolomeu
de Messines
Salir
Barranco
Velho
525

Vila do Bispo
Sa de Espinhaço de Cão
Lagos
278
Alvor
Portimão
Lagoa
Algoz
Paderne
Alcantarilha
Boliqueime
281
282
283
de Alportel
Vila R

Cabo de São
Vicente
(Cape
St Vincent)
Sagres
Pta de Sagres
276
Burgau
Piedade
279
Tavoeiro
Albufeira
280
Quarteira
Faro
Estói
Moncarap
Olhão
Rio Formosa

Cabo de Santa Maria

Santa Cruz de Tenerife
Las Palmas

23

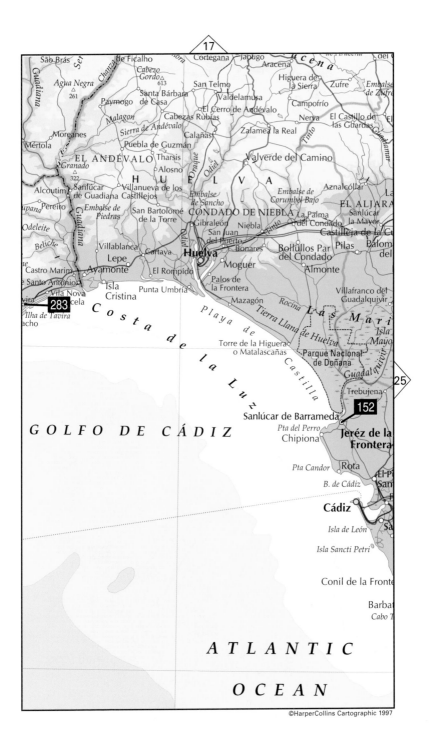

São Brás
Agua Negra
261
Cabezo Gordo
613
de Ficalho
Cortegana
Jabugo
Aracena
Higuera de la Sierra
Zufre
Embalse de Zufre
Paymogo
Santa Bárbara de Casa
San Telmo
Valdelamusa
Campofrío
Malagon
Cabezas Rubias
El Cerro de Andévalo
Nerva
El Castillo de las Guardas
Moreanes
Sierra de Andévalo
Calañas
Zalamea la Real
Mértola
Granado
322
EL ANDÉVALO
Tharsis
Alosno
Valverde del Camino
Alcoutim
Sanlúcar de Guadiana
Villanueva de los Castillejos
HUELVA
Embalse de Corumbel Bajo
Aznalcóllar
EL ALJARA
Pereito
Embalse de Piedras
San Bartolomé de la Torre
CONDADO DE NIEBLA
La Palma del Condado
Sanlúcar la Mayor
Odeleite
Beliche
Villablanca
Cartaya
Gibraleón
Niebla
Castilleja de la C
Castro Marim
Lepe
Huelva
San Juan del Puerto
Bonares
Bollullos Par del Condado
Pilas
Palom
del
Santo António
Ayamonte
El Rompido
Moguer
Almonte
Vila Nova cela
Isla Cristina
Punta Umbria
Palos de la Frontera
Villafranco del Guadalquivir
Ilha de Tavira acho
Mazagón
Rocina
Las Mari
Isla Mayo
Playa de la
Tierra Llana de Huelva
Costa de la Luz
Torre de la Higuera o Matalascañas
Parque Nacional de Doñana
Guadalquivir
25
Trebujena
Castilla
152
Sanlúcar de Barrameda
Pta del Perro
GOLFO DE CÁDIZ
Chipiona
Jeréz de la Frontera
Pta Candor
Rota
B. de Cádiz
El-P San
Cádiz
F
Isla de León
Sa
Isla Sancti Petri
Conil de la Fronte
Barbat
Cabo T
ATLANTIC
OCEAN

283

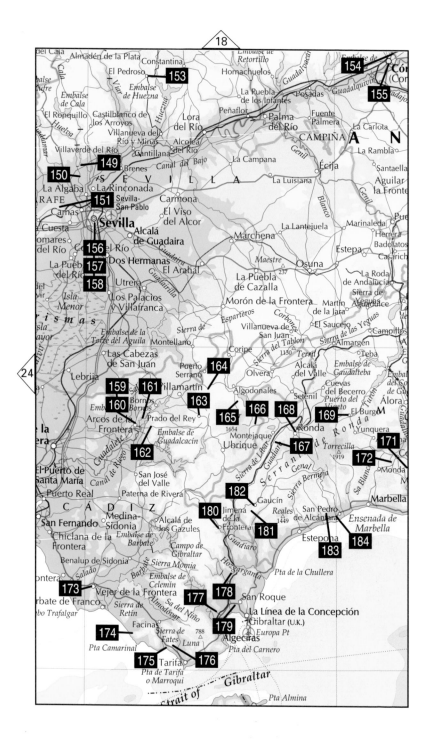

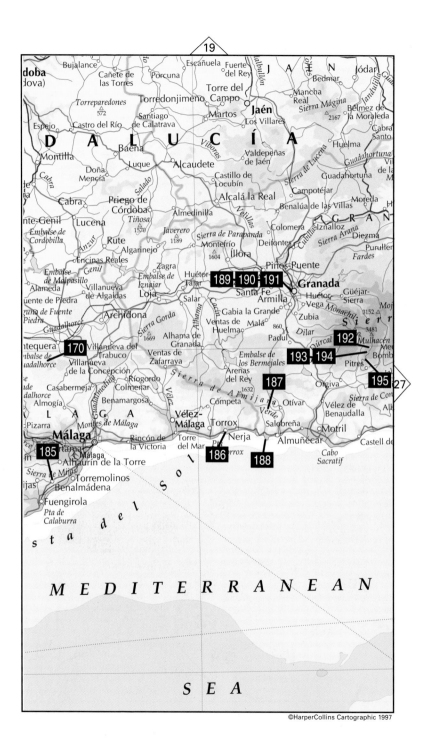

©HarperCollins Cartographic 1997

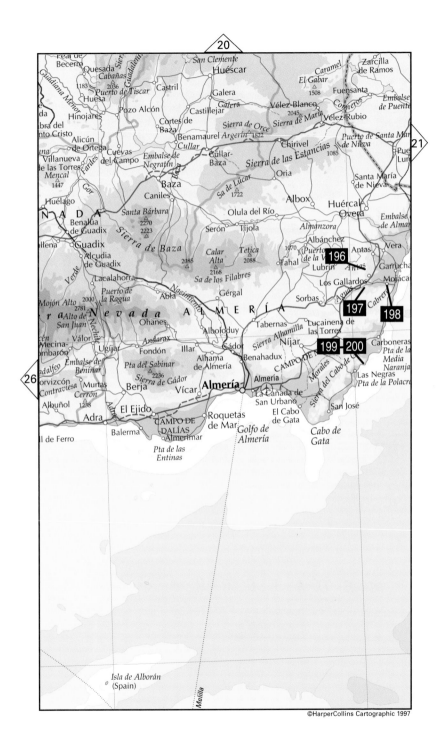

*"For centuries there were miracles
and apparitions to be seen at every
turn of the road to Santiago; you
could meet angels, beggars, kings
and status-seekers – the
Plantagenet King Edward I on
horse-back, St. Francis of Assisi
walking barefoot and a certain
Flemish wayfarer who is reputed to
have carried a mermaid around
with him in a tub."*

FREDERIC V. GRUNFELD - *Wild Spain:
A Traveler's and Naturalist's Guide*

Galicia

Pazo de Souto

Sisamo
15106
Carballo
La Coruña

Tel: (9)81 756065
Fax: (9)81 756191

Management: Carlos Taibo Pombo

We are proud to have such places in our guide. It is hard to find more charming or kindly hosts. Carlos and his father José have recently opened their fine old Galician manor house to guests. It has stood here for 300 years near the rugged north coast, lost among fields of maize. The vast sitting room has a lareira (inglenook) fireplace, exposed stonework and heavy old beams. The dining area, similar in design, has tables up on a gallery, all subtly lit. Outside is a large garden and from the terrace there are fine views across the surrounding farmland. A splendid granite staircase leads up to the guestrooms — we preferred those on the first floor to the smaller attic ones. It is all spick and span, the furnishings are new and lots of locals were dining there when we visited (fresh fish daily from the nearby fishing village of Malpica). If you fancy cooking for yourself, you can use the guest kitchen for a small supplement. All this and the wild beauty of the north coast besides. Carlos is most helpful and has impeccable English.

Rooms: 5 doubles with bath & wc + 5 doubles with jacuzzi.
Price: D/Tw with bath 7500-10000 Pts; D/Tw with jacuzzi 9000-11500 Pts.
Breakfast: included.
Meals: Lunch/Dinner 1500-1750 Pts (M); 3000-3500 Pts (C).
Closed: Never.

How to get there: From La Coruña C552 (or A9) to Carballo. From here take road towards Malpica, then hotel is signposted.

1

Map No: 1

Pousada Rosalía

Calle Los Angeles
15280
Brión
La Coruña

Tel: (9)81 887580
Fax: (9)81 887557

Management: Andrés Martínez

Named after Galicia's most famous poetess, many of whose verses were penned in this area, Pousada Rosalía was opened for 'Holy Year' in 1993. Since then it has established its reputation as a reliable staging-post. The hotel is basically an old granite farm-house with a modern extension housing most of the bedrooms. You enter by a rather grand wrought-iron gate then through to the patio which is bounded by a series of intimate eating areas — very snug for dining in the colder months. Meals are served in the courtyard in summer. The food — lots of regional fare — is certainly good value and there are often barbecues. Pride of place in the restaurant goes to the ubiquitous lareira, the vast inglenook fireplace typical of old Galician farm-houses. Most of the rooms are smallish, with modern prints, wooden or tiled floors and stained pine furniture; the bathrooms are roomy, however. The décor is modern, generally greens and pinks. We particularly liked the few rooms in the old part of the building. Horse-riding can easily be arranged.

Rooms: 31 with bath & wc.
Price: D/Tw 3900-6600 Ps.
Breakfast: 350 Pts.
Meals: Lunch/Dinner 1200-1500 Pts (M),
3000-3500 Pts (C).
Closed: Never.

How to get there: From Santiago N650 towards Pontevedra; before leaving city, right on C543 towards Noía. After going through Brión, hotel signposted to left.

Hostal Hogar San Francisco

Campillo del Convento San Francisco 3
15705
Santiago de Compostela
La Coruña

Tel: (9)81 572564
Fax: (9)81 571916

Management: Aniceto Gómez Nogueira

Few hostelries can be quite as appropriate as the San Francisco. This old monastery, parts of it nearly five centuries old, is very near the cathedral and the beautiful medieval heart of Santiago. It may not be quite as grand as THE hotel on the Obradoiro square but its cloister (now a lovely meditative space with palm trees, roses and fountain), its very fine old refectory and the almost monastic peace that envelops you once you pass the gate are powerful enticements to stay. The guestrooms, up a couple of good old granite staircases, are mostly at the front of the building; you can see the cathedral from some. They are simply furnished; religious prints adorn the walls and the floors are marble. So close to a high point of religious fervour, their rather austere decor feels right; you can forgive the size of the singles: they were once monks' cells. It would be a fitting privilege to dine in the cavernous refectory with both Santiago and San Francisco looking on from their respective altars. The menu is a mix of Galician and traditional Spanish with fish a speciality.

Rooms: 70 with bath & wc.
Price: S 6000-6900 Pts; D/Tw 7900-9700 Pts; Tr 9700-11000 Pts; Ste 14500-15500 Pts.
Breakfast: 550 Pts.
Meals: Lunch/Dinner 1900 Pts (M).
Closed: Never.

How to get there: Take 'Salida Norte' from motorway. Follow signs to centre and cathedral. Hotel next to Monumento de San Francisco, close to the Faculty of Medicine.

Casa Grande de Cornide

Cornide (Calo-Teo)
15886
Santiago de Compostela
La Coruña

Tel: (9)81 805599
Fax: (9)81 805751

Management: María Jesús Castro Rivas

This very special B&B just 15 minutes' drive from Santiago is surrounded by exuberant Galician green. Casa Grande is like a good claret — refined, select, for lovers of the real thing and worth paying a bit more for. José Ramón and María Jesús are both lecturers (he writes books, including one on the Way to Compostela) and a love of culture is evident throughout their home. It has a large collection of modern Galician paintings, a huge library and decoration that is a spicy cocktail of old and new: exposed granite, designer lamps, wooden ceilings, and — all over — the paintings. A place to come to read, to paint (!) in the beautiful mature garden or to ride out from the house (four bikes free of charge for guests). The studied décor of the lounges and library is also to be found in the bedrooms and suites, some of which are housed in a separate building. They have all mod cons and the same mix of modern and old furnishing; there are books, ornaments, more paintings and little details, like handmade tiles in the bathrooms, that make the house special.

Rooms: 2 with bath & wc, 1 with shower & wc; 4 suites.
Price: D/Tw 10000-12000 Pts, Ste 12000-14000 Pts.
Breakfast: 950 Pts.
Meals: None.
Closed: 15 Dec-10 Jan.

How to get there: From Santiago N550 towards Pontevedra. After 7km, just after Cepsa petrol station, turn left and follow signs.

Pazo de Sedor

Castañeda
15819
Arzua
La Coruña

Tel: (9)81 193248
Fax: (9)81 193248

Management: María Jesús Saavedra Pereira

One of a number of Galician pazos to open to guests, Pazo de Sedor is indeed a grand place to stay on the road to or from Santiago — or anywhere, come to that. It is an imposing, 18th-century country house surrounded by wooded hillsides and fields of maize and grazing cattle. Inside, you get a definite sense of its aristocratic past: the rooms are big and a wide wooden ballustraded staircase joins the two floors. The building's most memorable feature is the enormous open fireplace (lareira) that spans one whole wall of the dining room with a bread-oven at each side. The bedrooms are a real delight; they are high-ceilinged, decorated with family antiques, have embroidered bedcovers and curtains and shining wooden floors; half of them have their own balcony. One room has beautiful Deco beds; all are big enough to take an extra bed when families are staying. Meals are as authentic as the house: Galician with many of the veg home-grown and a chance to try the local cheese and cold sausage. ¡Fabuloso!

Rooms: 6 with bath & wc.
Price: Tw 9000 Pts inc VAT.
Breakfast: 500 Pts.
Meals: Lunch/Dinner 2000 Pts (M).
Closed: Never.

How to get there: From Lugo N540 then N547 towards Santiago de Compostela. At km57 right to Pazo.

5

Map No: 1

Hotel San Marcus

Plaza Porta Sobrado de los Monjes
15132
Sobrado
La Coruña

Tel: (9)81 787527

Management: Manuel and Elisa Carreira

Manuel's welcome is effusive... and genuine. He loves Spain but after years in London loves the English and their language as dearly! He has now come home to create his shangri-la beside the pilgrim's path to Santiago and opposite one of the oldest Cistercian monasteries in Europe. It is a smart, modern hotel of human proportions. Manuel treats every guest with the personal attention that he considers basic to the art of hostelry. His rooms are like wedding cakes — some of you might leave the icing but few would fail to appreciate the filling. Every detail counted when he was designing and furnishing the hotel. Furniture was specially made, bathrooms were carpeted and you may recognise some of the fabrics as Laura Ashley. Room 16 is particularly grand with its great canopied bed. Four rooms have a sitting area in the covered gallery. Outside is a carefully-planted garden. But the cherry on this cake is the fabulous prize-winning food — lots of Galician specialities with fish to the fore. Those map-book people rate it and so do we.

Rooms: 12 with bath or shower & wc.
Price: S 3000-4000 Pts; Normal D/Tw 5000-6000 Pts; water bed 7000-10000 Pts.
Breakfast: 475 Pts.
Meals: Lunch/Dinner 2400 Pts (M); approx. 4000 Pts (C).
Closed: Jan.

How to get there: From Lugo NVI west towards La Coruña. At La Castellana, left onto LC231 to Tejeiro and then Sobrado. Hotel opposite monastery.

Hotel Pazo El Revel

36990
Villalonga
Pontevedra

Tel: (9)86 743000
Fax: (9)86 743390

Management: Luis Ansorena Garret

The caring eye of Don Luis Ansorena Garret, owner of this lovely old pazo, watches over the Revel. This was one of the first palace-style hotels to open in Galicia and its reputation has grown with the years. The stately façade and huge gates that greet you on arrival whet the appetite; and the surrounding gardens are a feast in themselves with exuberant stands of hydrangea. The palm, plum and citrus trees add an exotic touch and there's a bracing whiff of sea air penetrating this rich greenery. You enter the house via a grand entrance hall; here, as throughout the Revel, the granite, the beams and the tiled floors are warmly authentic. Sitting and dining rooms are large and airy and there is an attractive terrace with wicker furniture. The bedrooms are properly equipped, have tiled floors and 'rustic' furnishing, and are good value. Both staff and owner will bend over backwards to look after you. There is bar service here and plenty of good seafood restaurants just a short drive away. But book ahead.

Rooms: 22 with bath & wc.
Price: S 6650-7650 Pts; Tw 10650-11650 Pts.
Breakfast: Buffet included.
Meals: None.
Closed: Oct-May.

How to get there: From Pontevedra, Vía Rápida to Sanxenxo. There, towards A Grove and A Toxa. Through Villalonga; at end of village turn left following signs to El Revel.

Map No: 1

Residencia Galicia

Anceu-Ramis
36829
Pontecaldelas
Pontevedra

Tel: (9)86 767231
Fax: (9)86 767231

Management: Angela Bareuther

Reaching the Residencia Galicia is a real adventure; along a narrow road, through the tiniest of hamlets, then on down... to the very end. One understands why Angela Bareuther chose this spot for a country guest house and pottery. The 19th-century buildings have been restored to give seven rooms with their own cooking facilities and a further four that share a kitchen. As you might expect, their decoration has a large ceramic element! All have views, some out across forest, others down to the nearby Eiras reservoir. There is a huge guest sitting room with its own bar area as well as a terrace, a large garden and a swimming pool. Angela has clearly taken Galicia to her heart and after some 14 years here she knows the area and its people well and will happily direct you to its loveliest spots. Between October and April she gives weekend pottery courses. If you don't fancy preparing your own food there is a fine old tavern nearby for a special meal out. All of this in the most memorable of rural settings — with good fishing.

Rooms: 11 'apartment-rooms' with shower, wc & cooking facilities.
Price: S 5000-5500 Pts; D/Tw 6000-7000 Pts inc VAT.
Breakfast: Self-catering.
Meals: Self-catering.
Closed: Never.

How to get there: From Pontevedra, C531 towards La Cañiza; through Puente Caldelas. 4km beyond, right just before Caritel and follow signs.

Pazo Viña Mein

Lugar de Mein-San Clodio
32420
Leiro
Orense

Tel: (9)88 488400/(9)08 887059
Fax: (9)88 488400

Management: Javier Alen

Here, far off the beaten track in the beautiful Ribeiro vineyards, you are disturbed only by the silence. The guestrooms are among the largest we saw in Spain, with beds and bathrooms to scale, terracotta floors, antique furniture and carefully chosen fabrics and prints. One has a double door onto the terrace where you can sit and soak up the quiet beauty. The living room and dining area work as well as the guestrooms. Wood and granite complement one another; in the enormous lounge there is a traditional lareira, that huge fireplace large enough to seat a whole family on its side benches during cold winters. Nowadays central heating means you won't need to, but you can expect a fire in the hearth. There is a good selection of literature — Javier Alen also owns a bookshop in Madrid. In the warmer months you can dine out on the terrace; with regional dishes and wines from the state-of-the-art bodega next to the pazo. Bikes are there for exploring the surrounding green. This is good value, and there is nothing to explode your lullaby.

Rooms: 3 with bath & wc + 2 two-bedroom apartments.
Price: D/Tw 7000 Pts; Apt10000 Pts.
Breakfast: Included.
Meals: Lunch/Dinner 3000 Pts (M); 3000-4000 Pts (C) on request, minimum 4 persons.
Closed: Never.

How to get there: From Orense N120 towards Vigo. At km596 right towards Carballiño. Continue 10km then right towards San Clodio then on to Viña Mein.

Map No: 1

Finca Río Miño

Las Eiras
36760
O. Rosal
Pontevedra

Tel: (9)86 621107
Fax: (9)86 621107
E-Mail: bfe2262@mail.telepac.pt

Management: Tony & Shirley Taylor-Dawes

The green hills and rivers of northern Portugal and Galicia are dear to Tony and Shirley Taylor-Dawes. They know the people, villages, food and wines like few others; they even write books about them. Perhaps their passion for fine wine led them to this 250-year-old farm with its terraced vineyards and bodega carved in solid rock. And what a position, up on the bank of the Miño with views across to Portugal. In the vast garden are two pine-clad lodges built by Tony. They are simply furnished, have their own small kitchen (although breakfast can be provided), lounge and two bedrooms. Best of all are the terraces which have the same wide view over the river. In the main house there is another room with bathroom, a sitting room with pretty Portuguese furniture, a breakfast room and an unforgettable terrace with a rambling passion fruit providing extra shade. Don't miss dinner where port is king, whether in sauces for meat or in puddings like 'sozzled apricots' or 'Duero lemon haze'. There's a pool-with-a-view, or river beaches at the end of the farm track and the Atlantic just five miles away.

Rooms: 2 lodges for 2-4 with bath & wc.
Price: Lodge for two 9500 Pts; Lodge for three/four 11500 Pts. Book early.
Breakfast: From 500 Pts.
Meals: Gourmet Dinner from 4000 Pts incl. port tastings (M).
Closed: Never.

How to get there: From Vigo N550 to Tuy. La Guardia exit then C550 for about 15km. Just after km190, left at 'Restaurante Eiras' sign, over next crossroads, signposted after 1.5km to left.

Hotel Convento de San Benito

Plaza de San Benito s/n
36780
La Guardia
Pontevedra

Tel: (9)86 611166
Fax: (9)86 611517

Management: Antonia Baz Gómez

Ten years ago, San Benito was still occupied by Benedictine nuns. To stay here now you need take no vows, although you might feel inspired by the cloistered patio to retire from the world. It is a beautiful building whose full and sensitive restoration by young, dynamic owners has produced one of Spain's most special small hotels. The decoration is perfect: stained-glass windows, old benches and trunks, religious paintings, an old confessional.... even some of the Order's furniture. The crockery bears the monastery's coat of arms, there are cut flowers and, in the grand old entrance, there may be (taped) Gregorian chant. The guestrooms, in a new annexe, have had the same care lavished upon them. They are large and light with attractive wooden furniture and all mod cons; some look out over the harbour (203 for example), some have a small terrace. (This is hardly a noisy spot but they are double glazed to guarantee a peaceful night). The two charming hosts, a pretty fishing harbour and generous pricing are a recipe for a memorable stay.

Rooms: 24 with bath & wc.
Price: S 4100-5500 Pts; D/Tw 5900-8400 Pts; Ste 8000-11200 Pts.
Breakfast: 550 Pts.
Meals: Lunch/Dinner 2200 Pts (M), 3500 Pts (C)
Closed: Never.

How to get there: From Vigo C550 to Bayona and La Guardia. There, follow signs to port — hotel on left on the way down.

Pazo de Villabad

Villabad
27122
Castroverde
Lugo

Tel: (9)82 313000
Fax: (9)82 312063

Management: Luis Abraira and Teresa Arana

Opened in 1994 in a delectably quiet corner of Galicia, the Pazo de Villabad is the kind of place where you sigh and say "If only there were more like this...". You are welcomed by mother and son into a very grand family home — NOT a hotel. All the furniture and paintings that decorate bedrooms, sitting and dining rooms are family heirlooms. There are stacks of lovely pieces in the big, airy bedrooms — old brass or walnut beds, dressers and old tables; in the corridors there are statues, a chaise longue and family portraits above the grandest of stairwells. Endearingly, the rooms are named after beloved family members — Aunt Leonor, Great-grandmama. But most seductive is the lovely breakfast room with a gallery and an enormous lareira (inglenook) fireplace where you can feast on cheeses, home-made cakes and jams and pots of good coffee. The heart and soul of it all is Señora Teresa Abraira, a hugely entertaining and sprightly lady, so determined to get it right that she studied rural tourism in France before opening her own house. Her creation is magnífico.

Rooms: 6 with bath & wc.
Price: S 10000 Pts; D/Tw 12000 Pts.
Breakfast: 900 Pts.
Meals: Dinner on request — 2500 Pts excl. wine.
Closed: Never.

How to get there: From Lugo NVI towards Madrid. At km484.4 left to Castroverde. There C630 towards Fonsagrada and after 1km left to Villabad. House next to church.

Pousada Torre de Vilariño

Fión 47
27548
Escairón/O Saviñao
Lugo

Tel: (9)82 452260
Fax: (9)82 452260

Management: Antonio García Beltrán

Many monasteries were founded here in the Middle Ages beside the Sil and Miño rivers. It is still an area for rest and contemplation but the hostelries open to would-be converts no longer require a hair shirt. It is fitting that this lovely ivy-clad 18th-century building should now be an inn since one stood on this site 600 years ago. The organic warmth of wood is everywhere in the nine guestrooms. There are dried flowers and religious images to remind us we are in the land of Santiago. In the mature garden Antonio Beltrán points with pride to what he believes to be the oldest box tree in Europe. Most of all we liked the dining areas, two inside the pousada and another in a converted outbuilding decorated with a fine collection of old farm implements. Thick cocido stew, squid and bacalao are among the great regional dishes served here, followed by home-made puddings, all reinforced by wines from the bodega; they are proud of the recently-created local A.C.'Ribeira Sacra'. Bikes can be hired for visits to monasteries, churches or pazos.

Rooms: 9 with bath & wc.
Price: D/Tw 5000-6000 Pts inc. VAT.
Breakfast: Full 400 Pts.
Meals: Lunch/Dinner 1500 Pts (M).
Closed: Never.

How to get there: From Orense N120 towards Monforte. At km535 left towards Ferreira & soon right towards Escairón. Continue through hamlets until Vilariño is indicated left, then follow signs.

13

Casa Grande de Trives

Calle Marqués de Trives 17
32780
Poboa de Trives
Orense

Tel: (9)88 332066
Fax: (9)88 332066

Management: Adelaida Alvarez Martínez and Alfredo Araujo Alvarez

Sometimes grand family homes converted to receive guests cease to be either 'grand' or 'family'. Not so Trives; here the balance between caring for you and respecting your intimacy is just right. This noble old village house (it has its own chapel) was one of the first in Galicia to open to guests. Like good claret it has improved with time. The rooms are in a separate wing of the main building, big and elegantly uncluttered with lovely wooden floors and the best of mattresses. There is a sitting room with books where you can have a quiet drink, and a truly enchanting garden beyond for the warmer months. Breakfast is taken in the quite unforgettable dining room; here the richness of the furnishings, the cut flowers and the classical music vie with the grand buffet breakfast, a real feast. There are home-made cakes, fruit, big pots of coffee, croissants... it all makes its way up from the kitchen via the dumb waiter. Lovely china adds to the elegance of the meal. A marvellous place and a most gracious welcome by mother and son; Grand Cru Galicia!

Rooms: 7 with bath & wc.
Price: S 6200 Pts; D/Tw 7700 Pts; Tr 9200 Pts.
Breakfast: Buffet 750.
Meals: None.
Closed: Never.

How to get there: From Orense take C536 to Castro Caldelas. There, right towards Puebla de Trives. House in centre of village on right.

"From my first visit, simply being in Spain has always occasioned in me a kind of joy, a physical tingle which comes from a whole crop of elements: its light, its landscape and, most of all, its human rhythm, a manner of being that graces the place."

ALASTAIR REID - *Whereabouts: Notes on Being a Foreigner*

North Spain

Hotel Rural Casa Pedro

33776
Santa Eulalia de Oscos
Asturias

Tel: (9)8 5626097
Fax: (9)8 5626078

Management: María del Mar Fernández López and Pedro Martínez Rodríguez

The Oscos are a group of high mountain villages in western Asturias that have only recently attracted walkers in search of new pastures. It is a lovely, deepest green land of gorse, heather, rushing streams and long views. In one of the area's more attractive villages, the Casa Pedro is just the place from which to explore. Modern it may be but this stone and slate house blends well with the village architecture, built as it is with the traditional local building materials. The hotel sits high up above the road and has wonderful views. The young owners greeted us with genuine friendliness and we feel the rooms are worth every last peseta. They are medium-sized with smart, walnut furniture and good bathrooms; those at the front have the best views but all look out to the green beyond. The food is good, traditional fare (try the hake in cider) and eating here won't break the bank. A small hotel that, like its owners, is keen to please. There are wonderful walks straight out from the village and bikes available at the hotel.

Rooms: 6 with bath or shower & wc.
Price: D/Tw 5000-6500.
Breakfast: 400-600.
Meals: Lunch/Dinner 1200(M), 2000-2500(C).
Closed: Never.

How to get there: From Oviedo A66/A8 to Aviles then N632/634 along coast to Vegadeo. Here AS11 to Puerto de la Garganta; right at top to Santa Eulalia. Hotel in centre of village.

15

Hotel La Marquesita

Calle Principal
33654
San Martín de Oscos
Asturias

Tel: (9)8 5626002
Fax: (9)8 5626002

Management: María del Carmen Gutiérrez Mosqueira

Your very welcoming hosts are passionate about their area, its history, archeology and ravishing natural beauty. Few can know it better than they (her son is a mountain guide) and they ensure you get the utmost out of your visit. The hotel is small, unpretentious, utterly authentic. After difficult times during the Asturian depression of the last decades, the building was renovated and returned to its original purpose of receiving guests (hospedería) in 1994. The restaurant is a lovely room with slate details and a fine old grandfather clock. It has the reputation locally of being one of the very best places to eat. Three of the bedrooms look onto the street, three onto the garden. They are small, impeccably clean, with simple wooden furniture (the beds were in the family before they opened the hotel), lithographs by the owner and nice touches such as fresh apples (this is Asturias) and a few flowers. Such simple genuine hospitality will make your heart sing long after you leave. (Above is a photograph of a typical Oscos farmhouse. The small photo shows the hotel.)

Rooms: 6 with bath & wc.
Price: D/Tw 5000-7000 Pts.
Breakfast: 350 Pts.
Meals: Lunch/Dinner 1500 Pts (M).
Closed: Never.

How to get there: From Gijón A8, N632, N634 along coast to Vegadeo. There AS11 to Puerto de la Garganta and then AS13 through Villanueva de Oscos and on to San Martín de Oscos.

La Corte
33843
Villar de Vildas
Somiedo
Asturias

Tel: (9)8 5763131

Management: Adriano
Berdasco Fernández

Villar de Vildas is a tiny hamlet, literally at the very end of the road. At the western flank of the Somiedo park — where some of the last bears in Europe roam free — you could find no sweeter place from which to discover some of the many beautiful walks of the Pigüeña valley. Your inn is a 19th-century farm-house of wood and stone, carefully reconverted by Adriano to create a small guesthouse and restaurant. You enter by a small courtyard and up old stone steps to a handsome wood-floored and ceilinged guest lounge. There's a handsome hearth, plus books and a galleried balcony that catches the afternoon light. A narrow wooden spiral staircase brings you up to your rooms; ask Adriano for a hand getting cases up. There are only five rooms (there's also an apartment next door) and they vary in size; two have dormer windows looking to the stars and peaks, all have good bathrooms and comfy beds. There are durries, pine furniture; all of it sparkling clean. The restaurant is just as welcoming; low-ceilinged, beamed and with basket lamps. Expect to meet the locals who come for the Asturian cooking — or just a drink. If you like the Alps, but think that they are over-walked, this is for you.

Rooms: 5 with bath & wc + 1 apartment.
Price: D/Tw 6500 Pts; Apt 10000 Pts inc. VAT.
Breakfast: 450 Pts.
Meals: Lunch/Dinner 1350 Pts (M); 2000 Pts (C).
Closed: Jan.

How to get there: From Oviedo take N634 west. Just before Cornellana left on AS15 to Puente de San Martín. Here AS227 south to Aguasmestas. Here, right to Pigüeña and climb on up via Cores to Villar de Vildas.

Hotel Casa del Busto

Plaza del Rey Don Silo 11
33120
Pravia
Asturias

Tel: (9)8 5822771
Fax: (9)8 5822772

Management: Alberto Mencos Valdés, Jesús Ranera Solano

This very fine old nobleman's mansion, which once belonged to the famous liberal politician Jovellanos, was restored and converted three years ago into a small hotel by its two sophisticated young owners. They spent years doing it and now run courses in furniture restoration — many of their lovely pieces come from their own workshop. Ceilings are high, floors are rustically tiled or wooden, the staircase is marble and, most unusual, some walls are original tabique (wattle and daub). Some doors have warm-coloured ragged paintwork, there are tapestries, sculptures and chandeliers and, despite so much grandness, a relaxed atmosphere. The dining area is in the delightful interior courtyard and the guestrooms give onto the gallery above, each room with its own special touch (the suite has a jacuzzi too). The decoration is a triumph of nobility and simplicity. The owners will help you organise your visits, even occasionally go with you, and they sometimes hold 'gastronomic days'. A high-class yet friendly place to stay.

Rooms: 11 twins with bath & wc + 1 suite.
Price: Tw 6890-9010 Pts; Ste 8360-11010 Pts.
Breakfast: 500 Pts; English breakfast also served.
Meals: 1500 Pts (M), 3000 Pts (C).
Closed: Never.

How to get there: From Oviedo, N634 to Grado. There take AS237 to Pravia. In village centre.

Hotel Casa España

Plaza Carlos I
33300
Villaviciosa
Asturias

Tel: (9)8 5892030/5892682
Fax: (9)8 5892682

Management: María José Lorda

When rich emigrants came home after working in Central and South America many of them built grand houses with their earnings — these are the Casas de Indianos that you stumble across in far-flung corners of green Asturias. Casa España is one of them. It catches the eye with its display of colonial wealth in arched stone doorways, balconies and projecting eaves. It stands at the heart of the busy little town of Villaviciosa, looking out onto the main square, and was opened for paying guests in 1995. The rooms are on two floors, reached by the wide central staircase. They are mostly large, high-ceilinged and have lovely wooden floors. The furniture is nearly all made of wood, too; many of the pieces are original, period antiques and there are original oils in some of the rooms. Bathrooms are big, all with full-length baths. The bar/restaurant downstairs is lively throughout the day; this is where (continental) breakfasts are served as well as snacks at other times. Although there is no restaurant there are lots to choose from close by.

Rooms: 12 with bath & wc + 2 suites.
Price: D/Tw 6500-8500 Pts; Ste 8500-10500 Pts. In Aug min stay 6 days.
Breakfast: 600 Pts.
Meals: Snacks and light meals in hotel bar.
Closed: Never.

How to get there: From Santander A67/N634 towards Oviedo. Just after Infiesto (about 40km before Oviedo) right on AS255 to Villaviciosa. In centre of town.

La Quintana de la Foncalada

Argüero
33314
Villaviciosa
Asturias

Tel: (9)8 5876365
Fax: (9)8 5876365

Management: Severino García and Danièle Schmid

This honeysuckle-clad farm-house at the heart of the coastal mariña area of Asturias is down to earth and delightful. Severino and Danièle believe that on a country holiday you should learn about its people and traditions, so they encourage you to try potting (potters worked here in the 18th century) and help with the Asturian ponies or the organic veg patch. Nearly everything is home produced: honey, cheese, juices and jams. The inside of the house is much as you would expect from such people, with light, cheerful and uncluttered bedrooms (smallish bathrooms) and table lamps and other things made by Severino himself. You are welcome to make yourself hot drinks in the large kitchen. Upstairs there is a guest lounge with wicker furniture and masses of information on walks and visits. Severino, who loves his land and people, will happily advise you on the best beaches (and there are some lovely ones), where to eat and the best excursions from La Quintana by bike or pony. A perfect place for a family holiday.

Rooms: 4 with bath & wc + 2 suites with bath & wc.
Price: D/Tw 5000 Pts; Ste 9000 Pts .
Breakfast: 400 Pts.
Meals: Dinner 1500 Pts (M) — low season only.
Closed: Never.

How to get there: From Gijón N632 towards Santander. At Venta de las Ranas left onto AS256 towards Tazones. After 5km, in Argüero, Foncalada is signposted.

Map No: 3

20

El Correntiu

Ma Luisa Bravo Torano
Sardalla, 42
33560
Ribadesella, Asturias

Tel: (98) 5861436
Fax: (98) 5861436

A traditional Asturian house on nine acres of kitchen garden with fruit trees and centuries-old cork trees. A small stream runs through the grounds; escorentia means 'place that collects rain water'. Old farm buildings have been converted into self-contained units, including two old grain silos now incorporated into a charming apartment for two or three. All the conversions are exquisite: elegantly simple, almost Scandinavian in their crisp use of wood, plain colours, discreet lighting and space. Each unit has its own kitchen garden (really) from which you may pick to your heart's content. One has a sitting-room and fireplace; all have books, games, sheets and towels ... everything you might need. Ribadesella is a fishing village at the mouth of the river Sella, with a magnificent beach.

Rooms: Two cottages: one with 2 rooms and 2 bathrooms; one with double bedroom, sofabed and bathroom. House (for 4/5) 9000-11000 Pts; house (for 2/3) 7000-9000 Pts.
Breakfast: None.
Meals: None.
Closed: Never.

How to get there: From Ribadesella head for Gijón on N632. After bridge turn left on the local road signed 'Cuevas-Sardalla'. From here it is 2km to El Correntiu.

Map No: 3

Casa Ana

Comedor de Aldea-Alojamiento
Carretera Nacional 632 KM15
33344
Cerracín-Caravía, Asturias

Tel: (9)8 5853010

Management: Rafael Guardiola Blanco

Turn off the busy coast road, follow a lovely winding lane to its end and next to a gently flowing river you will find this old Asturian farm-house. The sea is only a mile away but the foothills of the Sierra del Sueve Park beckon. This is a superb base for walkers; Rafael's enthusiasm about the many walks or rides straight from the farm is infectious. The bedrooms, in a converted outbuilding, are large, filled with light and simply furnished — just right for families. Wood, beams and stone add to the natural feel. And then there's the food... the owners assured us that it is simply 'the most delicious and best value' to be found in the north of Spain! The ingredients certainly sound enticing; stacks of homegrown organic fruit and veg, meat reared on the farm and lots of fresh fish and seafood. Why not try your first Asturian fabada, a thick bean stew rather like cassoulet? There is a bar in an old horreo (a raised maize-store typical of this region), and only the susurrus of the countryside to keep you awake.

Rooms: 6 family rooms with bath & wc + 2 family rooms sharing bath & wc.
Price: D/Tw 6800-8000 Pts; D/Tw sharing 5100-6000 Pts.
Breakfast: 400 Pts.
Meals: Lunch/Dinner 1000-3000 Pts (M), 2000 Pts (C).
Closed: Never.

How to get there: From Ribadesella N632 towards Gijón. After 15km at Caravía follow signs for La Cabaña, in hamlet of Cerracín.

Hotel El Carmen

El Carmen s/n
Ribadesella
Asturias

Tel: 98 586 12 89
Fax: 98 586 12 48

Management: José Ruisánchez Rodrigo

This small rural hotel of stone and wood in traditional local style sits in a little valley with fine views over the Sierra de Santianes from all sides. The elder son's wife is an expert restorer and the family did the furniture restoration themselves. The sitting-room has an open fire, stone walls and tiled floor; there is a reading room — and table games too. The tiny village has just 30 inhabitants but there is a restaurant only 100 yards away; try the local cider. If you are keen to go boating down the river Sella, or to hike, the hotel will set it up for you. José, the owner, inherited the local shop and has run it with his wife for 40 years. His sons built this splendid hotel and it is run with the same integrity. Don't miss a walk in the Picos de Europa, only 20 miles away and there are lovely walks from the hotel too.

Rooms: 2 triple, 2 double + 4 twin.
Price: D/TW 6000-7800 Pts, Tr 8000-9800 Pts. Extra bed 1500 Pts
Breakfast: 550 Pts.
Meals: None.
Closed: Never.

How to get there: From Ribedesella take N632 west (signposted 'Gijón por la Costa'). After just 1km left at sign for Hotel El Carmen.

23

Hotel Aultre Naray

Peruyes
33547
Cangas de Onis
Asturias

Tel: (9)8 5840808
Fax: (9)8 5840848

Management: Pilar Celleja and Fernando Mateos

Asturias' grand casonas date from a time when returning emigrants invested the gains of overseas adventures in fine and deliberately ostentatious homes. The transition from grand home to fine hotel has been an easy one at Aultre Naray. The name means, "I'll have no other" — as hidalgos would declare to their heart's desire and what Pilar and Fernando would have YOU exclaim after a visit. Amid the greenest green, looking up to the high peaks of the Escapa sierra, this is a splendid base for exploring Asturias. Furnishing and decoration is '90s-smart; you might not know of interior designer Paco Terán, but those in fashionable Madrid society would. Here he has lovingly married print, fabric and furniture with the more rustic core elements of beam and stone walls. No expense has been spared; ever slept beneath a Christian Dior duvet before? We marginally prefer the attic rooms but all are design-mag memorable. Perhaps the biggest treat is breakfasting out in milder weather on the terrace, with a choice of crêpes, home-made cakes, or even eggs and bacon. And there are lots of good places to eat nearby.

Rooms: 10 with bath & wc.
Price: S 6000-8500 Pts; D/Tw 7800-11000 Pts.
Breakfast: 750-1000 Pts.
Meals: Dinner 2000 Pts (C).
Closed: Never.

How to get there: From Oviedo towards Santander at first on motorway, then N634. After passing Arriondas at km335 turn right towards Peruyes. Climb for 1km and the hotel is on your left just before you arrive in the village.

Hotel Halcón Palace

Cofiño (Parres)
33548
Arriondas
Asturias

Tel: (9)8 5841312
Fax: (9)8 5841313

Management: Leo Benz

Wise are those who visit this soul-stirring area of Spain and wiser still who stay in the Halcón Palace. Amazingly, a few years ago the building was abandoned, overrun with vegetation and doomed to ruin... until this Spanish-Swiss couple arrived with the energy and conviction to create their dream hotel. The chief protagonist here is the incomparable view that claims all your gaze as you sit on the terrace or at your bedroom window. There are century-old trees in gardens dripping with colour — this part of Asturias enjoys a micro-climate. Indoors, the gentle good manners of your two hosts communicate themselves to the very building. The dining rooms are elegant but still conducive to long, lazy meals and here as in other communal areas antique and modern furnishings combine well. The rooms are smart, sparkling clean and guests are spoiled with the very best mattresses and that view from every room. Finally, there is a cosy little bar for an apéritif before dinner.

Rooms: 14 with bath & wc.
Price: S 7000-9500 Pts; D/Tw 9000-13000 Pts.
Breakfast: Included.
Meals: 1100 Pts (M), 3000-4000 Pts (C).
Closed: Never.

How to get there: From Arriondas take SA260 towards Colunga. After 5km turn left following signs for hotel.

25

Hotel Posada del Valle

33549
Collida
Arriondas
Asturias

Tel: (9)85841157
Fax: (9)5841559

Management: Nigel and Joann Burch

Nigel and Joann Burch's love of Spain is more than a passing romance; they lived and worked in eastern Spain for the best part of twenty years. But they longed for greener pastures and after two long years of searching the hills and deep valleys of Asturias they found the home of their dreams — a century-old farmhouse just inland from the rugged north coast with inspirational views out to rock, wood and meadow. And already they are nurturing new life from the soil while running a small guest house; the apple orchard is planted, the flock grazing on the hillside and the first guests delighting in the sensitive conversion that has created one of the area's most beguiling small hotels. Rooms are seductive affairs with polished wooden floors below, beams above and carefully matched paint and fabric. Perhaps most memorable is the glass-fronted dining room — here the menu pays homage to the best of things local. You are close to the soaring Picos, the little-known beaches of the Cantabrian coast and some of the most exceptional wildlife in Europe. Do book a second or third night here ...

Rooms: 8 all en suite
D/Tw 6800-9000 Pts
Breakfast: 700 Pts
Meals: 1,900 Pts
Closed: 16 Oct-14 March.

How to get there: From Arriondas,
AS-260 towards Colunga & Mirador del Fito. After 1km right towards Collia & Torre. Go straight through Collia (do not take right hand turn to Ribadesella). The hotel is 300m on the left-hand side after the village.

Map No: 3

25A

La Quintana

Granda de Arriba
33546
Parres (Arriondas)
Asturias

Tel: (9)8 5922320

Management: Marta Iglesias

This gorgeous Asturian farm-house is more than 200 years old and... Simón Bolívar's nanny *might* have lived here! There are other reasons for staying at La Quintana, however. It is tucked away in the prettiest of hamlets, a heavenly setting in the rolling green of the hinterland. Marta and Marcelino's restoration work to create four guestrooms shows total respect for the building's past. The rooms are a delight: heavy beams, stone, antique furniture and one truly splendid wrought-iron bedstead. The doubles share a massive bathroom; the twin has its own, separate from the room. One of the bathrooms is specially designed for disabled guests. There are enticing views through the fruit orchards that surround the farm to the hills beyond — lucky people may see deer or wild boar; you will hear owls at night. The former kitchen is now a cosy wooden-floored sitting room — the old bread oven is in one corner. A dream place for walkers — paths lead straight from the house to connect with routes up towards Covadonga... and both rooms and food are marvellous value.

Rooms: 3 sharing bath & wc + 1 with own separate shower & wc.
Price: D/Tw 3500-5500 Pts.
Breakfast: 300 Pts.
Meals: Dinner 1000 Pts inc. cider or wine.
Closed: Never.

How to get there: From Arriondas N634 towards Oviedo; after 2km in Ozanes left towards Tospe and Llerandi. After 3.6km signposted on right.

Map No: 3

Hotel Peñalba

La Riera s/n
33589
Cangas de Onís
Asturias

Tel: (9)8 5846100
Fax: (9)8 5846046

Management: Roberto González González

Just beside the road from Cangas to Covadonga, Peñalba is an attractive old village house. In 1989 it won a prize for its conversion from private home to hotel; the traditional elements of local architecture — wood, slate and heavy beams — have been successfully married to more innovative features like a spiral staircase that leads up to rooms on the first floor and in the attic above. The rooms are smallish but attractive, all the nicer because the owners were not tempted to spoil them with television sets. Ochre colours, wooden floors (and wooden ceilings in the attic rooms) and dried flower arrangements add further warmth. You will feel the same sense of intimacy downstairs in the bar and restaurant and dining à la carte or from the set menu will please both palate and purse. It would be a treat to be here in autumn when the valley is dressed in russet, red, green and gold, perhaps to ride into the mountains in the company of the young owners. Praise has been heaped on the Peñalba and we enjoyed Roberto's ebullience.

Rooms: 8 with bath & wc.
Price: D/Tw 5000-7000 Pts; Q 6000-12000 Pts.
Breakfast: 450 Pts.
Meals: 1500 Pts (M), 2000 Pts (C).
Closed: Never.

How to get there: From Ribadesella N634 towards Oviedo. In Arriondas N625 to Cangas de Onís then AS114, AS262 towards Covadonga. Hotel in La Riera on right.

La Casona de Mestas

Las Mestas
Carretera Cangas de Onís-San Juan de Beleño
33557
Mestas de Ponga, Asturias

Tel: (9)8 5843055
Fax: (9)8 5843092

Management: Nieves Uzal Alvérez and Jorge Luis González

Surrounded by soaring peaks, set beside a mountain torrent, Casona de Mestas is at the heart of one of Spain's most beautiful mountain ranges. As it is also friendly, comfortable and fairly priced, it is fast acquiring a reputation among walkers. But even if you prefer just gazing at these glorious mountains, it would be a fine place to stay. The rooms are unpretentious and just right; they are light with simple wooden furniture and most of them have writing desks. (There are no television sets!) Really good mattresses and the sound of water guarantee a blissful night's rest. Water is the essence of Mestas; it is built beside a hot spring whose 30°C waters are channelled directly to the hotel's pool and 'hydro-massage' baths. From the glass-fronted restaurant there is a tremendous view and, to cap it all, excellent regional cooking: game is the speciality. Jorge and Nieves, the hotel's young owners, are most thoughtful hosts and the scenery is stupendous.

Rooms: 14 with bath & wc.
Price: S 4200-5400 Pts; D/Tw 6000-7700 Pts inc. VAT.
Breakfast: 600 Pts.
Meals: Lunch/Dinner 1500 Pts (M), 3000 Pts (C).
Closed: 20 Jan-1 March.

How to get there: From Cangas de Onís N625 towards Riaño/Puerto del Pontón. After 10km right towards Beleño on AS261. Hotel on right after 13km.

Hotel Torrecerredo

Barrio Vega
33554
Arenas de Cabrales
Asturias

Tel: (9)8 5846640
Fax: (9)8 5846640

Management: Pilar Saíz Lobeto

Torrecerredo is just outside the busy town of Arenas de Cabrales, a hub for walkers and sightseers visiting the Picos. If you are searching for that 'room with a view' look no further. The views are stunning — much more so even than the photograph suggests — a 'double glory for hearts and eyes'. The hotel is a rectangular, modern building on a hillside just outside the town. The bedrooms are spartan but perfectly adequate; we preferred those on the first floor at the front. What we liked most here was the pine-clad dining/sitting room where guests are treated to the owner's simple home cooking — the perfect thing when you return from a day in the mountains. Walking is the main activity here; Jim, Pilar's partner, is a mountain guide and walkers come from England to walk with him. Few know the area as intimately as he and Pilar; they are generous with time and advice on routes and can help plan excursions including nights in mountain refuges, canoeing, riding, climbing or caving. Good value: no frills.

Rooms: 16 with bath & wc.
Price: S 4000 Pts; D/Tw 6500 Pts.
Breakfast: 400 Pts.
Meals: Lunch/Dinner 1200 Pts.
Closed: Never.

How to get there: From Santander N634 towards Oviedo then left on N612 towards Potes. In Panes C6312 (AS114) to Arenas de Cabrales. Through town and right after Hotel Naranjo de Bulnes. Signposted.

Map No: 3

Hotel Rebeco

Carretera Fuente Dé s/n
Fuente Dé
39588
Camaleño, Cantabria

Tel: (9)42 736600/01/02
Fax: (9)42 736600

Management: Ottomar Casado Polantinos

What the photograph doesn't show are the mountains that rise sheer behind the hotel. The setting is spectacular enough to defy description but just imagine walking on wild paths at over 1000 metres up through yew, beech and oak woods where brown bears used to roam and the 'chamois' antelope is still protected. The hotel, which is just next to the cable-car, is a heavy old mountain house of stone and great timbers with balconies, geraniums, arches and beams — stacks of character and an appropriately uncluttered interior. The rooms are all slightly different, the emphasis being on plain walls, rich-textured materials, rugs and polished wood furniture. Those with mezzanines are ideal for families with children. It is all impeccable and simple and would be equally pleasing winter or summer. There are three dining rooms — others know this is a good eating house... and the Rebeco is justifiably proud of its cooking, based on the very varied list of regional specialities such as local trout, meats, sausages and cheeses — delicious!

Rooms: 30 including 11 duplex, with bath
& wc.
Price: S 5500 Pts; D/Tw7500 Pts; Tr
9200 Pts.
Breakfast: 500 Pts.
Meals: Lunch/Dinner 1500 Pts (M), 3500
Pts (C).
Closed: Never.

How to get there: From Santander
A67/N634 towards Oviedo. Left at Unquera onto N621 to Potes. In Potes follow signs to Fuente Dé.

30   Map No: 3

Hotel El Coronel

33840   **Tel:** (9)8 5763700
Somiedo
Asturias

Management: María Llanos García and Segismundo Lorences Fernández

Several generations of Segismundo's family have raised cattle in this tiny valley, right at the very top of one of the highest passes in Somiedo. It is beautiful up here at any time of the year; when the snows are down, when the first Alpine flowers break through, but perhaps most memorable of all when autumn sets the mountainsides alight. There are wonderful walks in all directions; do consider this as a base if you are walking, or if you simply enjoy the contemplation of high places. The building is no great beauty, but come at a weekend and you'll soon see that the place's reputation has been made in the kitchen. Try the classic Asturian fabada — the local cassoulet taste-alike — and end the feast with a glass of home-made wild strawberry liqueur. Portions are enormous, but you should have worked up an appetite with a hike (or cross-country skiing in winter?). Rooms are modern, with good beds, views and decent bathrooms; those on the first floor are big enough, but those in the attic are cramped. Brilliantly priced and positioned but ask for that room 'en la primera planta'.

Rooms: 11 with bath & wc.
Price: D/Tw 4000-5000 Pts.
Breakfast: 300Pts.
Meals: Lunch/Dinner 1000-1500 Pts (M); 1500-2000 Pts (C).
Closed: Never.

How to get there: From Oviedo take N634 west. Just before Cornellana left on AS15 to Puente de San Martín. Here AS227 south through Aguasmestas, Pola de Somiedo and on up to El Puerto. Hotel on left side of road.

Hotel Valle de Lago

Valle de Lago
33480
Somiedo
Asturias

Tel: (9)8 5763611/5763711
Fax: (9)8 5763711

Management: Manuel Lopez Espiña

Brothers Manuel and Pepe have been at the helm of the Valle del Lago for just a few years, but have already established its reputation as one of Asturias' most delectable small hotels. The drive up is unforgettable; the road twists and climbs then twists and climbs again until you arrive at this tiny village. All about is rock and peak and mountain pasture; come and stay a week and Pepe will help you plan a different walk every day. Come for the wildlife; 'though you won't see bears, at least you know they're out there'. Within the hotel things are almost as special as without; the bar-cum-lounge is bright and welcoming, with open hearth, comfy sofas, books and a growing collection of modern art. The dining room is just as intimate; here Manuel's gastronomic artistry takes centre stage. Most dishes are Asturian, presentation is a match for flavours, and your hosts know their wine; 'the best list in Asturias,' says Pepe. The nicest rooms are the two up in the attic with mansarded ceilings, but all of them have comfortable beds, snazzy fabrics and are equipped for winter and summer. Amazing value.

Rooms: 10 with bath & wc.
Price: S 5550 Pts; D/Tw 6990 Pts; Attic rooms extra 1000 Pts.
Breakfast: 800 Pts.
Meals: Lunch & dinner 1500 Pts (M); approx. 4000 Pts (C).
Closed: Never.

How to get there: From Oviedo take N634 west. Just before Cornellana left on AS15 to Puente de San Martín. Here AS227 south to Pola de Somiedo. Through village and follow signs to Valle de Lago. Hotel to left as you pass through village.

Map No: 3

La Casona de Villanueva

33590
Villanueva de Colombres
Asturias

Tel: (9)8 5412590
Fax: (9)8 5412514

Management: Nuria Juez and Angel Gascón

If we are allowed to have favourites Villanueva is one of them. Angel and Nuria left successful city careers in search of their rural idyll. First they found the right building, a grand old 18th-century village house in the quietest of hamlets close to the Cantabrian coast. Next came a year of external restoration work and then the interior decoration. And what decoration! — each and every corner has been carefully studied, there are warm pastel colours on the walls, paintings and etchings, antiques everywhere. There are exposed granite lintels, heavily-shuttered windows, attractive fabrics and lots of plants. And smaller details like home-made jams at breakfast, cut flowers to grace the table or classical music to accompany your meal. Nuria is passionate about her lovely walled garden and rightly so; it has fish ponds, flowers and vegetables. Both your hosts speak good English and gladly help you plan your visits to, for example, Romanesque churches, little fishing villages and the soaring Picos de Europa.

Rooms: 6 with bath & wc + 2 suites.
Price: S 6000-7000 Pts; D/Tw 7500-9000 Pts; Ste 12000-13000 Pts.
Breakfast: 650 Pts.
Meals: Dinner on request approx. 2500 Pts.
Closed: Never.

How to get there: From Santander N634 towards Oviedo. At km283 left towards Colombres. Through village then 2km to Villanueva. Signposted in village.

Map No: 4

33

Hotel Don Pablo

El Cruce
39594
Pechón
Cantabria

Tel: (9)42 719500
Fax: (9)42 719500

Management: Pablo and Magdalena Gómez Parra

Don Pablo enjoys a beguiling spot between the two estuaries on the outskirts of the hamlet of Pechón. The sea is just a few hundred yards away and a track snakes towards it through green fields from the hotel. This is all the creation of kindly ex-banker Pablo and his wife Magdalena who never faltered in their conviction that 'it could be done'. Theirs is a well-dressed hotel; downstairs is a very spick and span little dining room where breakfasts include fresh fruit juices and Cantabrian cakes. Stone, antiques and oak beams decorate the inside, greenery adorns the outside where there is a terrace for sitting out when it's warm. There is a large sitting room with an oversized television. The bedrooms, of medium size, have nice wooden beds and chests, good bathrooms and splendid oak ceilings. We especially liked the attic rooms looking out to the Cantabrian Sea. This is a modern hotel with looks — and a heart.

Rooms: 35 with bath & wc.
Price: S 5900-7400 Pts; D/Tw 6900-8900 Pts; Tr 8600-11300 Pts inc. breakfast in high season.
Breakfast: high season included; low season 500 Pts.
Meals: None; restaurant next door.
Closed: Never.

How to get there: From Santander A67/N634 towards Oviedo. 9km after San Vicente de la Barquera right to Pechón. Hotel on right as you leave Pechón.

Hotel Esmeralda

Calle Antonio López 7
39520
Comillas
Cantabria

Tel: (9)42 720097/720015
Fax: (9)42 722258

Management: Gilberto Fernández

A short drive from Santillana, between the towering Picos de Europa and the rugged northern coast of Cantabria, Comillas is an endearing little place. Right at the top of the town the bright awnings and grand façade of the Hotel Esmeralda beckon you in. This is every inch a family hotel; the Fernández brothers and their mother will want you to feel, as they do, that this is your home. The inside of the building retains the feel of a grand 19th-century village house. To one side of the main hallway is a small bar; the dining room leads off from here. Meals are memorable affairs; red peppers stuffed with hake might not be on the menu when you stay but expect the food to be GOOD. There is a very complete wine list, too. Downstairs there is a small sitting/reading area with the original staircase leading up to the rooms; and most attractive they are, too, with their original tiled floors and cavernous bathrooms. Some rooms at the front of the building have balconies.

Rooms: 17 with bath & wc.
Price: S 5000-6000 Pts; D/Tw 7000-8600 Pts; Tr 8500-10100 Pts.
Breakfast: 550 Pts.
Meals: Lunch/Dinner 2000 Pts (M); 3000 Pts (C).
Closed: Feb.

How to get there: From Santander A67 towards Oviedo then C6316 via Santillana to Comillas. Second building on right as you enter old part of town.

Hotel Central

Calle General Mola 5
39004
Santander
Cantabria

Tel: (9)42 222400
Fax: (9)42 363829

Management: Carlos Martín

'Something different' is the Central's motto — and it certainly is engagingly different. Its leitmotiv — and its delight — is BLUE, echoing from the blue façade to the blue and white suite to the height-of-fashion partly-blue doors and views out (from the top floor...) to the blue sea. In an old building with the occasional uneven floorboard, it is at the hub of the fine old town of Santander, on a pedestrian street for nocturnal peace, just 200m from the ferry. It was completely restored, in 'Deco' style, 5 years ago. One of the owners is an interior designer and the bar area is a work of art in itself, decorated with 'foreign' objects (moose head, sledge, hockey stick for Canada, cricket bat for Britain, jazz instruments for New Orleans), old cabin trunks and an ancient hotel switchboard, a 'centralita'. The management team is as light-hearted and travel-minded as the decor. King Alfonso XIII and his large family spent pre-war summers here that were unsurpassed in elegance and high living. Modernity and memories are well married at the Central.

Rooms: 41 with bath & wc + 1 suite.
Price: S 6600-9240 Pts; D/Tw 10010-14520 Pts; Ste 20000-30000 Pts.
Breakfast: Included.
Meals: Snacks in cafeteria all day.
Closed: Never.

How to get there: Head to Main P.O — 'Correos Central' — and from there to Plaza Porticada. Unload outside hotel and staff will show you where to park.

Map No: 4

Hostal Mexicana

Calle Juan de Herrera 3
39002
Santander
Cantabria

Tel: (9)42 222350/54

Management: María Eufemia
Rodríguez

The photograph says it all: at the Mexicana you feel you are in a different era. This modest little hostal first opened its doors in 1955 (when the picture was taken!) — and has been run by the family of María Eufemia ever since. A kinder and more gentle family you could not hope to meet. You would probably not write home about the rooms but you WILL have a comfortable night here. The rooms are simple and the furniture is unmistakably Spanish, the bathrooms spick and span. The hostal is excellent value considering that you are right in the town centre. But what we liked most about the Mexicana was its little restaurant; it reminded us of an English seaside B&B with its cornices, deliciously dated 50s furniture and sense of timelessness. As you might expect, the food is simple home cooking. Do consider the Mexicana if you are looking for something not too grand. Santander has the charm of a slightly down-at-heel port; watch boats on the quay, admire the Cantabrian Cordillera on a clear day, eat fish-of-the-day in authentic sailors' restaurants.

Rooms: 31 with bath & wc.
Price: S 2400 Pts; D/TW 3800 Pts.
Breakfast: 340 Pts.
Meals: Lunch/Dinner 1800 Pts (M).
Closed: Never.

How to get there: In town centre very close to Plaza del Ayuntamiento (town hall); underground parking in square; reduction for Mexicana clients.

La Tahona de Besnes

Besnes (Peñamellera Alta)
33578
Alles
Asturias

Tel: (9)8 5415749
Fax: (9)8 5415749

Management: Sarah and
Lorenzo Nilsson

In a valley of chestnut, oak and hazelnut with a crystalline brook babbling by, the Tahona de Besnes is a number of old village houses carefully converted into a lovely country hotel. The main building was once a bakery, another a corn mill, a third a stable. At the heart of it all, the bakery-restaurant is prettily decorated with dried flowers, chequered table cloths and old farm implements. There is also a charming terrace beside the brook. Specialities here include pote (Asturian bean stew), regional cheeses, wild mushrooms and dishes cooked in cider. Rooms and apartments are decorated to match their rustic setting; there are comfy beds, good bathrooms and nothing too fancy. This is a wonderful base for a very active, or simply interesting, holiday. The hotel has plenty of literature on the area and can arrange for you to ride, walk, canoe, fish or take trips out by jeep. When you finally drag yourself away, make sure you take a local cheese and a bottle of honey-liqueur, or other goodies from the bakery.

Rooms: 13 with bath & wc.
Price: S 5120-6720 Pts; D/Tw 6400-8400 Pts; Apmt for 2: 9000-11000 Pts; Apmt for 4: 11000-15000 Pts.
Breakfast: 750 Pts.
Meals: Lunch/Dinner 1850 Pts (M); 3000 Pts (C).
Closed: Never.

How to get there: From Santander N634 towards Oviedo; after 67km left to Panes. In Panes right towards Cabrales; after approx.10km right towards Alles and follow signs.

38

Casa Gustavo Guesthouse

Aliezo
39584
Tama Potes
Cantabria

Tel: (9)42 732010 (Bookings UK 01629 813346)

Management: Lisa and Michael Stuart

In the beautiful Liébana valley lies the tiny hamlet of Aliezo where you will find an old farm-house — Casa Gustavo. Your young English hosts are not typical ex-pats; Lisa and Mike love their adopted land, have learned its language and know its footpaths like few others. Within the thick stone walls of their house are low timbered ceilings and wood-burning stoves; this is home with a heart. For home it is; don't expect hotelly trimmings like hairdryers, television sets or telephones here. They believe that what visitors like best is a hot meal, a hot shower and a good bed at the end of a day. The house is deliciously organic; some rooms are small, some large, some have balconies, one an en-suite bathroom and all are shuttered. Redstarts nest beneath the eaves. There are dogs and cats, a cosy lounge, magazines and books. But Mike and Lisa agree that no matter how lovely their home, the real reason to be here is Nature herself and her Picos mountains. A superb place for ornithology, botany and walking.

Rooms: 1 twin room with bath & wc; 2 twins, 1 double, 1 quad, sharing a bathroom.
Price: S 2000-3000 Pts; D 2500-3000 Pts; Tw 2500-3500 Pts.
Breakfast: Included.
Meals: Dinner 2000 Pts (M); packed Lunch 500 Pts.
Closed: Never.

How to get there: From Santander A67/N634 towards Oviedo. Left at Unquera onto N621 towards Potes. Shortly before Potes, through Tama then after 200m left to hamlet of Aliezo.

Map No: 4

39

"The best fish in Spain - the best fish in Europe! Basque cooking lets the quality of the ingredients shine through undisguised and what we have available to us is remarkable... fish from the Cantabrian sea, mushrooms and game from the Pyrenees, vegetables from the Navarra valley and wines from the Rioja..."

JUAN MARI ARZAK - *Basque chef*

Basque Country
– Navarre

Atalaya Hotel

Passeo de Txorrokopunta 2
48360
Mundaka
Vizcaya

Tel: (9)4 6177000
Fax: (9)4 6876899

Management: Maria Carmen Alonso Elizaga

Atalaya has long since earned its laurels as one of the friendliest and most 'family' of Vizcaya's small hotels; the Spanish daily El País gives it no less than 10 out of 10 for service! You couldn't better its position, tucked away at the heart of the village of Mundaka, a stone's throw from the lively fish market and just yards from a beach at the edge of a deep inlet carved by the Cantabrian sea. The house speaks of the optimism of the early years of the century; its open, galleried frontage lets in the ever-changing light and lets you contemplate sand, sea and the adjacent church tower of Santa María. The owners — kind, straight-forward folk — care deeply for their hotel; you'll probably meet with them when you arrive and they'll find time to help you plan visits. We would choose a room with a sea view, but they're all worth a night; medium-sized, carpeted and with modern prints, they are spick-and-span, quiet and comfortable — and have more gadgets than you need, plus king-size beds. Atalaya would be a good place to spend a last night before the ferry (car and belongings safe in the free car park); there are good fish restaurants within walking distance.

Rooms: 14 with bath & wc + 1 suite.
Price: S 7100-8300 Pts; D/Tw 10900-12500 Pts; Ste 12900-14900 Pts.
Breakfast: 950 Pts.
Meals: None.
Closed: Never.

How to get there: From Bilbao BI-631 via Mungia to Bermeo. There, right on BI-635 to Mundaka; left into village centre. Hotel near Santa María church.

Urresti

Barrio Zendokiz
48314
Gautegiz Arteaga
Vizcaya

Tel: (9)4 6251843

Management: María Goitia

This is a dream come true for María and José María, Urrresti's two young owners, who launched themselves wholeheartedly into the restoration of the old farm-house which was near to ruin when they first arrived. Outside it still looks like a 17th-century farm-house; inside it is more modern. Breakfast is served in the large sitting/dining room, and good value it is, too; cheese, home-made jam, fruit from the farm and plenty of coffee. For other meals guests have free rein in a fully-equipped kitchen. The smart, impeccably clean bedrooms upstairs have parquet floors and new, country-style furniture; some have their own balcony and number 6 is especially roomy with a sofa-bed. The house stands in lush green and lovely countryside with the sea not far away — and Guernika, too. There are old forests of oak and chestnut to be explored, perhaps on the three bikes available for guests. The whole area is a Natural Park and many come here just for the birdlife (visitors are constantly astonished by the birdlife in Spain).

Rooms: 6 with bath & wc.
Price: D/Tw 4700-5500 Pts.
Breakfast: 450 Pts.
Meals: None (use of kitchen 600 Pts).
Closed: Never.

How to get there: From Guernika take road towards Lekeitio; after 6km left towards Elanchobe. House on right after 1.2km.

Txopebenta

Barrio Zendokiz
48314
Gautegiz-Arteaga
Vizcaya

Tel: (9)4 6254923/
(9)89 581727 (Mobile)
Fax: (9)4 6254923

Management: Juan Angel Bizzkarra

Between Guernika and the rugged north coast, in an area of great natural beauty, Txopebenta is one of the most remarkable of a growing number of first-class B&Bs in the Basque country. The house bears witness to the boundless energy and optimism of its owner Juan 'Txope' Bizzkarra. He decided that to create a guest house at his 19th-century farm-house he would have to add another floor; and he did so by careful use of old railway sleepers as good sound lintels, stairs, benches and roof supports. The whole house now breathes an air of solid wellbeing. The sitting/breakfast room is ideal for a convivial breakfast with delicious local cheese and fresh fruit juice. The rooms at the top are low-ceilinged and particularly cosy. There is a terrace where you can sit in summer. Your hosts certainly love their land; they will want you to visit it all. Don't miss the 'painted forest' in the Oma valley and the Biosphere Reserve of Urdabai with its spectacular birdlife — and there are beaches within walking distance.

Rooms: 6 with bath & wc.
Price: D/Tw 5000-6000 Pts; Tr 6500 Pts.
Breakfast: 450 Pts.
Meals: None.
Closed: 24-25 Dec.

How to get there: From Guernika take road towards Lekeitio and after 6km left towards Elanchobe. House on right after 0.8km.

Mendi Goikoa

Barrio San Juan 33
48291
Axpe-Atxondo
Vizcaya

Tel: (9)4 6820833
Fax: (9)4 6821136

Management: Agurtzane Telleria and Iñaki Ibarra

'Donde el silencio se oye' — (where you can hear the silence) — is the way the owners like to describe their hotel. Peaceful it is, and utterly beautiful. Mendi Goikoa is one of a new breed of chic country hotels which provide Cordon Bleu cooking and a bed to match. The hotel is two 19th-century farms — big, handsome buildings in a huge meadow with panoramic views from every room. The main restaurant is vast and high-ceilinged — it was the old barn — and absolutely packed with antiques. The emphasis is on traditional Basque dishes with a few of the chef's own innovations. There is a smaller breakfast room and a real gem of a bar in the other building. It is a popular venue for the suit-and-tie brigade though you won't feel uncomfortable if you are not one of them. A wedding-feast place, in fact, but don't be put off. The guestrooms are as good-looking as the dining room with beams, exposed stones, some lovely old pieces, lots of carpet — and utterly seductive views. And there are lovely walks up to (or towards!) the surrounding peaks to work up an appetite for dinner.

Rooms: 12 with bath & wc.
Price: S 8500 Pts; D/Tw 12500 Pts.
Breakfast: 700 Pts.
Meals: Lunch/Dinner 2000 Pts (M), 5500 Pts (C).
Closed: 22 Dec-8 Jan.

How to get there : From A8 exit 17 for Durango. From there BI-632 towards Elorrio. In Atxondo right to Axpe; house up above village, signposted.

Map No: 5

43

Hostal Alemana
Calle San Martín 53
20007
San Sebastián
Guipúzcoa

Tel: (9)43 462544
Fax: (9)43 461771

Management: Luis and Roberto
Garagorri Esnoz

If visiting the North of Spain do spend at least one night in San Sebastián; people here will tell you that there is nowhere quite as beautiful. La Concha, a sweep of golden sand, is the centre of life and, just one street back from the promenade, Hostal Alemana is ideal if the grander hotels are not your thing. The hostal occupies the upper floors of an elegant turn-of-the-century townhouse. The Garagorri family has run a hostal here for more than thirty years and it was given a thorough face-lift in 1992. The rooms have been designed with business people in mind, with credit-card keys and trouser presses that we might not need. But we do appreciate their generous proportions, good beds and large bathrooms. The breakfast room is handsome indeed: the light pouring in from the three windows in its curved wall will take your mind off the taped music pouring in from elsewhere. It would be tempting to use this as a last stop before the ferry and have a final dinner at one of the seafront restaurants.

Rooms: 21 with bath & wc.
Price: S 5500-7200 Pts; D/Tw 7700-8900 Pts.
Breakfast: 525 Pts.
Meals: None.
Closed: Never.

How to get there: From motorway take exit for Ondarreta; continue towards town centre. Hostal is 2km from motorway exit.

Arotz-Enea

Apartado 99
20280
Hondarribia
Guipúzcoa

Tel: (9)43 642319
Fax: (9)43 642319

Management: Jenobeba and Santos Etxebeste Aranberri

A short distance from the beautiful town of Hondarribia and nestling in a green valley, this is a very smart country B&B. Parts of the farm date back to the 14th century; it has all been given new life by Santos and Jenobeba since they decided to open their home to guests. It is most seductive; the road twists and turns and then the house comes into view, a building of fine proportions with a marigold-filled garden. Like a Swiss chalet, it has timbers and balcony and hills rising up behind. Beyond the heavy old doorway the interior lives up to expectations: a cosy little sitting/dining room with antiques, cut flowers, perhaps a bowl of fruit, terracotta floors and old beams. (There is lots of wood.) The bedrooms, as cosy as they are big, are among the loveliest we have seen — difficult to explain; go and see! There are home-made jams to accompany the croissants and bread at breakfast — and all in the very quietest, greenest of spots. A superb first or last night stop-over when travelling to or from France.

Rooms: 5 with bath & wc.
Price: S 4000-6400 Pts; D/Tw 5000-8000 Pts; Tr 6750-10800 Pts.
Breakfast: 500 Pts.
Meals: None.
Closed: Never.

How to get there: From Irún towards Hondarribia. Just before airport left into Amute. After 400m, sign on left for Llobregat. From here follow white arrows painted on road surface.

Map No: 5

45

Iketxe

Apartado 343
20280
Hondarribia
Guipúzcoa

Tel: (9)43 644391
Fax: (9)43 644391

Management: Patxi Arroyo and Fátima Iruretagoiena

Another enchanting B&B in the rolling green Basque country. Very near the lovely town of Hondarribia yet entirely rural, Iketxe is a house that matches its owners: quiet, unpretentious and utterly Basque. You can only wonder at the energy of Patxi who built his home virtually single-handed and made much of the furniture too. He finished it all just over four years ago but you might not guess that Iketxe is a new house, so faithfully has local building tradition been respected. The rooms are beautiful; first there are the views and then the decoration — wood floors, bright kilims, handsome bathrooms and no two of them alike. Floors are terracotta and two of the upstairs rooms have their own balcony. It would be hard to choose but ours would probably be number 1. We were glad that there was no television to break the spell. Fátima will happily help at breakfast time when it comes to planning your visits or recommend one of the many restaurants in Hondarribia. Hats off to Patxi for realising his dream and sharing it with us all.

Rooms: 5 with bath & wc.
Price: D/Tw 5000-6000 Pts; Tr 6750-8100 Pts.
Breakfast: 400 Pts.
Meals: None.
Closed: Never.

How to get there: From Irún towards Hondarribia. Just before airport left into Barrio Arkoll then left at sign to Llobregat. After approx. 1km at Chapel of Santiagotxo, follow signs to Iketxe.

Map No: 5

Maidanea

Barrio Arkoll
Apartado 258
20280
Hondarribia, Guipúzcoa

Tel: (9)43 640855
Fax: (9)43 640855

Management: Rosamaría Ugarte Machain

Maidanea, one of the first B&Bs to open in this beautiful corner of the Basque country, is a chalet-style farm-house on a hill looking over the river to France. It is a traditional Spanish home with a mix of old and new furnishing, tiled floors, lace curtains, a collection of old plates, plants and books, and religious images over some of the beds. It has been much restored — you probably wouldn't guess it was more than 400 years old. There is a big, galleried sitting/dining room for breakfast, a relaxed meal served as late as you like; the silence of the place and good mattresses encourage late starts. The bedrooms, on the first and attic floors, are modern and medium-sized. Señora has lavished much care on details such as her dried flower arrangements and her hand-embroidered sheets and cushions. Some rooms have the view across to France and number 4, our favourite, has its own balcony. The whole house is utterly spotless, there is a good mature garden and the old streets of nearby beautiful Hondarribia to discover.

Rooms: 6 with bath & wc.
Price: D/Tw 5000-6000 Pts.
Breakfast: 400 Pts.
Meals: None.
Closed: Never.

How to get there: From Hondarribia take Irún road and just past airport turn right. Through Amute, on towards Bekoerrota; signposted.

Venta de Donamaría

Barrio Ventas 4
31750
Donamaría
Navarra

Tel: (9)48 450925/450708
Fax: (9)48 450708

Management: Elixabet Badiola & Imanol Luzuriaga

A mouth-watering address! Donamaría is tucked away off to one side of a pass through the mountains between France and Spain, within striking distance of Pamplona. Your hosts are sophisticated, amusing folk whose love of the finer things in life is given ample expression in their guesthouse. These two old village houses (guestrooms in one, restaurant in the other) are packed full of objets d'art, antiques, old toys, dried flowers and a few surprises to boot; it all creates an intimate, relaxed atmosphere, much of it tongue-in-cheek. This is most certainly a place to linger over lunch or dinner; connoisseurs rave about the food: traditional Navarre dishes with 'a French touch and modern elements'. The tradition is long: there has been a restaurant here for almost 150 years. The rooms are all that you'd expect — big with antique furniture, timbered ceilings, lots of dried flowers and richly-coloured fabrics. Mother, father and daughter welcome you most graciously into their home. It is, by the way, set among old oak forests where the heart soars at every turn.

Rooms: 5 with bath or shower & wc.
Price: D/Tw 7000 Pts.
Breakfast: 500 Pts.
Meals: 1500 Pts (M), 3500 Pts (C).
Closed: Never

How to get there: From San Sebastián motorway towards France then N121 to San Esteban (Doneztebe). Here NA404 towards Saldías. Venta in village of Donamaría on right.

Venta Udabe

Valle de Basaburúa
31869
Udabe
Navarra

Tel: (9)48 503105

Management: Laura Ganua and Javier Fernández

On the edge of a tiny Navarrese village, Venta Udabe is the creation of two dedicated young folk who have revived its 300-year-old tradition of hostelry. It is a beautiful little rustic inn, every detail designed for its aesthetic appeal. The large timbered dining room has ochre walls, a fireplace and antiques lovingly restored by Laura. There are two sitting rooms, one downstairs with a fireplace and one up with peace and quiet. There are dried flowers everywhere and masses of old farm implements. The bedrooms have been designed with the same affection, books and flowers echoing the warmth of the wooden furniture and floors. Rooms at the front are slightly smaller and give onto a (quiet) road. Javier describes Udabe's cuisine as 'Navarrese, with imagination'. Its reputation is spreading and it is generously priced. Breakfast is a feast of fruits, yoghurt and home-made jams, after which you may ride out, on a bike or a horse, into the deepest green of the Navarre hills.

Rooms: 8 with bath & wc.
Price: S 5200-6200 Pts; D/Tw 6500-7500 Pts; Tr 8500-9500Pts.
Breakfast: Included.
Meals: Lunch/Dinner 1600 Pts (M), 2500 Pts (C).
Closed: Mon-Thurs except in summer and public holidays.

How to get there: From Pamplona N240A towards San Sebastián. Then A15 towards San Sebastián. At km118 turn right then immediately left where sign says to Lizaso then on to Udabe. Venta on left as you go through village.

Hostal Las Palas

Urrutia 49
31680
Ochagavía
Navarra

Tel: (9)48 890015
Fax: (9)48 890015

Management: Milagros Navarro.

Beside a rushing river high up on one of the passes between France and Spain, Las Palas would be perfect for memorable first or last nights in Spain. Ochagavía is the prettiest of mountain villages, a honeypot for walkers and cross-country skiers. The guesthouse is a handsome old building and has recently been given a complete face-lift by its young owners. Centre-stage here is the food. Milagros studied New Basque Cuisine and everything is home-made with only the best ingredients. It is wonderful value, too, unlike Nouvelle Cuisine elsewhere. The rooms are simple and follow the twists and turns of the old house. They are on the small side, their decoration simple; there are no televisions and three of them have flower-filled balconies looking out to the river. Throughout the house there are old framed photographs of Ochagavía and the surrounding region; the whole place has a lovely homely feel to it; the staff are kind and easy-going and will help all they can if you base yourself here for a walking holiday. ¡Nos gusta!

Rooms: 5 with bath & wc.
Price: S 3300-4000 Pts; D/Tw 4300-5000 Pts; Tr 5300-6000 Pts.
Breakfast: 450 Pts.
Meals: Lunch/Dinner 1500 Pts (M), 2000-2500 Pts (C).
Closed: Nov.

How to get there: From Pamplona N240 towards Jaca. Left onto N178 via Lumbier, Escaroz to Ochagavía. Hostal beside river over stone bridge.

Aragon –
Catalonia

Casa Ruba

Calle Esperanza 18-20
22630
Biescas
Huesca

Tel: (9)74 485001
Fax: (9)74 485001

Management: Ramón and Jesús Ruba

Casa Ruba, a small, utterly Spanish hotel right in the centre of Biescas and with a long tradition of receiving guests, claims to be the oldest hotel in the Aragonese Pyrenees, though this is not immediately apparent: it has recently had a complete façade-lift. Faithful (Spanish) clients come back year after year, not for chic décor but because they know they will be welcomed as friends. The scale and atmosphere are human and there is a lively bar packed with local folk. A pine-clad restaurant serves regional and classic Spanish fare (a lot of game and locally-farmed trout) and the wine list is varied and extremely good value, like the food. The rooms, as unpretentious as the two brothers who own and run Casa Ruba, are medium-sized, clean, with smallish bathrooms (half-tub baths) and occasionally a view. Most feel slightly dated but don't let this put you off; you are a short drive from the magnificent Odesa National Park, many beautiful Romanesque churches and Benedictine monasteries and you are even within striking distance of the ski-runs.

Rooms: 33 with bath & wc.
Price: S 3000-3400 Pts; D/Tw 4100-4700 Pts.
Breakfast: 475 Pts.
Meals: Lunch/Dinner 1700 Pts (M), 3000 Pts (C).
Closed: Oct-Nov.

How to get there: From Zaragoza N330 via Huesca to Sabiñanigo and then N260 to Biescas. Hotel in town centre.

Map No: 6

Casa Frauca

Carretera de Ordesa s/n
22374
Sarvisé
Huesca

Tel: (9)74 486353/486182

Management: Carmen Villacampa

So close to the border, this delightful little roadside hotel could very well be a French townhouse with its neo-classical pilasters, symmetrical design and pale pink wash, but inside it is faithful to its Spanish Pyrenean environment and has all the right timbers, tiles, sloping ceilings and pieces of rustic furniture. We especially took to the round window with its two semi-circular shutters. The owners are a kind and homely couple who like caring for their guests and they keep their house clean and warm. There is an intimate, rather smoky little bar for close encounters with the locals and a dining room where regional dishes will nourish the active visitor — lots of salads and vegetables, good stews and roasts, and plenty of everything. Sarvisé is in an extraordinary valley of abandoned villages that was due to be dammed... and never was, thank heavens! Enjoy the wooded hillsides, rugged rocks and rushing streams, or the snow and ice in winter.

Rooms: 12 with bath & wc.
Price: S 3000-4500 Pts; D/Tw 3500-4500 Pts; Tr 4300-5500 Pts.
Breakfast: 400 Pts.
Meals: Lunch/Dinner 1400 Pts (M); 2500-3500 Pts (C).
Closed: Never.

How to get there: From Lérida N240 towards Barbastro then N123/C318 to Ainsa. Then N260 towards Biescas to Sarvisé. Hotel on left in village.

La Choca

Plaza Mayor 1
22148
Lecina de Bárcabo
Huesca

Tel: (9)74 343070/(9)08 633636
Fax: (9)74 343070

Management: Ana Zamora Figuera and Miguel Angel Blasco Franco

Lecina de Bárcabo is for lovers of high places: a tiny hamlet in a rugged, wild part of Huesca perched at the edge of a limestone outcrop. Miguel Angel and Ana left teaching to restore this lovely old fortified farm-house and... to farm rabbits. But glorious La Choca cried out to be shared so they opened the house as a farm-school and later as a guesthouse. You will be captivated by the indescribable beauty of the views, the utter tranquillity of the hamlet. We fell asleep to the hooting of an owl and awoke to the sound of a woodpecker! The public rooms have stone walls and ancient timbers; the bedrooms are also rustically simple... and television-free. Three of them are big enough for a family and one has its own terrace. And you'll eat well here (often to the strains of classical music): home-made jams at breakfast, regional dishes with a French influence at other meals — and Ana's own recipes, too. Cave paintings nearby, bikes to be rented in the hamlet and gorgeous walks straight out from the house into the Sierra de Guara National Park.

Rooms: 9 with bath & wc.
Price: S 3000-3210 Pts; D/Tw 4670-5000 Pts inc. VAT.
Breakfast: 450 Pts.
Meals: Lunch/Dinner 1400 Pts (M); 2500-3000 Pts (C).
Closed: Nov.

How to get there: From Huesca on N240 towards Lérida. After village of Angües towards Colungo. 15km after Colungo left towards Lecina de Bárcabo. House first on left entering village.

Hotel San Marsial

Carretera Francia s/n
22440
Benasque
Huesca

Tel: (9)74 551616
Fax: (9)74 551623

Management: Marisa and Ramón Garuz

Benasque is a pretty place in the Aragonese Pyrenees, a centre for winter sports or for walking once the snows melt (no, it is not eternally snowbound). The San Marsial is an immensely warm, friendly little hotel with a smile at reception and rooms of human proportions, all lovingly created just a few years ago. A successful combination of slate floors, beamed wooden ceilings and rustic furniture makes it feel like a home from home, a place to linger over dinner or a good book. Wood is the basic material: many of the pieces were made or installed by the carpenter owner. The bedrooms are very smart — many have attractive handpainted bedheads; there are wooden floors and ceilings and matching curtains and bedcovers. 10 rooms have their own small terrace; all of them are light, medium-sized and have good bathrooms. In corridors, sitting and dining rooms there is a veritable museum of old farm implements, skis, chests... and in the middle a lovely hearth diffusing yet more warmth. The nearest ski stations are only 5km away.

Rooms: 24 with bath & wc.
Price: S 4200-8500 Pts; D/Tw 6500-11800 Pts.
Breakfast: Included.
Meals: Lunch/Dinner 1850 Pts (M), 3600 Pts (C).
Closed: Never.

How to get there: From Lérida N240 to Barbastro then N123 to Graus. From here C139 to Benasque. Through village and hotel on left.

Map No: 7

54

Hotel Valarties

Calle Mayor 3
Arties
25599
Valle de Arán, Lérida

Tel: (9)73 644364
Fax: (9)73 642174

Management: Irene España Plagues and Andrés Vidal España

A short distance from the ski stations and high-mountain walks of the upper Arán valley and against a backdrop of (snowy) soaring peaks, Hotel Valarties, which opened just ten years ago, is generally recognised as one of the very best places to stay — and most certainly to dine — in this part of the Pyrenees. The hotel is away from the centre and has an enormous garden. The rooms are very plush, have all mod cons, nice parquet floors and excellent mattresses. We would choose one of the attic rooms with sloping wooden ceilings to match the parquet floors; half of them look out across the garden. Downstairs there's a small sitting room, breakfast room and bar but the heart of the hotel is the attractive dining room. Andrés Vidal has really won his colours here with his fine 'cocina de autor' cuisine. He describes his art as 'refined — with a slight modernist touch'! Whether you choose the (surprisingly cheap) set menu or delve into the à la carte, your meal will be a feast fit for a King. (Whenever he is in Arties, this is where he dines!)

Rooms: 25 with bath & wc + 2 suites.
Price: S 5700 Pts; Tw 8750 Pts; Tr 11500 Pts; Ste 13500 Pts.
Breakfast: 950 Pts.
Meals: Lunch/Dinner 3900 Pts (M), 5000-6000 Pts (C).
Closed: 1 May-mid June and Oct-Nov.

How to get there: From Lérida N230 to Vielha. Here C142 to Arties. Hotel on right as you enter village.

Map No: 7

Besiberri

Deth Fort 4
25599
Arties
Lérida

Tel: (9)73 640829
Fax: (9)73 644260

Management: Carmen Lara Aguilar

Besiberri is exactly the kind of place we longed to find when we began our research: small, intimate, family-run, in a beautiful setting, with caring owners. It is a chalet-hotel, a pretty, flower-clad building beside a rushing stream and the first sight of it is a delight. Then you are greeted by Carmen's kindly smile and know you have chosen well. You enter through a small sitting room with the dining area off to one side. There's an open hearth, a beamed ceiling, dried flowers and a collection of pewter jugs. Wonderful to warm yourself in front of a blazing fire after a day on the ski slopes. Upstairs there are some first-class guestrooms, cheerfully decorated with wood used to good effect, very good beds and views beyond the window boxes. At the end of each floor there is a balcony with chairs, up above the river. Spoil yourselves and take the suite at the top of the building; it has windows to both sides, its own balcony, a small lounge and a very plush bathroom. And just yards away is one of the best restaurants in the Pyrenees.

Rooms: 16 with bath & wc + 1 suite.
Price: D/Tw 7500-9500 Pts; Ste 14000 Pts.
Breakfast: Included.
Meals: None.
Closed: Never.

How to get there: From Lérida N230 to Vielha then C142 to Arties. Signposted off right as you enter village.

Banhs de Tredos

Apartado de Correos 170　　　　　　**Tel:** (9)73 253003
Vielha
25530
Valle de Arán, Lérida

Management: Ricardo Pérez and Aurora Escarate

Banhs de Tredos is a new spa-hotel with a difference, not one of those turn-of-the century crumbling ghosts where a sense of terminal illness seems to hover. Tredos breaks radically with tradition, mixing designer chic with thermal cures, those who come for the waters with those who come for the walking, refusing to bow to the gloomy spectre of spa-hotel food as a logical progression from school dinners. You CAN take the cure here: 33°C-spring water is piped directly to a hydro-massage bath; but most of us would come for the incomparable beauty and isolation — you take a long track that winds up and up... and on up to 6000 feet! Few places as glorious for walking as this. The rooms are superb; lovely fabrics, pine-clad ceilings, designer furniture, old prints of the Pyrenees. It is all very comfy, very 90s. You eat in the tiny sitting/dining room. Staff are willing, friendly and attentive and it is altogether a wonderful spot.

Rooms: 6 with bath & wc + 1 large suite
(2 bedrooms, 2 bathrooms & lounge).
Price: D/Tw 14000 Pts; Ste 28000 Pts.
Breakfast: Included.
Meals: 1 meal 2650 Pts p.p; 2 meals 5000
Pts p.p.
Closed: Never.

How to get there: From Lérida N230 to
Vielha and then C142 towards Baqueira. In
the middle of Salardú, right at sign for Baños de Tredos (go very slowly or you'll miss it). 8km of track to hotel.

Casa Coll
25527
Barruera
Lérida

Tel: (9)73 694005
Fax: (9)73 694005

Management: Josep Lluís Farrero Moyes

This 300-year-old village house is one of the most 'basic' lodgings that we have included here but, although it is has none of the finery of some of our grander hotels, it will be just perfect for some. Barruera is a few kilometres from the entrance to the Aigües Tortes National Park, a place of soaring peaks, glaciers and lakes that the young owner of Casa Coll knows like no-one else. He runs a mountaineering shop in the village and will help you plan your sorties. The house is hidden away in a narrow cobbled street with room to park just opposite. An old stone staircase leads up to the simply-furnished sitting room and the two kitchens which have all you need to do your own cooking. We liked the bedrooms; one really quite small, another large enough for a whole family. It is all furnished with family bits and pieces — everything, from crockery to wooden floors to old chests of drawers, wears the patina of time. There is a walled garden, ideal for dining after a day of walking. Blissfully quiet. It's well worth dispensing with the en-suite bathroom to stay here.

Rooms: 1 double with bath & wc + 4 sharing bath & wc. Kitchen for guests 250 Pts.
Price: D 1800 Pts p.p.; D sharing 1600 Pts p.p. inc. VAT.
Breakfast: Self-catering.
Meals: Self-catering.
Closed: Never.

How to get there: From Lérida N230 towards Vielha. Just after Pont de Suert, right towards Caldes de Boi. As you enter Barruera sports shop 'Besiberri' is on right. Ask here for keys and directions.

Casa Guilla

Santa Engracia
Apartado 83
25620
Tremp, Lérida

Tel: (9)73 252080/(9)09 368473
Fax: (9)73 252080

Management: Richard and Sandra Loder

This is a matchless position, a veritable eagle's nest. As you soar higher and higher to the tiny hamlet perched high on a rocky crag you can only wonder at the valour of those who first chose to build here. Richard and Sandra Loder have a head for heights and after returning from Africa patiently set about restoring the buildings that make up Casa Guilla — a fortified Catalan farm-house, parts of which are nearly 1000 years old. The house is a labyrinth: it twists and turns on many different levels. There are two sitting rooms — one large with an open hearth, another smaller with books and local info. The bedrooms are simply but cosily furnished; there are terracotta tiles, heavy old beams, low ceilings... all deliciously organic. And the food... big breakfasts with home-baked bread, generous dinners with lots of game and that incomparable view from both dining room and terrace to accompany it. Caring and informative hosts in a fascinating part of Catalonia; geologists, lepidopterists, ornithologists and botanists are in their element here! A superb place.

Rooms: 1 double, 3 twins + 1 triple sharing 3 shower rooms.
Price: Half-board only 6000 Pts p.p inc. VAT.
Breakfast: Included.
Meals: Dinner included.
Closed: Never.

How to get there: From north take C147 from Pobla de Segur towards Tremp. After 5km right into Salás de Pallars, then right at school following signs to Santa Engracia. After 5.6km fork left for village. House near church. (or see No. 60)

Casa Mauri

Santa Engracia
25636
Tremp
Lérida

Tel: (9)73 252076
Fax: (9)73 651778

Management: Anne and Mike Harrison

Few villages in Spain can match spectacular Santa Engracia for setting; from its rocky ledge you look across to hill, gorge and mountain — all of it changing with each passing hour. Just arriving here you feel a sense of adventure, of discovery. The heady magic of the place soon worked its spell on Anne and Mike who have gradually restored and renovated a group of 200-year-old houses. Guests can choose between the house and the apartamento. Either would be perfect for a family — or the house for a group of friends. Rooms come with radiators and wood-burners, attractive wooden furniture; pine and beam and pointed stone walls, rugs and bamboo lamps lend warmth. A place where you'd want to stay several nights. To do? — if you should tire of that grandest of views you could follow dinosaur footprints, visit Romanesque churches, bird-watch or, most obviously, choose between any number of fabulous walks in the area — you may see wild horses and boar. Rooms and dinner are both excellent value, Mike and Anne happy in their role of hosts.

Rooms: 1 house with 3 bedrooms sharing 2 shower rooms; 1 apartment with 2 bedrooms sharing 1 bathroom.
Price: S 2000 Pts; D/Tw 4000 Pts.
House (for 6) 30000-60000 Pts weekly.
Breakfast: 500 Pts; cooked breakfast 700 Pts
Meals: Lunch/Dinner 1400 Pts (M) or self catering.
Closed: Never.

How to get there: From Tremp north towards La Pobla de Segur on C147, past turn-off to Talarn. 300yds later turn left under viaduct for Santa Engracia. 10km of good track to village. Park and walk up to house; house last on left.
(or see No. 59)

Map No: 7

60

Hotel Can Boix

Can Boix s/n
25790
Peramola
Lérida

Tel: (9)73 470266
Fax: (9)73 470266

Management: Joan Pallarés Oliva

No fewer than ten generations of the Pallarés family have lived and worked at Can Boix; three of them have turned this seductively located inn into something of an institution in Catalonia. But this is not a family to sit back on its laurels; as you'll see from the photo, innovation and renovation have led Can Boix solidly into the '90s with Joan as head man. Come, if only for the food; it is a celebration of what is locally grown or raised. Presentation is superb, and accompanying views are as scrumptious as the meal. Guest bedrooms are big and modern, yet nevertheless cosy, thanks to the wooden floors and furniture; they all have terraces (see photo) — large, mirrored, fitted wardrobes and every mod-con. Bathrooms are marbled, double-sinked, plush; tubs will hydromassage you if the sauna and high pressure showers of the gym have not worked their magic. This is a blissfully peaceful spot; cycle or ride into the spectacular foothills of the Pyrenees. An immensely friendly hotel which cares equally for both business person and traveller.

Rooms: 20 with (hydromassage) bath & wc.
Price: D/Tw 16000 Pts.
Breakfast: Buffet 900 Pts.
Meals: Lunch/Dinner 2800 Pts (M); 4800 Pts (C).
Closed: Never.

How to get there: From Barcelona towards Lleida on N11. Exit for Cervera/La Seu d'Urgell, Andorra. Through Cervera to Ponts; there right on C1313 to Oliana. 3km after Oliana, after bridge, left to Peramola. 4km to hotel.

Masia del Cadet

Les Masies de Poblet
43449
L'Espluga de Francolí
Tarragona

Tel: (9)77 870869
Fax: (9)77 870869

Management: Mercedes Vidal

Close to Poblet Monastery (founded in the 12th century to commemorate the Christian reconquest of Catalonia from the Moors), on the edge of the village, this fine Catalan farm-house was already standing when Colombus sailed West to get East but has been fundamentally transformed to create one of the region's smartest small hotels. It all sparkles; the day we visited there were three girls busily cleaning the reception area! Mercedes Vidal was born here and has lavished much love on her house. Guests are pampered from the moment they arrive; you'll find a small bottle of the region's moscatel wine and a local biscuit (carquiñol) on your bedside table. Some of the rooms have balconies and two have their own terrace; the furniture is all modern as are the prints on the walls. There are two sitting rooms downstairs and a pretty tiled bar. A love of things local is also reflected in the dining room: choose from a tempting array of regional dishes and taste the region's best wines. Then taste more in the well-stocked bodega — just the place for wine-lovers.

Rooms: 12 with bath & wc.
Price: S 4500 Pts; D/Tw 6500 Pts; Tr 7200 Pts.
Breakfast: 575-700 Pts.
Meals: Lunch/Dinner 1850-2500 Pts (M), 2500-3000 Pts (C).
Closed: Nov.

How to get there: Exit 9 from A2/E90 motorway. Into Montblanc, then to L'Espluga de Francolí, then towards Poblet via village of Las Masias. Hotel signposted to left as you arrive in Las Masias.

Map No: 7

62

Can Borrell

Retorn 3
17539
Meranges, La Cerdanya
Gerona

Tel: (9)72 880033/(9)29
794758
Fax: (9)72 880144

Management: Antonio Forn Alonso

Can Borrell is one of the most gorgeous of the many gorgeous places to stay in this part of the Pyrenees. High up to one side of the valley, tucked away in a tiny village with meadows in front and mountains beyond, this farm-house is nearly 200 years old. Inside it is exactly as you might hope: stone, beams, slate floors, an open hearth, dried and fresh flowers. Its restoration and conversion are utterly faithful to local tradition, not over-pretty, but just right. It has the warmth and intimacy of a little Cotswolds pub! The rooms welcome you with fabulous views and excellent beds. They vary in size because they follow the idiosyncrasies of an old house and are suitably uncluttered by televisions. When it comes to sitting down to dinner expect something out of the ordinary. The cooking here is, in the owner's words, 'traditional Catalan — with a special touch'. Hardly surprising that Can Borrell should have a widespread reputation and we include it here wholeheartedly.

Rooms: 7 doubles and 1 twin with bath & wc.
Price: S 6000-7000 Pts: D/Tw 8000-9000 Pts; Tr 10000-11000 Pts.
Breakfast: 700-850 Pts.
Meals: Lunch/Dinner 3000 Pts (M); 4000-6000 Pts (C)
Closed: 7 Jan-30 Apr exc. w/e.

How to get there: From Barcelona A18 via Terrassa and Manresa then C1411 to Berga. Through Tunnel del Cadí then on towards Andorra. After approx 5km right towards Puigcerdá. In Meranges village, signposted.

Hotel del Lago

Avenida Dr Piguillem 7
17520
Puigcerdà
Gerona

Tel: (9)72 881000
Fax: (9)72 141511

Management: Bartolomé Pascual Tubau

In such a quiet setting, just beside the lake from which it takes its name, this pretty rose-coloured hotel has been run by the Tubau family for more than fifty years. A stay here is deeply restful. There is a large flower-filled garden, shady spots beneath the trees and an unusual hexagonal dining room that is built almost entirely of wood, very light and a charming place for breakfast in the cooler months. Although no dinners are served, there are several restaurants just a short walk from the hotel. It came as no surprise to learn that the faithful return here year after year, many of them during the skiing season. The Lago is within easy reach of some of the best Catalan runs and some French slopes too: the border is less than a mile away. The guestrooms are carpeted and prettily decorated with floral prints — pinks and salmons mostly — for bedcovers and curtains. They are smaller than average but honestly priced. It all has a home-from-home feel and your hosts will treat you as family friends.

Rooms: 13 with bath & wc + 3 suites.
Price: S 6000-6500 Pts; Tw 9000-9500 Pts; Ste 12000-14000 Pts.
Breakfast: Buffet 800 Pts.
Meals: None.
Closed: Never

How to get there: From Barcelona A18 via Terrassa and Manresa then C1411 to Berga. Through Tunnel del Cadí then right to Puigcerdà. Hotel signposted in town; next to the lake.

Cal Pasto

Calle Iglesia 1
Fornells de la Mutanya-Toses
17536
Gerona

Tel: (9)72 736163
Fax: (9)72 736163

Management: Josefina Soy Sala

Josefina and Ramón are quiet, gentle folk. Their family has farmed in this valley for generations and they are devoted to it. Two rooms next to their house were opened to guests and more recently Ramón's parents' former home was converted to create a further 6 guestrooms. These are spotlessly clean and simply furnished; all have tiled floors, a very Spanish choice of fabric and good beds. Our favourites were those in the attic where wooden ceilings create a cosier feel. The breakfast room is slightly soulless but don't be put off; you will be served a grand breakfast and afterwards will probably be asked to visit the Museo del Pastor (shepherd's museum) — a testimony to the work of four generations of Ramón's family on the surrounding mountainsides. The trans-Pyrenean, Mediterranean-to-Atlantic footpath runs right by the house and you may feel inspired to do part of it. In the evening, choose between Josefina's cooking and the quiet little restaurant next door.

Rooms: 7 doubles or triples + 1 quadruple all with bath or shower & wc.
Price: S 3500; D/Tw 5000 Pts; Tr 6250 Pts.
Breakfast: 600 Pts.
Meals: Dinner 1400 Pts.
Closed: Never.

How to get there: From Ripoll N152 north through Ribes de Freser and on towards Puigcerdá. Fornells de la Muntanya signposted on left (km133.5) after steep climb. House in village by restaurant.

Map No: 8

Hotel Calitxó

Passeig el Serrat s/n
17868
Molló
Gerona

Tel: (9)72 740386
Fax: (9)72 740746

Management: Josep Sole Fajula

A second hotel close to Camprodón with more than just a hint of the Tyrolean chalet. Entering this pretty mountain village, over 3000 feet up in the Pyrenees, you'll see the Calitxó set back from the road. It has an attractive balconied facade brightened by the pots of geraniums adorning each and every balcony. You enter through the restaurant; the day we visited there was a merry atmosphere and nearly all the diners were local — always a good sign. The menu is pure Catalan and all ingredients are fresh from the market. The fillet steak in cream sauce with wild mushrooms is mouth-watering and prices here are more than reasonable. The rooms are all you need: generous-sized with locally-made wooden furniture, and each has a view out to the surrounding mountains. Some have their own balconies. Señora's friendly welcome, even though she was very busy attending her restaurant clients, melted our reserve and we liked her small, unpretentious hotel. Walking, skiing and the beautiful Romanesque churches close by are irresistible.

Rooms: 26 with bath & wc.
Price: S 4200-5350 Pts; D/Tw 5250-6400 Pts; Ste 8925-11025 Pts.
Breakfast: Buffet 950.
Meals: Lunch/Dinner 2500 Pts (M); 3500 Pts (C).
Closed: Never.

How to get there: From Ripoll C151 to Camprodón, and continue on C151 to Molló.

Hotel Grèvol

Carretera Camprodón a Setcases
Vall de Camprodón
17869
Llanars, Gerona

Tel: (9)72 741013
Fax: (9)72 741087

Management: Antonio Sole Fajula

Less than two hours drive from Barcelona, close to ski slopes, mountain trails and a whole series of Romanesque churches, El Grèvol will at first sight make you wonder if you aren't in the Swiss Alps. Carved pine balconies, exposed stonework, slate and wood floors, wooden furniture all provide the perfect setting for the après-ski. There are high ceilings, a free-standing central hearth, a light and airy feel over all. As you'd expect of a four-star hotel, the guestrooms have all the trimmings. Those on the first floor give onto the balcony that runs round the building; attic rooms have pine ceilings and dormers and smaller balconies. The communal areas have great warmth; food is regional/international/haute-cuisine — 'it tastes good and looks good' was the owner's comment. Or you can order more snacky food in the bar. So close to Camprodón, all kinds of activities can easily be organised including — ¡claro! — skiing in season. The hotel itself has an indoor swimming pool and a bowling alley — less seductive, perhaps, than the mountains.

Rooms: 34 with bath & wc + 2 suites.
Price: D/Tw 12150-15650 Pts; Ste 19250-25000 Pts.
Breakfast: Buffet included.
Meals: 3700 Pts (M); 4100-4500 Pts (C).
Closed: Never.

How to get there: From Barcelona A7 towards France, then N152 via Vich to Ripoll. There C151 to Camprodón. Hotel is 1500m from Camprodón on the road to Setcases.

Casa Etxalde

Rocabruna
17867
Camprodón
Gerona

Tel: (9)72 130317

Management: Satya and Iñaki Tablado

What magnificent walking country this is — and what a gorgeous place to stay is the Etxalde, 3000 feet up in a vast deciduous forest. It is a tall, proud building that looks across a beautiful valley to the castle of Rocabruna. A Frenchman built and then abandoned it but Satya and Iñaki Tablado have breathed new life into it after months and months of careful restoration work. The house is next to one of the long-distance paths and keen walkers love it here. Although no food is provided guests have their own fully-equipped kitchen and you can buy the hosts' homegrown (organic) veg in season; make sure to try their cider and jams too. The rooms are reached by an outside staircase at the back; whether you are in the tower kitchen/diner or any of the bedrooms they all have the same tremendous view, as does the cosy little lounge (lots of local info here). Two of the rooms have balconies, all are attractively but simply furnished and the bathrooms are perfect, with dried flowers, floral prints, tiled floors. Two warm, relaxed and friendly hosts.

Rooms: 4 with shared bath & wc + 1 triple/quadruple with own bath & wc.
Price: 3000 Pts p.p. if sharing facilities; 3500 Pts p.p. in large room with bath and wc.
Breakfast: Self-catering.
Meals: Self-catering.
Closed: Never.

How to get there: From Camprodón C151 towards France. After 3km right towards Rocabruna/Beget. After 4.5km track to house signposted on right.

Map No: 8

68

Mas el Guitart

Santa Margarida de Bianya
(La Vall de Bianya)
17813
Gerona

Tel: (9)72 292140
Fax: (9)72 292140

Management: Lali Nogareda and Toni Herrero

El Guitart is right up with the avant-garde of a new, dynamic approach to rural tourism. Lali and Toni are young and enthusiastic hosts; he left television, she left designing, to launch themselves with gusto into the restoration of this old dairy farm. Thanks to their hard work and good taste they have succeeded in creating one of Catalonia's very best small B&Bs. We loved the rooms; each is decorated in a different colour with Lali's stencilling to match; there are wooden floors and beams, old beds and washstands, rugs, decent bathrooms and good views. We especially liked the Blue room. The dining and sitting rooms are decorated in similar vein; breakfast is Catalan, with juice, jams and home-made sausage, and good dinners are also served. An excellent place to stay a few days and, with Toni's help, set out to explore the mountains. He has researched and marked new walking routes in the valley. Exceptional hosts, home and countryside.

Rooms: 4 with bath & wc + 2 two-bedroom apartments.
Price: D/Tw 6000 Pts; Apmt 9000 Pts (min. stay 2 nights) inc. VAT.
Breakfast: 500 Pts.
Meals: Dinner on request 1300 Pts.
Closed: Never.

How to get there: From Gerona C150 to Besalú. Continue on C150 to Castellfollit de la Roca. Here follow signs Ripoll/Camprodón. House signposted in Vall de Bianya.

Map No: 8

Mas Salvanera

17850
Beuda
Gerona

Tel: (9)72 590975
Fax: (9)72 590975

Management: Rocío Niño Ojeda and Ramón Ruscalleda Calicó

This solid 17th-century Catalan farm-house has been transformed into a very smart country hotel. In a blissfully quiet part of the lovely wooded Pyrenean foothills, Mas Salvanera is a rare treat. The guestrooms, in an old olive mill next to the main house, are named after signs of the zodiac. Our favourite was Cancer but they are all very smart, large and beamed with antique furniture lovingly restored by Rocío — her dried flower arrangements add an extra touch to the studied décor and the bathrooms are generous. The main building has an old well, vaulted ceilings and open hearths, more antiques and lots of exposed stone. Upstairs there is the guest dining room, dominated by the grand 18-place dining table. Breakfast here from the buffet any time you want. Lunch and dinner are created with huge flair by your dynamic hostess; paella and rabbit are two of her regional specialities. There is a quiet walled garden with a pool among the olives — a fine place for a siesta. Six bikes for guests' use when you're feeling more energetic.

Rooms: 8 rooms sharing 4 bathrooms.
Price: B&B 4750 Pts p.p; half board 6750 Pts p.p; full board 8500 Pts p.p.
Breakfast: Included.
Meals: Lunch/Dinner 2500 Pts.
Closed: Christmas Day.

How to get there: From Figueres N260 towards Olot/Besalú. Before Besalú right at sign for Maia de Montcal. House signposted from here along 1.6km of track.

Hotel Playa Sol

Pianc 3
17488
Cadaqués
Gerona

Tel: (9)72 258100/258140
Fax: (9)72 258054

Management: José Lladó and Esther Kaenzig

The Playa Sol sits snugly in a small cove looking out across the bay of Cadaqués. The Lladó family have owned and managed it since it opened more than thirty years ago and clearly take pride in their creation. The hotel leans heavily towards family holidays; there are bikes, a small-tennis court and putting green as well as a pool set in a terraced olive grove behind the hotel. In summer guests can dine in the garden. At the front there is a terrace with tantalising views of the glittering sea. We would certainly always choose a room with sea-view and terrace. Those we saw were a decent size and you learn to love the air conditioning in the Catalan summer. But it is the sheer beauty of the setting that will seduce you. This would be a quiet base for exploring the narrow streets of Cadaqués and its many restaurants and art galleries or the beautiful hinterland, recently declared a National Park.

Rooms: 50 all with bath & wc.
Price: S 8900-10900 Pts; D/Tw sea-view 12900-16900 Pts; D/Tw north-facing 10900-13900 Pts; Tr sea-view 15500-19900 Pts.
Breakfast: Buffet 1200 Pts.
Meals: None.
Closed: 17-27 Nov and 7 Jan-13 Feb.

How to get there: From Figueras C260 towards Rosas then GE614 to Cadaqués. Left at sea-front, signposted at end of beach on left.

Map No: 8

El Molí

Mas Molí   **Tel:** (9)72 525139
17469
Siurana d'Emporda
Gerona

Management: Maria Sanchís Pages

El Molí is a modern building; but it more than earns a place in the 'special' category alongside its older Catalan neighbours. Although open for just over a year, it has already been awarded a Diploma for B&B excellence. Its position couldn't be better; you are just 7km from wonderful Figueras and the Dalí museum, while a half hour drive will bring you to the beach. The house is modelled on the traditional Girona 'mas'; inside, its tiled floors, wooden furniture and big rooms with views out across the farm are ample compensation for sharing a bathroom (although at the time we go to press, more are on the way). But the heart of the house is Maria; don't miss dinner (wonderful value) and conversation with her and husband Josep; veg, chicken and beef come straight from the farm and there's an infusion of hierbas to end your feast. At breakfast, try the home-made yoghurt and jams. Ask to see the old ice-well in the garden; it was built in Roman times. This would be a good place to break the journey travelling north or south and Maria can help organise cycling routes out from the farm.
Rooms: 4 sharing 2 baths & wcs (en-suite for 1998).

Price: D/Tw 4000-4600 Pts; Tr 6000-
6900 Pts; Q 8000-9200 Pts.
Breakfast: 600 Pts.
Meals: 1100 Pts (M).
Closed: Never.

How to get there: Coming from the
North on A9 take exit 4 towards La Escala,
then turn right to Siurana d'Emporda.
Arriving in village, El Molí is signposted.

Map No: 8   **72**

Can Jou

La Miana
17854
Sant Jaume de Llierca
Gerona

Tel: (9)72 190263
Fax: (9)72 190263

Management: Rosa Linares and Mick Peters

You will remember arriving at Can Jou: all the way up the track to the farm you sense you are leaving the mundane, the ordinary, behind you. Round a final bend and there it is, high on a hill looking out over miles and miles of thick forest of oak and beech. Small wonder that Mick and Rosa were inspired to revive this old Catalan farm; first by working the land, then by giving the house a family (they have four children), thirdly by restoring the old barn so they can now share the beauty of it all with their guests. The guestrooms are simple, furnished with a mix of old and new; six have their own balcony and bathrooms while four larger rooms share three bathrooms. This would be a fine place for a family holiday; there is the farm to explore (ducks, turkeys, cattle and sheep), horses to ride (a perfect place for learners and there are marked forest bridleways for experienced riders), a river beach nearby for swimming. Rosa's regional cooking will have you dining in every night and many of the ingredients come straight from the farm. Close to the house is a spring-filled rock pool — if you're heading back to Nature, head for here.

Rooms: 6 doubles with bath & wc + 4 family rooms sharing 3 bathrooms.
Price: B&B 4000 Pts p.p; half board 5500 Pts p.p; full board 6500 Pts p.p. Family rooms B&B 3500 Pts p.p; half board 4500 Pts p.p; full board 5500 Pts p.p.
Breakfast: Included.
Meals: Lunch and/or Dinner included.
Closed: Never.

How to get there: From Figueres N260 to Besalú and to Sant Jaume de Llierca. Left into village, and then 2nd left into Calle Industria. Continue for 6km along track to house — marked at all junctions.

Map No: 8

Rectoria de la Miana
17854
Sant Jaume de Llierca (Sant Ferriol)
Gerona

Tel: (9)72 190190/223059

Management: Frans Engelhard

At the heart of a vast stand of beech and oak, at the end of 6 kms of rough and winding track, La Miana nestles in a setting of incomparable beauty. History is very present here: in the Middle Ages there was a fortified manor-house; in the 1300s a rectory was built complete with vaulted ceilings, escape tunnel and chapel. It took courage and vision for Frans Engelhard to embark on its restoration. But his dream of a house open to all, a place for theatre and workshops where the creative impulse could be given free rein, is fast being realised and from the ruins has emerged an extraordinary and beautiful hostelry. No two rooms are alike. They have pastel walls, they are furnished almost exclusively with antique furniture, there are bright kilims and each old handmade floor tile is a work of art. In the vaulted dining room downstairs you will have a genuine Catalan breakfast, and regional dishes for lunch or supper. The walking here is wonderful, there is riding at a nearby farm and La Miana has bikes. Or just abandon yourself to the hushed loveliness of it all. Perhaps better for walkers than for those seeking easy comfort.

Rooms: 9 with bath/shower & wc.
Price: Half board 4500 Pts p.p; full board 5500 Pts p.p inc. VAT.
Breakfast: Included.
Meals: Lunch and/or Dinner included.
Closed: Never.

How to get there: From Figueres N260 to Besalú and Sant Jaume de Llierca. Left into village then 2nd left into Calle Industria. 6km along track to house following signs to Can Jou — marked at all junctions. Rectory just past Can Jou farmhouse.

Can Fabrica

Santa Llogaía del Terri
Cornellà del Terri
17844
Pla de Estany, Gerona

Tel: (9)72 594629
Fax: (9)72 594629

Management: Marta Casanovas Bohigas and Ramón Caralt Elias

On top of a hill with heart-stopping views sits the 17th-century farm-house that Marta and Ramón have restored and brought back to life, not least by planting trees and farming their 17 acres of land. They have created a blissful corner of peace and quiet whence to explore the nearby villages and Romanesque churches. If you are here in summer, do visit the Dali museum by night! Ramón is an engineer, Marta a designer. They are an exceptionally friendly young couple with environmentalist leanings and want you to discover the treasures of their area; there are four bicycles for hire and a wealth of walking and cycling routes. The bedrooms are smallish, simply furnished with old pieces and lamps, while soft materials set off the bare stone walls. The food is good home cooking, often with produce from the farm, and you will have Can Fabrica honey on the breakfast table as well as the traditional Catalan ingredients of tomato, oil and garlic. A lovely place and lovely people; stock up on farm produce before you move on.

Rooms: 6 with bath or shower & wc.
Price: S 3200 Pts; D/Tw 6400 Pts; Tr 9000 Pts inc. VAT.
Breakfast: Included.
Meals: Dinner 1800 Pts (M).
Closed: Christmas-Easter.

How to get there: Leave A7 at exit 6 onto C150 towards Banyoles. After approx. 8km right towards Cornellà del Terri/Medinya. After 2.5km left to Santa Llogía; through village, 400m of track to house on left.

75

La Tria
08589
Perafita
Barcelona

Tel: (9)3 8530240
Fax: (9)3 8530240

Management: Maite Tor

This area of the Pyrennean foothills remains puzzlingly 'undiscovered'; as you wander through beautiful old Perafita you'll meet few visitors. But it is lovely. Snug in the green countryside just a short walk from the village, this 17th-century Catalan mas will quicken your passion for the natural world. Gentle-mannered Maite is a painter and her sensitivity is reflected in the simple, country-style decoration; rooms are fresh, light and uncluttered. The place is really more geared to self-catering lets — there are two kitchens — but Maite will happily prepare you a Catalan (or continental) breakfast if you wish, and there are two cheap-and-cheerful restaurants in Perafita. In the main farm-house are an enormous wooden-floored dining room and two lounges, one very cosy with open hearth. The whole place is blissfully quiet and would be ideal for families; there's an enormous, carefully tended garden and a dairy farm to explore — Maite and husband Lluís enjoy showing guests round. Central heating means you'll be comfortable at La Tria in the cooler months, too. The area is known for its many Romanesque churches.

Rooms: 8 with bath & wc.
Price: D/Tw 4000 Pts.
Breakfast: 400 Pts or self-catering.
Meals: None.
Closed: First 2 weeks of July.

How to get there: From Barcelona N152 to Vic. By-pass town to west then turn off for Sant Bartolomeu del Grau. There towards Perafita; La Tria signposted to left before arriving in village.

Map No: 8

76

Mas Banús — Casa Rural

El Banús
08519
Tavérnoles
Osona, Barcelona

Tel: (9)3 8122091
Fax: (9)3 8887012

Management: Antonio Banús

This grand Catalan farm-house, nearly five centuries old, has always been the seat of the Banús family — their family tree proudly graces a corner of the sitting room, taking the lineage back to 1214. It is a noble but sympathetic house, with a lovely overgrown garden, lots of mature trees and the farm estate beyond. You enter by a very grand old arched doorway; within are vaulted ceilings, great flagstones and an impressive staircase up to the guestrooms. And what lovely rooms they are! Beamed, decorated with family heirlooms, they are in what once was the granary to the main house. No matter that they share bath or shower rooms; Antonio Banús insists that the last thing he wanted was to create a hotel atmosphere. We really fell for a corner room, number 8. On the same floor there is a large, peaceful sitting room, a perfect place to settle down with a good book. The dining room is a treat: more antiques... and farm-fresh eggs for breakfast. Dinner is a chance to try good Catalan country food. Boating, cycling and riding nearby and lots of Romanesque churches.

Rooms: 5 sharing 4 bath/shower rooms.
Price: D/Tw 4000 Pts; Tr 5500 Pts; Family room 7000 Pts.
Breakfast: 600 Pts.
Meals: Dinner 1500 Pts (M).
Closed: Second week Sept.

How to get there: From Vic C153 towards Roda de Ter. After approx. 5km right towards Tavérnoles (signposted for Parador); El Banús on right after 2km.

Map No: 8

El Jufré

Tavertet
08511
Osona
Barcelona

Tel: (9)3 8565167

Management: Josep Ruquer and Lourdes Rovira

The medieval hill-top villages of this part of Catalonia rival some of those in Provence. Simply driving up to Tavertet past craggy limestone outcrops and stands of forest is memorable; once you arrive and look out over the plain far below you can only gasp at the grandeur of what lies before you. Stay with Josep and Lourdes and their two young children in their VERY old house: parts of it date back to 1100. It was rebuilt in the 1600s and has been refurbished to create the guesthouse. You'll like your room here; there are eight of them, happily marrying the old (beams, exposed stone) and the new (good beds, lighting and bathrooms). We would opt for one that looks straight out over the craggy ledge that is El Jufré's perch. There is a terrace on which to linger over a 'fino' and a restaurant next to the house, a friendly place with good, simple fare and a special reduction (it's cheap anyway) for guests of Josep and Lourdes. For lovers of utter tranquility and high places and those glad to trade car for foot.

Rooms: 8 with bath & wc.
Price: S 3500 Pts ; D/Tw 5600 Pts inc. VAT.
Breakfast: Included.
Meals: Dinner 1100 Pts (M).
Closed: Christmas.

How to get there: From Vic C153 towards Olot to L'Esquirol/Santa María Corco. Here, right to Tavertet. House on left as you enter village.

Xalet La Coromina

Carretera de Vic s/n
17460
Viladrau
Gerona

Tel: (9)3 8849264
Fax: (9)3 8848160

Management: Gloria Rabat

Once here, you will wax as lyrical as the Coromina's staff about the stunning Parque Natural del Montseny: its woodlands are grandiose, water runs, flows and falls everywhere, indigenous trees and plants flourish, some of them rare. It is a place for a back-to-nature walking holiday. The building dates from the turn of the century when wealthy Catalan families first built themselves summer residences away from the sticky city. It has kept its elegant exterior while being thoroughly modernised inside. The ancient/modern mix is visible in the decoration too: the little sitting room has an old fireplace, all bedrooms have their own personality with an antique in each, English and French prints for curtains and bedcovers, good bathrooms and yet more stupendous views. The Coromina prides itself on its food and on using local products in season. You can expect delicious mushroom dishes made with local setas just as they spring up after the rain. A gentle small hotel in a spectacular setting.

Rooms: 8 with bath & wc.
Price: S 7100 Pts; D/Tw 8900 Pts; Tr 9900 Pts.
Breakfast: 900 Pts.
Meals: Lunch/Dinner 1750 Pts (M), 3000 Pts (C).
Closed: 8-31 Jan.

How to get there: From Barcelona A17 towards Girona/France. Then N152 towards Vic/Puigcerdá. Just before Tona, right on BV5303 then left on GE520 to Viladrau.

Hotel Aigua Blava

Platja de Fornells
17255
Begur
Gerona

Tel: (9)72 622058/624308
Fax: (9)72 622112

Management: Joan Gispert-Lapedra

Its design and management make the Aigua Blava feel half its size, AND it is 4-star comfortable. The bedrooms, all in different styles, occupy several terraced wings with fine gardens, sea views and delicious hidden coves below — so rugged a piece of coast is almost unspoilable. Run by the same family (the manager started at 15), nourished by the same chef (his son is training to take over), tended by the same gardener for 45 years, the hotel has a strong tradition of personal attention. You will breathe deeply in the sweet-smelling pinewoods, bask beside the huge pool or plunge from its diving-boards, enjoy fresh lobster in the dining room while delighting in the sight of the small fishing port or sip a cool drink at the smart snack bar on the uncrowded beach. All is top quality but no amount of money can buy the sense of hospitality that comes naturally to the family and their staff. No groups are taken and customer loyalty is strong. The village, too, is one of the prettiest on the Costa Brava, so you should book ahead if you can.

Rooms: 86 in total — twins with bath & wc, some terraces, some suites.
Price: S 8000-10400 Pts; D/Tw 10400-12500 Pts; D/Tw terrace 12000-17100 Pts; D/Tw lounge 13800-18000 Pts; Ste 16500-22000 Pts.
Breakfast: 1500 Pts.
Meals: Lunch/Dinner 3500 Pts (M), 4000-5000 Pts (C).
Closed: 9 Nov-15 Feb.

How to get there: From Gerona C255 to Palafrugell. From there GE650 to Begur. Signposted on entry to village.

Map No: 8

80

Hotel Llevant

Francesc de Blanes 5
17211
Llafranc
Gerona

Tel: (9)72 300366
Fax: (9)72 300345

Management: Familia Farrarons Puic

On the pedestrians-only sea-front in a busy little village, Llevant is a family-run hotel with many a devotee returning year after year. We were instantly won over by the kind smile that greeted us. The building is 60 years old but you could never tell; everything sparkles here from bathroom to crockery to the sea that almost laps its way to the door. The Puic family are proud of their creation, constantly improving and refurbishing; the bedrooms are very smart, with every mod con. But what makes it all special enough to earn a place in this guide is the restaurant/terrace. The promenade here is always animated, highly so at the evening 'paseo time', and beyond all this the sea is a constant backdrop; what better place to watch the world go by than this terrace, with the hotel's much-praised cooking as an accompaniment? The beach at Llafranc is sandy, clean and safe — we walked from end to end in September without seeing a scrap of paper! Good value at any time of the year, particularly so in the low season.

Rooms: 24 with bath & wc.
Price: S 5100-11500 Pts; D/Tw 8900-16800 Pts.
Breakfast: Buffet 900 Pts.
Meals: Lunch/Dinner 2200 Pts (M); 4500 Pts (C).
Closed: Nov.

How to get there: From Barcelona A7 north to exit 9 (San Feliu); past San Feliu and Palamos to Palafrugell. Here follow signs to Llafranc; hotel in centre of village right on sea-front. Park in street.

Hotel Sant Roc

Plaça Atlàntic 2
17210
Calella de Palafrugell
Gerona

Tel: (9)72 614250
Fax: (9)72 614068

Management: Teresa Boix and Bertrand Hallé

If only there were more hotels like Sant Roc on the Costa Brava. For it remains, in many parts, a stunning stretch of coastline and this quiet little hotel could restore your faith in seaside holidays in Spain. It is very much a family affair — not just family-owned and run but also a place where guests are valued like old friends (some return year after year). The setting is marvellous: a perch at the edge of a cliff amid pine, olive and cypress trees. From terrace and dining room there are views across the bay and its brightly-painted boats to the pretty village beyond. The sea is ever with you at Sant Roc, its colours changing with every hour. The nicest rooms are those with seaward terraces, of course, but we liked them all, their most striking feature being hand-painted beds and an abundance of original oil paintings. With Franco-Catalan owners you would expect something special from the kitchen and justifiably — the food is good and Bertrand and Teresa are charming hosts. There is a path from the hotel down to the beach and longer walks around the bay.

Rooms: 42 with bath or shower & wc + 6 suites.
Price: S 5920 Pts, sea view 6720 Pts; D/Tw 7600 Pts, sea view 8400 Pts; Ste 11760 Pts.
Breakfast: 900 Pts.
Meals: Lunch/Dinner 2750 Pts (M), 3500 Pts (C).
Closed: Mid Oct-end Mar.

How to get there: From Barcelona A7 north to exit 9 (San Felieu). Then past San Felieu and Palamos to Palafrugell. Here follow signs to Calella and then to hotel.

Map No: 8

82

Hotel Diana
Plaza de España 6
17320
Tossa del Mar
Gerona

Tel: (9)72 341886/341116
Fax: (9)72 341103

Management: Fernando Osorio
Gotarra

Although long ago discovered by the sun-and-sea brigade, Tossa del Mar still retains some of its charm, especially in the Vila Vela; wander up for wonderful views at sunset or sunrise. Visit out of season and stay at the Diana. The building is said to have been built by one of the Gaudí school; it certainly is a beautiful example of Spanish Art Nouveau. The hotel is surprisingly luxurious, considering such modest prices; chandeliered, bannistered and columned — the building hasn't forgotten its youth. There are old pieces in public rooms, like grandfather clocks, oils, gilt mirrors and the original tiled floors. Although some are modern, most bedrooms have period furniture; our favourites are those with a terrace looking out across the bay. Bathrooms have recently been revamped and thoroughly modernised. The hotel's patio looks out across the beach to the dancing waves but breakfast inside is just as much fun, amid ferns and wicker tables and chairs; the windows and doors would make any artist sigh!

Rooms: 21 with bath & wc.
Price: S 4400-6600 Pts; D/Tw 6050-9350 Pts;
Sea view extra 1050 Pts.
Breakfast: Buffet 825 Pts.
Meals: None.
Closed: Never.

How to get there: From Barcelona A7 towards France. Exit 9 towards Lloret de Mar; on past Lloret north to Tossa del Mar. Hotel on sea front; you'll recognise it!

83

Map No: 8

Oriol Riera
Veïnat Pibiller
17412
Maçanet de la Selva
Gerona

Tel: (9)72 859099
Fax: (9)72 851316

Management: Dolors Bosch Llinás

A special place, for those who are happy to forego some minor comfort in order to enjoy an authentic Catalan home. If you're happy to share a shower room and conversation at table, then stay as a guest of Dolors at her 200 year-old Catalan farmhouse. It is, she rightly points out, "una casa muy bonita". This is the antithesis of those credit-card hotels we so dislike; pull in off the busy NII and the ivy-clad frontage of Oriol Riera offers rest for sore eyes. Inside, decoration is as personal as in any family home: pictures of Dolors' family, sporting trophies on a shelf above a lace-clad dresser, dried flowers hanging down from the old beamed and planked ceiling. There are two dining rooms; dressers display the family china, there's a high-chair for younger children and, in one corner, a stone staircase leads up to the bedrooms — large enough to accommodate extra beds should the need arise. You'd be a fool to miss dinner; again we leave the last word to Dolors who describes it as, "familiar — calidad de primera clase".

Rooms: 4 sharing bathroom & wc.
Price: D/Tw 5000 Pts.
Breakfast: 600 Pts.
Meals: Lunch/Dinner 1400 Pts (M).
Closed: Never.

How to get there: From A7 take exit 9 for Massanet de la Selva. Towards Barcelona on NII; at km691.5 turn left at sign (careful-brow of hill!) and you'll see Oriol Riera to the right.

Nouvel Hotel

Santa Ana 18-20
08002
Barcelona

Tel: (9)3 3018274
Fax: (9)3 3018370

Management: Gabriel Carulla

Few of Barcelona's hotels have been functioning continuously since the Belle Époque. The Nouvel is aware that its laurels are already won but hasn't yet sunk into complacency. It was fully refurbished for the 1992 Olympics: you'll see 90s designer furniture and marble floors alongside the original chandeliers, cornices, mirrors and lovely Art-Nouveau doors. The staircase is a beauty — walk all the way up to the light and modern breakfast room on the fifth floor. Each bedroom has a slightly different feel (we loved those with period geometric floor tiles, eg 361 and 367); they are large and airy with high ceilings, furnished with a mix of old and new. Some have balconies onto the street but don't worry about noise here — for a city-centre hotel it is remarkably quiet. As you would expect of a 3-star establishment there is air conditioning in summer and decent-sized bathrooms throughout. But what makes it extra special is its position at the smarter (Catalunya) end of the Ramblas, the hub of the city. Superb value in the low season.

Rooms: 66 all with bath & wc + 1 suite.
Price: S 7500-10000 Pts; D/Tw 9300-13950 Pts; Ste 15000-18000 Pts.
Breakfast: 700 Pts.
Meals: None.
Closed: Never.

How to get there: From North on A7 take 'Ronda Litoral'. Exit 23 then Diagonal/Passeig de Gracia to Plaza Catalunya; nearest Parking SABA just off Plaza. Hotel in first street on left off Las Ramblas.

Hotel Adagio

Calle Ferran 21
08002
Barcelona

Tel: (9)3 3189061
Fax: (9)3 3183724

Management: Tomas Medina

In a lively narrow street of the 'Gothic' quarter, hard by the Ramblas, the Adagio is an excellent choice if you are visiting Barcelona with little to spend. The building is 1900s but you might think it newer; like many of the city's hotels it was given a very thorough face-lift for the 1992 Olympics. It is a tidy little place — the reception is clean and light with young and smiling staff; those we met spoke very good English and obviously enjoyed working there. Downstairs there is a bright sitting/dining area with simple tables and chairs and modern paintings; the buffet breakfasts are served here. Rooms are surprisingly well equipped for their price; spotlessly clean, most of them have a small balcony onto the street. The hotel is deservedly popular with younger travellers and there is masses of information (and help) at reception on what to do and see. This is the sort of place for striking up friendships with fellow travellers; intimate, family-run, and with many of the city's more interesting sights a short walk away.

Rooms: 38 with bath & wc.
Price: S 5500-6500 Pts ; D/Tw 6600-8800 Pts.
Breakfast: 600 Pts.
Meals: None.
Closed: Never.

How to get there: From South up Ramblas to Plaça del Teatre then right to Plaça Sant Miquel. Here left into Carrer de Ferran and hotel on left. For the car: Parking Intelligente on Rambla dels Caputxins.

Hotel Roma Reial

Plaza Real 11
08002
Barcelona

Tel: (9)3 3020366
Fax: (9)3 3011839

Management: Pascual Tarrasón

Roma Reial is excellent value if you want to stay on a tight budget in what is probably Spain's most interesting city. The hotel is in a corner of the Plaza Real, a pedestrianised square just yards away from the Ramblas in a lively, Bohemian part of the old town. The furnishing of the rooms here is unremarkable but the view from those looking onto the square IS — ask for one with a balcony. They are perfectly comfortable; they have telephones, central heating and are medium-sized, as are the bathrooms. In short they have all that you could expect for the price in such a brilliantly central position. No breakfast is served at the hotel, but there are lively cafés on the square that do breakfast; or walk to the Ramblas and do some people-watching over your café con leche. Most of the guests here are young, many of them backpackers, and the hotel is deservedly popular with its young clientèle; book ahead and get that room with a view!

Rooms: 52 rooms with bath & wc.
Price: S 3800 Pts; D/Tw 6000 Pts; Tr 7500 Pts inc. VAT.
Breakfast: 450 Pts.
Meals: None.
Closed: Never.

How to get there: On A7 from North, follow signs 'Ronda Litoral'; take exit 21 (immediately after a tunnel) signposted Ciudad Bella. Enter Las Ramblas and park in Parking Alarcón; 2nd street on right.

87

Map No: 8

Hotel La Santa María

Paseo de la Ribera 52
08870
Sitges
Barcelona

Tel: (9)3 8940999
Fax: (9)3 8947871

Management: Ute Voigt

The charms of Sitges are many; no surprise that it was for many years a fashionable resort town with wealthier Catalans. The crowd is more international now but the town has kept its intimacy and life centres on the promenade and beach. At the heart of it all is the Santa María. There is a bright awning and a terrace; within is the dining room, a small sitting and bar area and the bedrooms — all under the caring eye of Señora Ute, the hotel's indefatigable owner-manager. The rooms with their own balconies and a view across the palm trees to the bay beyond are well worth the extra. They are well furnished with mostly wooden beds, tables and desks; one or two have their original tiled floors and old furniture and some are large enough for a whole family. All of them have prints of Sitges; there may well be fresh flowers. But let's not forget the food; as you'd expect, lots of seafood and fish from the day's catch... and much more besides. Certainly a place where you should book ahead, especially in the season. The hotel has its own car park.

Rooms: 70 with bath & wc.
Price: S 7500-9000 Pts; D/Tw 9000-11000 Pts; D/Tw facing sea 9500-15400 Pts.
Breakfast: Buffet included.
Meals: Lunch/Dinner 2200 Pts (M), 3000 Pts (C).
Closed: 12 Dec-mid Feb.

How to get there: From Barcelona A16 motorway through Tuneles de Garaf. Take the SECOND exit to Sitges, follow signs to Hotel Calipolis. The Santa María is on sea-front.

Los Palacios

Calle Los Palacios 21 **Tel:** (9)78 700327
44100
Albarracín
Teruel

Management: Valeriano Saez

Albarracín is one of Teruel's most attractive walled towns; its narrow streets tumble down the hillside beneath the castle and eventually lead you to the lovely main square and the cathedral with its ceramic-tiled main tower. Los Palacios is a handsome building just outside the city walls; its earthy colours seem to fix it to the hillside on which it stands. The 50-year-old building was recently given a very thorough face-lift to make way for the 'hostal'. The bedrooms are furnished with new wooden furniture; tiled floors are modern, too. The fabrics might not have been our choice but these are utterly Spanish rooms, impeccably clean and the views from their small balconies are second to none. It is good to escape from telephone and television; the owners are keen not to disturb their guests' utterly silent nights. The little breakfast room/bar area has views, too, and while busy preparing your breakfast the owners will happily chat about trips from the hostal. This little inn has few pretensions, is wonderful value and we recommend it wholeheartedly.

Rooms: 13 rooms with bath or shower & wc.
Price: S 2500 Pts; D/Tw 4500 Pts inc. VAT.
Breakfast: Included.
Meals: None.
Closed: Never.

How to get there: From Teruel N234 north towards Zaragoza. After some 7km left on TE901 to Albarracín. Here through tunnel and right after 150m and Hostal is first house on right.

Hotel Esther
44431
Virgen de la Vega
Teruel

Tel: (9)78 801040
Fax: (9)78 801059

Management: Miguel Andrés Rajadel García

The high mountains and hill-top villages of the Maestrazgo have only recently begun to awaken the curiosity of those in search of new pastures to walk and, when the snow is down, to ski. At the heart of this wild and beautiful area the modern little Esther is one of our favourite places. It is a purely family business — father, mother and son look after bar, reception and restaurant. The focus is the dining room; it is modern but a timbered roof, mounted ceramic plates and a lovely tiled picture of Jaca help to create intimacy. You can expect a memorable meal here; specialities are roast lamb and kid as well as jugged meats like turkey and rabbit. Try the junket with honey for dessert. There is a good choice of wines and you can trust Miguel's recommendations. Decoration is the same upstairs and down: tiled floors, simple wooden furniture. The bedrooms have small bathrooms and are irreproachably clean. Hotel Esther is another of the small hotels included here that prove that a modern hotel CAN have a heart. Honest prices for rooms and food.

Rooms: 19 with bath & wc.
Price: S 5000 Pts; D/Tw 7200 Pts; Tr 9000 Pts.
Breakfast: 440 Pts.
Meals: Lunch/Dinner 1600 Pts (M), 2500-3000 Pts (C).
Closed: 8-20 Sept.

How to get there: From Valencia towards Barcelona; at Sagunto left on N234 towards Teruel. TE201 to Mora de Rubielos then TE201 towards Alcalá de la Selva. 2km before Alcalá on right.

Fonda Guimera

Calle Agustín Pastor 28
44141
Mirambel
Teruel

Tel: (9)64 178269

Management: Pedro Guimera

Mirambel is one of the most beautiful of the hill-top villages of the Maestrazgo, a place so well preserved that when Ken Loach came to film 'Land and Freedom' it sufficed to move a few cars and the cameras were up and rolling for his 1930s drama. A lovely arch leads you through the town walls and straight into the village's main street; just along on your left is Fonda Guimera. The inn is six years old but you would never guess it; it is a lovely stone building that is utterly faithful to local tradition and fits perfectly between much older houses on both sides. On the ground floor are the bar and the restaurant which serves simple home-cooking. Upstairs the rooms are as unpretentious as the hosts but they lack nothing and are impeccably clean with simple wooden furniture and shutters. Bathrooms are smallish but with good-quality towels. The rooms at the back look out over terracotta roofs to the mountains beyond; a few have their own terrace. When leaving you may be tempted to question your bill; can it really be so little?

Rooms: 18 with bath & wc.
Price: D/Tw 2800 Pts inc. VAT.
Breakfast: 250 Pts.
Meals: Lunch/Dinner 1000 Pts (M), 1800 Pts (C).
Closed: Never.

How to get there: From Valencia A7 towards Barcelona ; exit for Vinarós. Here N232 to Morella; just before Morella, CS840 to Forcall. Here road to La Mata de Morella then Mirambel. Under arch and Guimera along on left.

Mas del Pi

44580
Valderrobres
Teruel

Tel: (9)78 769033/(9)08 836254

Management: Carmen and Ramón Salvans

This is the stuff of which back-to-nature dreams are made. High on a hilltop Mas del Pi is literally at the end of the road — your arrival will be a memory to savour. Ramón and Carmen have worked their 70-hectare farm for 12 years; there are vines, olives and almonds, ducks and chickens and a beautiful big vegetable patch. What better way for them to meet new people and share their love of the place than by setting up a small B&B? They are nevertheless firm believers in tradition: 200 years ago this was a coaching inn. Things here are definitely rustic; hosts and house are utterly authentic. They are proud of their simple guestrooms with their tiled floors, old furniture and views across the farm. At breakfast there are home-made jams and cakes and newly-laid eggs. We have fond memories of sharing dinner and easy conversation; nearly everything from meat to veg to wine to liqueur is home-produced. Outside there is the farm to explore and glorious walks, with the Pyrenean sheepdog to accompany you if you want. Children love it here.

Rooms: 4 with bath & wc; 2 sharing.
Price: 4000 Pts p.p inc. breakfast and dinner.
Breakfast: Included.
Meals: Lunch 1200 Pts; Dinner included.
Closed: Never.

How to get there: From Barcelona A7 north to exit 40 for L'Aldea-Tortosa. C235 to Tortosa then C230 towards Mora la Nova. After 16km left to Valderrobres. Just before village right to 'Ermita de los Santos'; Mas del Pi signposted up 3km of good track.

La Torre del Visco

Apartado 15
44580
Valderrobres
Teruel

Tel: (9)78 769015
Fax: (9)78 769016

Management: Piers Dutton and Jemma Markham

Bajo Aragón is one of Spain's best-kept secrets: beautiful, wild, unspoilt by tourism and stacked with natural and man-made treasures. Stay with Piers and Jemma and renew body and spirit in their superbly-renovated medieval farm-house. Standards of comfort, decoration and food are high, as is their gift for creating a relaxed atmosphere. Their farmland and forests protect the house from modern noise and nuisance in this exceptional walking country; peace is total inside and out — neither telephone nor television to disturb you in your room. After a day of discovery — your hosts will advise you, they have been here for years — settle with one of their 7000 books before a great log fire, delight in their eclectic taste where each piece of furniture, be it antique, modern or rustic, Art Deco or Nouveau, fits with the old tiles, beams and exposed brickwork. Dinner is a feast of own-farm produce, the Visco's bodega offers a fine choice of wines, breakfast in the great farm-house kitchen is renowned. Of course, famous people have made films here...

Rooms: 7 with bath & wc + 1 suite.
Price: S 15000 Pts; D/Tw 21000 Pts; Ste 30000 Pts inc. breakfast and dinner.
Breakfast: Included.
Meals: Lunch approx. 4000 Pts; Dinner included.
Closed: Never.

How to get there: A7 south towards Valencia. Exit junction 38 for L'Hospitalet de L'Infant y Móra. Follow signs to Móra la Nova, then Gandesa. There towards Alcañiz but left in Calaceite to Valderrobres. There left towards Fuentespalda and after 6km right. Follow track to house.

93

Map No: 15

Hotel Cardenal Ram

Cuesta Suñer 1
12300
Morella
Castellón

Tel: (9)64 173085
Fax: (9)64 173218

Management: Jaime Peñarroya
Carbo

The whole of the town of Morella is listed 'patrimonio artístico nacional' and you'll see why when you first catch sight of this fortress town girt about with its unbroken wall. In one of its grandest mansions you'll find a hotel as remarkable as the town. Just to one side of the colonnaded main street, it is a building whose proportions and upper storey of arched windows give it a Venetian air. You enter through a lovely arched doorway beneath the coat of arms of the Ram family; Jaime Peñarroya is passionate about his hotel and wild horses wouldn't drag him away. A wonderful vaulted stairwell sweeps you up to the guestrooms — and what rooms! They are big, with polished wooden floors; their bedheads, writing desks and chairs are all of carved wood. Bright bedcovers and rugs add a welcome splash of colour, and the bathrooms are attractive too. The food is for gourmets: lots of truffles are used and there are delectable home-made puddings. Discover the wild beauty of the Maestrazgo — superb walking country and still relatively unknown. Worth every peseta.

Rooms: 19 with bath & wc + 2 suites.
Price: S 4500 Pts ; D/Tw 7000 Pts;
Tr/Ste 9000 Pts.
Breakfast: 800 Pts.
Meals: Lunch/Dinner 1500 Pts (M),
4000-4500(Pts C).
Closed: Never.

How to get there: From Valencia A7
towards Barcelona; exit for Vinarós. Here
N232 to Morella. Up into old town; hotel in main street 200m from cathedral.

Map No: 15   **94**

> *"The light is brilliant, the atmosphere is preservative, the colours are vivid, so vivid that sometimes this seems like a painted country as the mauve and purple shadows shift across the hills, as the sun picks out a village here, a crag there, as the clouds scud idly across the candlewick landscape of olives or cork oaks and the red soil at your feet seems to smoulder in the heat."*

JAN MORRIS - *Spain*

East Spain

Hostería de Mont Sant

Subida al Castillo s/n
46800
Xátiva (Játiva)
Valencia

Tel: (9)6 2275081
Fax: (9)6 2281905

Management: Javier Andrés Cifre

This place has it all — Arab castle above and red-roofed city below, mountains and Mediterranean beyond, terraced gardens groaning with orange trees and 700 newly-planted palm trees. There is fascinating archaeology (Iberian and Roman shards, Moorish fortifications, Cistercian monastery walls — the history of Spain in a nutshell) and a Moorish irrigation system that has guaranteed water in all seasons since the 12th century. The mountain streams are channelled, refreshing the air as they go, into a 250,000-litre cistern under the garden. Señor Cifre's old family house has cool, beamed living areas with unexpected nooks, charmingly undecorated guestrooms (just natural materials, old tiles, antique furniture and no pictures "because the windows frame pictures enough") and a see-through kitchen! Pity the exposed cooks but enjoy the delicious food. Enjoy, too, the balconies, terraces and quiet corners. There is a marquee for receptions and a few log cabins are to be built under the pines but it will surely remain as friendly and peaceful as ever.

Rooms: 7 with bath or shower & wc.
Price: D/Tw 15000Pts inc. VAT.
Breakfast: Included.
Meals: Lunch/Dinner 4000-5000 Pts (C).
Closed: 15-30 Jan.

How to get there: From Valencia N340 towards Albacete. X(J)átiva exit, follow signs for old city/Castillo. Signposted.

95

La Casa Vieja
Calle Horno 4
46842
Rugat
Valencia

Tel: (9)6 2814013
Fax: (9)6 2814013/2813737
E-Mail lacasavieja@xpress.es

Management: Maris and Maisie Watson

Maris and Maisie have just recently taken over at the reins of this delectable B&B. This most peaceful of hideaways combines 400 years of old stones with a very contemporary idea of volumes and shapes. There are original arches, columns and capitals (it was probably a nobleman's house), vast twisty beams, ancient floor tiles, a well in the courtyard and... in a more recent vein... the swimming pool occupying most of the remaining patio space. A double-height sitting area faces an immense fireplace where deep sofas hug you as you sip your welcome fino before dining, indoors or out. The many antiques have been in Maris' family for as long as she can remember; for example, the 16th-century grandfather clock, Persian rugs, hand-carved mahogany table and the many oil paintings. Bedrooms are equally full of character, the beds firm, the night-time utterly village-quiet; kettles, tea and coffee remind you of home. Maris' cooking follows the seasons; expect market-fresh produce with interesting veggie alternatives but if there's some dish you'd particularly like to try, just ask.

Rooms: 5 with bath & wc.
Price: D/Tw 7000-9000 Pts inc. VAT.
Breakfast: Included.
Meals: Lunch — snacks only; Dinner 3000-4000 Pts (C).
Closed: Never.

How to get there: From Valencia A7 south then exit 60. N340 towards Gandia/Alicante. Exit onto CV60 towards Albaida. Exit for Terrateig/Montechelvo/Ayelo de Rugat/Rugat. Through Montechelvo; Rugat is 2nd village to left, signposted.

Hostal Mas de Pau

Carretera Alcoy
03815
Penáguila
Alicante

Tel: (9)6 5513111
Fax: (9)6 5513109

Management: José Antonio Zafra

Mas de Pau stands isolated on a hillside of the Penáguila valley amid groves of almond and olive trees. The farm-house is over two centuries old; it has been greatly restored to create a hotel for both business and pleasure — and most dapper it is, too. The restaurant is decorated in warm earthy colours; there are arches, heavy timbers and lots of exposed stone. There is also a cellar bar and a sitting room reserved for guests (the restaurant is open to non-residents) — a quiet corner to settle down with a good book. Bedrooms are on two floors; they are small (especially those on the attic floor) and bathrooms would be no good for a tango. But they do have handsome oak floors and the panoramic views from most of them help dissipate any cabin fever. You can swim every day of the year in the hotel's (large) heated pool and there are a sauna and tennis court (bring your own rackets). Beyond all these modern attractions, we wallowed in the SILENCE.

Rooms: 18 with bath or shower & wc.
Price: D/Tw 8500 Pts; Tr 10500 Pts.
Breakfast: Included.
Meals: Lunch/Dinner 1800-2000 Pts (M), 3200-3500 Pts (C).
Closed: Never.

How to get there: From Alicante A7 towards Valencia. Exit 67 onto N340 towards Alcoy. 3km before Alcoy right to Benifallim then on to Penáguila. Signposted.

Map No: 21

El Fraile Gordo

Apartado 21
03650
Pinoso
Alicante

Tel: (9)68 432211
Fax: (9)68 432211

Management: David Bexon

Multi-talented David Bexon — singer, interior designer, upholsterer and actor — has recently moved on to a new career as inn-keeper and chef-in-residence of El Fraile Gordo. He needed to draw on more of his Renaissance talents when he set about restoring this old farm-house. Why El Fraile Gordo (the fat Friar)? The house stands where brothers of the Franciscan order once lived and worked. Hard to imagine what confronted David when you see dining room, sitting-room, kitchen and bedroom; everything feels much older, thanks to the many antiques and old materials that he searched out when nursing the building back to life. But this is more than a simple farm-house; stained-glass windows, grand piano, statues, and original sculptures have added sophistication to lowly origins. Guestrooms are fresh, light, welcoming, with beds for big sleeps and glorious wrap-around views. There's a delightful walled garden, a terrace that captures the morning sun, inspired cooking and a host whose hospitality and kindness run far beyond the call of duty. Specialíssimo.

Rooms: 4 with bath & wc.
Price: D/Tw 6000-6500 Pts; Tr 'family room' 8500-9000 Pts.
Breakfast: Included.
Meals: Dinner 1500-2000(M); 3000-4000(M).
Closed: Never.

How to get there: From Alicante towards Valencia on A7; first exit on N330 for Madrid. Exit to Novelada; into centre, left at lights and at top A403 towards Algueña At end road left onto C3223 towards Fortuna. After 4km right towards Cañada del Trigo; house in hamlet after 700m.

Map No: 21

98

Hotel Els Frares

Avenida del País Valencià 20
03811
Quatretondeta
Alicante

Tel: (9)6 5511234
Fax: (9)6 5511234

Management: Pat and Brian Fagg

Brian and Pat left successful careers in the UK to head for the Spanish hills; five years on, their Herculean efforts have borne fruit at their village inn and restaurant. Villagers must have wondered what they were up to when they bought a hundred-year-old ruin! But now the attractive pastel façade of the building, and a constant flow of visitors, are adding life and colour to the village. If you are beguiled by mountains then visit Quatretondeta; just behind the village, the jagged peaks of the Serrela Sierra rise to over 2000 feet — the hotel takes its name from them. There are rooms with private terraces looking out across surrounding almond groves to those lofty crags. Good mattresses ensure good sleep, fabrics are bright and some rooms have their original floor tiles. There are wall friezes and floral prints and photos of the mountains; all quite 'satiny', but fun. We thought the cosy dining and sitting rooms just right for the hotel; you'd look forward to returning here after a walk, perhaps under the guidance of Brian. At table, choose from an extensive menu that celebrates local dishes and tapas yet still finds a place for imaginative veggie alternatives; many ingredients — from olive oil, to fruit, to herbs — are home-grown.

Rooms: 6 with bath & wc.
Price: D with terrace 7500 Pts; Tw 6500 Pts inc. VAT.
Breakfast: Included.
Meals: 1600 Pts (M), 3000 Pts (M-gourmet), 2500-3500 Pts (C).
Closed: Never.

How to get there: From Alicante N340 to Alcoy. Here AP3313 towards Callosa de Ensarria; after Benilloba left to Gorga. Here sharp right along unmarked road for 5km to Quatretondeta (on map spelt Cuatretondeta).

Hotel Apartamentos Don Pedro

Calle Mar del Norte 4
03724
Moraira-Teulada
Alicante

Tel: (9)6 6490351/55
Fax: (9)6 6490350

Management: Juan Antonio Ivars Ivars

If planning a traditional (family) seaside holiday in this area of Spain you might consider Don Pedro. Unusually for this guide book these are self-catering apartments; we include them because, in a seductively quiet part of Moraira, the architects have created a building sensitive to local tradition. There are eight apartments per floor, each with its own terrace. You go in through a small kitchen with cooker and refrigerator and pretty hand-painted Valencian tiles. The bedroom has terracotta floor tiles, geometric tiling on the walls and attractive wooden furniture including a (proper) writing desk; there is room for a third bed. French windows give the rooms a light and airy feel and from the balconies looking out across the pool you can just see the cliffs of the Costa Blanca. Included in the room price is a simple breakfast but you could supplement this rather meagre offering with a feast from your own kitchen. It is a blissfully quiet spot and there's a sandy beach just 1km away as well as the harbour at Moraira.

Rooms: 15 apartments with terraces & kitchens.
Price: 7000-12000 Pts; extra bed 2000 Pts. In Aug min. stay 1 week.
Breakfast: Included.
Meals: Self-catering exc. breakfast.
Closed: Never.

How to get there: Leave A7 at Benissa exit then follow signs to Teulada. Through village and on to Moraira. 500m before Moraira turn left at signs for Don Pedro.

*"Que bonito es no hacer nada y
luego descansar."*

*"How beautiful it is to do nothing
and then to rest afterwards."*

SPANISH PROVERB

West Spain

El Vaqueril

Avenida de Alemania 8
10001
Cáceres

Tel: (9)27 223446
Fax: (9)27 191001

Management: Beatriz Viernhes de Ruanu

The big skies and cork-oaked hillsides of Estremadura make it one of Spain's grandest visual feasts. Reached by a tree-lined drive, and at the heart of 320 hectares of cattle ranch, this imposing old farm-house stands amid carob, olive and palm trees. Its ochre and white frontage gives it a very southern face; the row of crenellations that top its façade look not a bit warlike. The house is classic cortijo; things gravitate towards a large central patio — the South's most effective technique for ensuring shade at any time of the day. No two bedrooms are the same; they are big, with domed ceilings and decorated with bright fabrics and the family antiques. There are pretty hand-painted tiles in bathrooms, framed etchings and prints, open hearths. You sense a designer's hand has been involved. Downstairs is a vaulted lounge with a riotous ceramic hearth and a cavernous, beamed dining room; beef comes from the farm, of course. Breakfast is as generous as the evening meal — there may be home-made cake — and, you may, once replete, cycle or walk out into the estate. Cáceres and Mérida are an easy drive. **(Note: address above is for correspondence and not that of farm).**

Rooms: 7 with bath & wc.
Price: Tw 7500-9000 Pts.
Breakfast: Included.
Meals: Dinner 2600 Pts (M).
Closed: Never.

How to get there: From Cáceres towards Alcántara on C523. El Vaqueril just before village of Navas del Madroño.

Hotel Huerta Honda

Avenida López Asne s/n
06300
Zafra
Badajoz

Tel: (9)24 554100
Fax: (9)24 552504

Management: Antonio Martinez Buzo

If you travel down through Western Spain it is worth a short detour to visit Zafra; there is a castle with a stunning Renaissance patio and many churches to drool over. And you must stay at the Huerta Honda. It is an unmistakably southern-Spanish hotel: tiles, geraniums, bougainvillea and fountains. The decor may be a trifle kitsch but it speaks of years of caring from its owner Antonio Buzo and we were soon won over. There is a guest lounge with wicker furniture, open log fire in winter and a superb hotch-potch of ornamentation — balsa parrots, geometric tiles, a mounted deer's head, statue-lamps. Next door are the dining rooms — the atmosphere is intimate, with ochre walls and heavy beams above beautifully laid tables. The Honda is famous for its hams and you might be tempted to splurge here (always worth it when the cook is Basque!) but there is a cheaper menu. The bedrooms are fun too. With balconies onto the plant-filled patio they have an eclectic mix of original paintings, hand-painted furniture, rugs and wickerwork.

Rooms: 40 with bath or shower & wc.
Price: S 6720-14000 Pts; D 7600-17500 Pts; Tr 10100-20000 Pts.
Breakfast: 700 Pts.
Meals: Lunch/Dinner 1500-3500 Pts (M).
Closed: Never.

How to get there: From Mérida south to Zafra. The hotel is in the city centre, near the Palacio de los Duques de Feria.

Mesón La Cadena

Plaza Mayor 8
10200
Trujillo
Cáceres

Tel: (9)27 321463

Management: Juan Vicente Mariscal Mayordomo

La Cadena (the Chain) was a privilege granted by Felipe II whereby, as with embassy status, those staying here had right of asylum from the guardia. The privilege no longer holds... but this unpretentious little place remains an excellent inn. It is right on the beautiful arch-rimmed Pizarro-graced Plaza Mayor. The rooms, all on the second floor, are refreshingly simple and good value: medium-sized with tiled floors, bright locally-woven rugs and twin beds. We were drawn to a room looking onto the square but from the rooms at the back you can see the mountains. The restaurant specialises in good solid Extremeño cooking; any remaining fried-food fans should try the Migas Extremeñas. There are wonderful chorizo sausages and other things porky. You can eat outside under the arches while in cooler weather it would be nice to eat in the Cadena's old dining room with its heavy old roof beams and tiled floors. Storks come to land here and Pizarro dreamed up his wild western conquerings in Trujillo all those centuries ago.

Rooms: 8 twins with bath & wc.
Price: Tw 5000 Pts.
Breakfast: 350-400 Pts.
Meals: Lunch/Dinner 1400 Pts (M).
Closed: 2 weeks in June.

How to get there: Follow signs for 'Centro Ciudad'. The hotel is on the main square.

Finca Santa Marta

Pago de San Clemente
10200
Trujillo
Cáceres

Tel: (9)27 319203/
(9)1 3502217
Fax: (9)1 3502217

Management: Marta Rodríguez-Gimeno and Henri Elink

Santa Marta is a fine example of an Extremadura lagar where the owner lived on the top floor and made oil in the basement. This one has been totally transformed by interior designer Marta Rodríguez-Gimeno and her husband Henri into a very special country inn. In the vaulted olive-pressing area there is now an enormous guest lounge and library; it is cool and elegant with estera matting, neo-mudéjar ceilings, interesting old furniture and subtle lighting. The rooms are a delight; some have antiques, some have hand-painted Portuguese furniture, no two are alike. Those in the 'other half', Finca Santa Teresa, may be rather more rustic with more locally-produced furniture but the effect is equally appealing. The whole house is a treasure trove of antiques, painting and good taste. Why so many South American bits and pieces? Henri was ambassador to Peru and it was sympathy for that Latin readiness to share that inspired him to open his home to guests. He and Marta do so with grace and charm. 30 hectares of peace and fabulous birdlife. Bring binoculars.

Rooms: 10 with bath & wc.
Price: D/Tw 8500 Pts.
Breakfast: Included.
Meals: Lunch/Dinner 2500 Pts. Book ahead.
Closed: Never.

How to get there: From Trujillo C324 towards Guadalupe. After 14km Finca is on the right where you see eucalyptus trees with storks' nests.

Hotel Rector

Rector Esperabé 10
Apartado 399
37008
Salamanca

Tel: (9)23 218482
Fax: (9)23 214008

Management: Eduardo Ferrán

Just a two-minute walk from the cathedral and hard by the Roman bridge this palacete or town mansion is one of the smartest small hotels we know and it is a joy to discover it in a city of such interest and ineffable loveliness. Much love and lolly have been lavished here — and the family antiques pillaged, to the delight of their guests! Wood is used to good effect throughout; there are sparkling parquet floors, stained-glass windows and old tapestries downstairs, inlaid bedside tables, writing desks and hand-crafted bedheads in mahogany and olivewood in the bedrooms. Wide corridors lead to large plush rooms which have the fittings of a five-star hotel. You might not need the telephone in the bathroom or the fax points, but you will certainly appreciate the double glazing, air conditioning and deep armchairs. In bathrooms the same luxurious note is held — marble, double basins, thick towels. The rooms are predominantly salmon-pink and blue and old prints add the final touch of class. Leave your car in the hotel car park and go walking.

Rooms: 14 with bath & wc.
Price: S 12000 Pts; D/Tw 17000 Pts; Tr 21000 Pts.
Breakfast: 1000 Pts.
Meals: None.
Closed: Never.

How to get there: From Madrid, follow signs round Salamanca towards Zamora. Do not take 1st bridge, pass Roman bridge

on right, take next bridge & turn right back along river. Hotel is on right after about 400m.

Palacio de Castellanos

San Pablo 58-64
37008
Salamanca

Tel: (9)23 261818
Fax: (9)23 261819

Management: Remedios Madrid

Just yards from Spain's finest central square, opposite the Dominican convent, is a luxurious part-15th-century hotel. Its centrepiece remains the beautiful cloister, now a drawing room covered by super-modern steel and glass. The restoration, a work of art in itself, has won prizes for its careful uncovering and embellishment of the old ceilings, stairwell and columns. Beneath the grand façade is a terrace café; within is another dining area. The menu is small but with a season-based choice of Basque and Navarre cooking. Staff are young and helpful and the hotel values tourists as much as businessmen. The bedrooms have all the extras; satellite TV, video, bathroom scales and 3(sic) phones in each... but this is no soulless monster; the whole hotel doubles as an 'alternative' art gallery showing young Catalan artists. This is one of our few 'chain' hotels but we have no doubts about including it; we were greeted with warmth and enthusiasm by its young manageress Remedios Madrid for whom people clearly come before pesetas.

Rooms: 58 & 4 duplexes with bath & wc.
Price: S 10000-14500 Pts; D/Tw 18200 Pts; Duplex 21500 Pts.
Breakfast: Buffet 1300 Pts.
Meals: Lunch/Dinner 2000 Pts (M); 4500 Pts (C).
Closed: Never.

How to get there: From Madrid, head for 'Centro Ciudad'/Plaza de Colón and ask for Los Domínicos (neighbouring monastery). Hotel has own parking.

La Posada de San Martín

Calle Larga 1
37659
San Martín del Castañar
Salamanca

Tel: (9)23 437036

Management: María Angeles del Valle

A few years ago, visitors to San Martín would come, look, enjoy.... and ruefully set off home. Now they can prolong the pleasure by staying in the posada. This grand old village house has been completely renovated by local artisans (and a little help from Brussels). You are definitely in a house: the sitting room and mezzanine dining room are family-sized; it is all deliciously cosy. Wherever possible old materials were restored and recycled and just about everything is local; the bedstead ironmongery, the lovely woven bedcovers and the dining room furniture. There are fresh-cut and dried flowers and lots of information on walks and visits. An attractive spiral staircase leads up to the rooms which are small but memorable with huge double beds — one 2 metres square, another a very grand four-poster with canopy. There is however, not much room to swing the proverbial kitty beside them. There is also a suite (one of the cheapest in Spain?) and even baby cots are available. At breakfast, try the local honey and cured hams. Great value.

Rooms: 5 with bath & wc.
Price: 'Normal' D/Tw 4500 Pts; 'Special' D/Tw 5500 Pts.
Breakfast: 350 Pts.
Meals: Lunch 1500 Pts (M); Dinner 1200 Pts (M).
Closed: Never.

How to get there: From Salamanca C512 to Vecinos then C210 to Tamames. Just after Tamames, left on C525 towards Béjar. After Arroyomuerto (17km), right to San Martín. Posada is in village centre — signposted.

Map No: 10

Hotel Doña Teresa

Carretera Mogarraz s/n
37624
La Alberca
Salamanca

Tel: (9)23 415308
Fax: (9)23 415309

Management: Fernando Rodríguez Puerto

The Doña Teresa is a sign of the new Spain where 'Rural Tourism' doesn't necessarily imply kipping in the hay. Although just recently completed, the building is thoroughly integrated thanks to its architects' scrupulously following the dictates of local tradition. The combination of terracotta, beams and wafer-bricking creates warmth throughout the downstairs areas. Arches and old cabin trunks soften the lines while the dining room introduces a hint of designer chic. Although the hotel caters for business folk as well as tourists, the rooms are exceptionally good value. They have all you need and maybe a lot you don't (jacuzzi, radio, hair dryer); most have either terrace or balcony. The beds were hand-carved in the village and we liked the bright bedcovers. There are also gym, sauna and sunbeds if that's your thing. In the middle of a glorious area of wooded hills, La Alberca is well worth a long detour and is a perfect place to recharge your batteries.

Rooms: 41 with bath & wc.
Price: D 6000 Pts; Tw 8000 Pts; Tw with terrace 10000 Pts.
Breakfast: 400 Pts.
Meals: Lunch/Dinner 1500 Pts (M or C).
Closed: Never.

How to get there: From Salamanca C512 to Vecinos then SA210 to Tamames then SA204 to La Alberca. There, take road towards Mogarraz — hotel is on left.

Finca La Casería

10613
Navaconcejo
Cáceres

Tel: (9)27 173141
Fax: (9)27 173141

Management: David E Pink & María Cruz Barona

This lovely old farm-house has been the home of Señora Barona Hernández' family for some 200 years. A monastery stood here originally and we all know that few have as keen a nose for a good site as the religious orders. The granite building stands in cherry groves one side of the lovely Jerte valley; be here at the end of March when blossom fills the valley or early summer when you can help to harvest the fruit! There are plums and figs and sheep and cows; between directing his guests to the extraordinary natural history or archeological spots of the area David Pink works hard at his smallholding. It is much more home than hotel (there is an abundance of dogs). The huge sitting room has books and an open hearth. Of the six guestrooms, mostly furnished with old pieces, the 'cuarto de arriba' has a screen and lovely wrought-iron bed which has recently celebrated its 166th birthday. Dinner or lunch is a relaxed occasion with home-made puddings to complement regional dishes. Many come to walk but you can fish for tench or swim in the nearby reservoir... or relax.

Rooms: 4 with own bath & wc, 2 sharing shower/bath & wc + 1 cottage.
Price: D/Tw 7000 Pts; D/Tw sharing 6000 Pts inc VAT. Cottage 10000 Pts (min. stay 2 nights).
Breakfast: Included; cottage self-catering.
Meals: Lunch/Dinner 2000 Pts (M); book ahead.
Closed: Aug.

How to get there: From Madrid E90 to Navalmoral de la Mata; C511 to Plasencia; N110 towards Avila. At km378.6 (about 27km from Plasencia), right at small sign for La Casería (3km before Navaconcejo).

Map No: 10

Antigua Casa del Heno

Finca Valdepimienta
10460
Losar de la Vera
Cáceres

Tel: (9)27 198077
Fax: (9)27 198077

Management: Graciela Rosso and Javier Tejero Vivó

The Casa del Heno stands superbly isolated on the southern side of the Gredos mountain range. Arriving along the 4km track that leads from Losar to this old shepherd's dwelling, your appetite is whetted for the feast to come. The 150-year-old building has been sympathetically restored by its young owners; there is much exposed stone, beams and use of cork in the decoration. Solar panels provide for a large part of the house's hot water. The eight guestrooms are just right; no television, good beds and views across the surrounding farm. Just 150 yards away is a crystalline river and beyond are the mountains begging to be walked. Horse-riding can be arranged, too. The whole of the valley is at its best in spring when the many thousands of cherry trees come into blossom. Predictably, you'll need to book well ahead if wanting a room at that time. Here too ornithologists can expect to see far more than just sparrows and pigeons. The owners welcome their guests as friends; there is good home cooking and barbecued meat is a speciality.

Rooms: 8 with bath & wc.
Price: D/Tw 7300 Pts.
Breakfast: Included.
Meals: Lunch/Dinner 2500 Pts (M);
2500-3000 Pts (C).
Closed: Christmas.

How to get there: From Madrid N V to Navalmoral de la Mata. Right onto CC904 to Losar de la Vera then take mountain track 4km to hotel.

"Children do not like Castilla, its flatness and harsh colours. But adults appreciate its beauty, dry and cruel as it is... there cannot be any rush here. Castilla's richness is nurtured daily as much by hard work as immense patience. The colours, bright reds and mauves, reflect the fights of lords, the tyranny of the clergy, the poverty of the plebian. The colours are the blood of Castilla."

CRISTINA DEL SOL - *Sueños*

Central Spain

Hostal El Milano Real

Hoyos del Espino
05634
Avila

Tel: (9)20 349108
Fax: (9)20 349156

Management: Francisco Sánchez Rico and Teresa Dorn

If you pass this small modern hotel by you miss a most special experience. With the Gredos range all about, the hotel feels rather like a Swiss chalet; this feeling is heightened by the carved wood of the balconies and the cosy atmosphere within. Up at the top, beneath the rafters, is a huge attic lounge and, down a floor, a second reading room. But the festivities really get under way in the dining room. The food brings people all the way out from Madrid; Basque/French influenced, and with some fine regional dishes, the restaurant wins a mention in all the famous guide books, Michelin included. Francisco ('Paco') knows his wine; he has a selection of 135 of his favourites to choose from and alongside each wine lists year, bodega, D.O. — then gives each his personal score out of ten! And when you wend your way to your room more treats are in store: decorated by Madrid's best, the fabrics, polished wooden floors, antique prints and views set the rooms solidly in the special bracket. Food and rooms are incredible value; worth a VERY long detour and the Gredos are another of Spain's better-kept secrets.

Rooms: 13 with bath & wc + 1 suite.
Price: D/Tw 7700 Pts; Ste 10500 Pts.
Breakfast: 450-1200 Pts.
Meals: Lunch/Dinner 2500 Pts (M);
3000-3500 Pts (C).
Closed: 3 weeks in Nov.

How to get there: From Avila towards Bejar/Plasencia. After 6km turn left towards Arena de San Pedro on N502, then right towards Barco de Avila on N500. Continue for 17km and signposted to right.

Map No: 10

Hostal Don Diego
Calle Marqués de Canales y Chozas 5
05001
Avila

Tel: (9)20 255475

Management: Miguel Angel Verguera

This sparkling little hostal, directly opposite the Parador and within the old city walls, is definitely a family affair. It is modest and unpretentious, offering you a clean room, a comfortable bed and a smile as you arrive. The smallish rooms are on three floors, each one named after one of the owner Miguel's children. His fourth child, Diego, gives the hostal its name. The bedrooms combine pine furniture with modern brass bedsteads; there are good bedcovers and plenty of blankets in winter. All the fittings are modern; half the rooms have baths, the others small shower rooms. Light sleepers would probably prefer a room at the back of the hostal. It is all unmistakably Spanish with more than a hint of kitsch. Although the hotel has no breakfast facilities the Parador opposite serves breakfast in a setting somewhat grander but less friendly than the hotel's. Or take a five-minute stroll up to one of the cafés in the Plaza to breakfast amid the hubbub of this lovely old town.

Rooms: 12 with shower or bath & wc.
Price: S 3000-3500 Pts; Tw 4800-5800 Pts; D 5000-6000 Pts.
Breakfast: None; Parador open opposite.
Meals: None.
Closed: Never.

How to get there: Entering Avila by Puerta del Carmen, follow signs to Parador Nacional. Hostal is opposite Parador.

Guts Muths

Calle Matanza s/n
Barrio de Abajo
24732
Santiago Millas, León

Tel: (9)87 691123
Fax: (9)87 691123

Management: Sjoerd Hers and Mari Paz Martínez

Santiago Millas and other villages in the area of La Maragatería drew their wealth from a virtual monopoly on the transport of merchandise by horse and cart throughout Spain. The coming of the railways put an end to all that. What remains of this past glory are some grand old village houses. Guts Muths is as fine an example as any. It is a big, solid house; you enter under an imposing arch to find yourself in a lovely flower and palm-filled courtyard. It is utterly peaceful. We take our hats off to Sjoerd and Mari Paz, the very sympathetic owners, for the easy-going intimate atmosphere they have created. Part of this is decorative flair — simple comfortable rooms where wood predominates; exposed stonework, dried and fresh flowers; an enchanting dining room where ceramic tiles, dark roof beams and an old bread oven are the backdrop for simply delicious regional dishes. The other part is Sjoerd's genuine enthusiasm that his guests get to love all this as much as he does; he'll regale you with history or take you out to explore the nearby gorges on foot, or mountain bike... or even attached to a climbing rope.

Rooms: 8 with bath & wc.
Price: D/Tw 8000 Pts; Q 12000 Pts.
Breakfast: Included.
Meals: Lunch 2000 Pts (M); Dinner 1850 Pts (M).
Closed: Never.

How to get there: From Astorga LE133 towards Destriana. After about 10km, left towards Santiago Millas, Barrio de Abajo — signposted.

113

La Posada del Marqués

Plaza Mayor 4
24270
Carrizo de la Ribera
León

Tel: (9)87 357171
Fax: (9)87 358101

Management: Carlos Velázquez-Duro

We think there are few places to stay in Spain quite as special as this old pilgrim's hospital, originally part of the Santa María monastery next door. Pass through the fine old portal and discover first a pebbled cloister and beyond a lovely mature garden with gurgling brook and big old trees. It reminded us slightly of an English rectory! Carlos Velázquez (his family have owned the posada for generations) and his wife graciously greet their guests before showing them to the superb bedrooms. They are set round a gallery on the first floor and are all decorated with family heirlooms — lovely Portuguese (canopied) beds, original paintings, old lamps and dressers. One has a terrace over the cloisters; all are quite enchanting. The sitting and games rooms downstairs are similarly furnished. Heavy old wooden doors, carved chests and tables and comfy armchairs and sofa in front of the hearth. There is a snooker table. Although the posada only serves breakfast, meals can be organised at a restaurant close by. Kind and erudite hosts and the most beguiling of settings.

Rooms: 11 with bath & wc.
Price: D/Tw 8000-9500 Pts inc VAT.
Breakfast: Included.
Meals: Special prices at restaurant nearby,
Dinner 1500 Pts (M), 2500 Pts (C).
Closed: Never.

How to get there: From León N120 towards Astorga. After 18km, right on LE442 to Villanueva de Carrizo. Cross river into Carrizo de la Ribera and ask for Plaza Mayor.

Casa Susarón

Calle Real 22
24855
Puebla de Lillo
León

Tel: (9)08 390400/
    (9)85 221918
E-mail:
susaron@cegijon.satelia.es.
Management: María Teresa
Fernández Rodríguez

Casa Susarón is a dream come true for this friendly young couple. Javier grew up in this small village at the southern flank of the mighty Picos. His new home was once the village bakery; the old kneading machine and oven speak of the building's past. The timbers and earthy colour of the frontage create a warm first impression; the house is tucked in beside the village church. We visited on a cold day and bedrooms were toasty warm; cut flowers, wafer bricking offset by warm ochre colours, old beams and the sheer peacefulness of the place make you feel instantly at home. Sitting and dining rooms are furnished with family bits and bobs, many recently restored by your hosts, and upstairs is a covered gallery; Javier is putting a library together for his guests. Rooms vary in size and configuration, following the original walls of the building. A couple of them are mezzanine; our favourite is the twin 'up the stairs on the left'. Bathrooms, likewise, vary in size; they too are nicely finished, with hand-painted tiles. The owners live next door but come in to prepare your breakfast in the morning. A wonderful base for skiing in winter, or walking at any time of year.

Rooms: 4 with bath & wc.
Price: D/Tw 5500-6500 Pts; Tr 8000 Pts.
Breakfast: 400 Pts.
Meals: None.
Closed: Never.

How to get there: From León N626 towards Boñar. Here follow on for Puerto de San Isidro until arrive in village of Puebla de Lillo. House on right near to church.

Map No: 3

Casa de las Campanas

34830
Salinas de Pisuerga
Palencia

Tel: (9)79 120118
Fax: (9)79 870450

Management: Isabel and Pedro Pablo López Duque

In a forgotten village in the little-known province of Palencia, Casa de las Campanas is one of a growing breed of rural hostelries which boldly dare to mix old and new, design and tradition. We think the mix has worked a treat here. Isabel and Pedro are sophisticated hosts yet receive guests with old-fashioned graciousness. The timbered dining room is well lit, with terracotta floors and — as throughout the house — carefully-chosen fabrics. Meals are generously priced; Isabel cooks well and in local tradition. An impressive modern spiral staircase winds up to the bedrooms. These, like the downstairs rooms, make good use of wood, traditional tiles and fabric. There are two sitting rooms on the upper floors; with sloping ceilings, good chairs and piles of books they seemed just the spot to settle down to read up on Palencia's many Romanesque churches. The most intriguing feature of the house is its unusual shutters (celosias or 'jealousies'), inspired by an old design that allowed young maidens to observe their heart's desire yet remain unseen.

Rooms: 6 with bath & wc.
Price: D/Tw 5500 Pts inc. VAT.
Breakfast: 300 Pts.
Meals: Lunch/Dinner 1400 Pts.
Closed: Never.

How to get there: From Santander A67 towards Oviedo then N611 south to Aguilar de Campoo. There towards Aguilar to Cervera de Pisuerga on P212. On right as you pass through village of Salinas de Pisuerga.

Posada de Santa María la Real

Carretera de Cervera s/n
34800
Aguilar de Campoo
Palencia

Tel: (9)79 122000/122522
Fax: (9)79 125680

Management: Arancha Moroso Mata and Elena Martín Milla

In a wing of the beautiful Cistercian monastery of Santa María la Real, eighteen guestrooms have recently been created by the local 'escuela taller' — a scheme that teaches traditional skills to the young unemployed. While they have been utterly faithful to local building and restoration techniques, they have dared to let 90s design play a part too; the result is an exceptional hostelry. On arrival you are struck by its peacefulness — monks have always had an 'ear' for this, after all. A pebbled patio leads you up to the entrance; the façade of timbers, stone, wafer bricking and eaves is beguiling. Once inside the building the marriage of old and new surprises and seduces. Every last corner has been carefully restored — and considered. There are pebbled and parquet floors; designer chairs and lamps snug beside hearth and beam. The design of the guestrooms followed the dictates of a tall building so they are small and 'mezzanine' and attractively decorated; we would willingly sacrifice space for charm and, let's not forget, we ARE in a monastery!

Rooms: 18 with bath & wc.
Price: S 5000-5300 Pts; D/Tw 6900-7300 Pts; Tr 8500-9100 Pts inc VAT.
Breakfast: Buffet included.
Meals: Dinner 1200 Pts (M).
Closed: 23-25 Dec.

How to get there: From Santander A67 towards Oviedo then N611 south to Aguilar de Campoo. On road that leads from Aguilar to Cervera de Pisuerga on left.

Map No: 4

El Convento

Calle Convento s/n
34492
Santa María de Mave
Palencia

Tel: (9)79 123611
Fax: (9)79 125492

Management: José Antonio Moral

You'll leave traffic, city, pollution and your cares far behind when you come and stay at El Convento. The Moral family laboured long and hard to nurse this 18th-century Benedictine monastery back to its former good health. The cloister, gardens and old stone walls remain as conducive to meditation as in the days when the brothers chose this peaceful site for their religious house. You reach the guest bedrooms, some in what were the monks' cells, via labyrinthine corridors; they are medium-sized, simply furnished in dark-wooded castellano style and most give onto the cloister. The two suites have curtained four-poster beds. You dine in the former chapter house where, once again, heavy antique furniture feels in keeping with the building's past. Cuisine is unashamedly traditional-Castillian; thick chick-pea or bean soups and many lamb-based dishes. Roast from a wood-fired oven is the house speciality, as are freshly-picked strawberries when in season. Don't miss the chapel; it dates back to 1208 and is considered one of the finest examples of Palencia's many Romanesque edifices. Exceptionally kind hosts.

Rooms: 23 with bath & wc + 2 suites.
Price: S 4000-4500 Pts; D/Tw 6000-7000 Pts; Ste 10000-12000 Pts.
Breakfast: 400 Pts.
Meals: Lunch/Dinner 1500 Pts (M); 2500-3000 Pts (C).
Closed: Never.

How to get there: From Aguilar de Campoo south towards Palencia on N611. After 5km, in Olleros de Pisuerga, left at sign for Santa María de Mave.

La Posada del Balneario
Camino del Balneario s/n
09145
Valdelateja
Burgos

Tel: (9)47 150220

Management: José Ramón Ríos
Ramos

The original spa hotel at Valdelateja first opened its doors in 1872, when the well-heeled would ride up from Burgos or down from Santander to take the waters. But spas ceased to be fashionable; then came the war and, by the beginning of the decade, the site lay abandoned. But after the Dark Ages, the Renaissance! — total rehabilitation of the two original buildings has produced one of Spain's loveliest small hotels. The setting is wild and wonderful; look out to woods of holm and evergreen oak that cling to the sides of the canyon cut by the river Rudrón. The building is rather 'Swiss-chalet', with wooden balconies, galleries and ornately carved eaves; inside wood is again the primary element, whether in darkened beam or polished parquet floor. The lantern-ceiling of the drawing-room — the former ballroom — is a real beauty. No two guest rooms are the same; some have antique bedsteads of wrought-iron, other beds are of padded fabric; all have big bathrooms with full-length baths. The dining room looks out to the river, a wonderful accompaniment to the home cooking; stuffed vegetables are the house speciality, the staff are bright and friendly.

Rooms: 21 with bath & wc.
Price: S 4900-5300 Pts; D/Tw 7000-8000
Pts; Ste 11500-12500 Pts.
Breakfast: 500 Pts.
Meals: Lunch/Dinner 1750 Pts (M);
2800-4000 Pts (C).
Closed: Never.

How to get there: From Burgos N623
towards Santander. Through San Felices
and just before Valdelateja turn right to Balneario; signposted.

Mesón del Cid

Plaza Santa María 8
09003
Burgos

Tel: (9)47 205971
Fax: (9)47 269460

Management: José Luis Alzaga

Few are the cathedrals to match that of Burgos and if you come to study this marvel of the Spanish Gothic stay at Mesón del Cid; from the rooms at the front you can almost reach out and touch the buttresses, pinnacles and grimacing gargoyles. The building once housed one of the first printing presses in Spain, established by an acolyte of Gutemberg more than 500 years ago, and the hotel takes its name from an illuminated manuscript of Mío Cid displayed at reception. This fine old townhouse is quite naturally considered THE place to stay in Burgos. We liked the bedrooms a lot; they are carpeted (right for winter), many have old wrought-iron bedsteads, all have prints, tables, plants and decent bathrooms. The suites are very grand; one has period furnishings, bronze taps and even an old-fashioned 'phone. No 302 would probably be our favourite. Good things await you in the restaurant where the setting is perfect for trying the traditional stews and roasts of the province.

Rooms: 25 with bath & wc + 3 suites.
Price: S 8500 Pts; D/Tw 14500 Pts; Ste 19500 Pts.
Breakfast: 900 Pts.
Meals: Lunch/Dinner 3500-4000 Pts (M), 4500 Pts (C).
Closed: Never.

How to get there: In old town directly opposite main entrance to cathedral on Plaza de Santa María. Car park next door.

Map No: 4

Hotel Arlanza

Calle Mayor 11
09346
Covarrubias
Burgos

Tel: (9)47 406441
Fax: (9)47 406359
E-mail: arlanza@ctv.es

Management: Mercedes Miguel Briones

Covarrubias is a charming old town, well off the tourist-beaten track and a must if you love places where tradition still counts. The heart of the old town is a colonnaded square — the Arlanza is on one side of it. Mercedes and Juan José, two of the friendliest and most charming hoteliers you will meet anywhere, have created a hotel to match the charm and intimacy of the town. You enter under the colonnade through an arched doorway. Inside, there are lovely terracotta floors, ceramic tiles from Talavera on the walls, old chandeliers, original beams and lintels. Downstairs it is rather dark as little light enters through the small original windows. By contrast, the bedrooms that give onto the square (see photo) are lighter. All the rooms are reached by an impressive staircase; they are large, with tiled floors, old lamps and rustic furniture. There is good regional fare in the restaurant and maybe a chance to talk with the owners; they visit the U.K. every year, know its farthest corners and speak the language, too.

Rooms: 40 with bath & wc inc. 2 suites.
Price: S 5500 Pts; D/Tw 9300 Pts; Tr 12300 Pts; Ste 9900 Pts inc. VAT.
Breakfast: 650 Pts.
Meals: Lunch/Dinner 1950 Pts (M), 3000 Pts (C).
Closed: 15 Dec-15 March.

How to get there: From Burgos N1 towards Madrid. In Lerma left on C110 towards Salas de los Infantes. Hotel in Covarrubias on Plaza Mayor.

Map No: 4

Hotel Tres Coronas de Silos

Plaza Mayor 6
09610
Santo Domingo de Silos
Burgos

Tel: (9)47 390047/390065
Fax: (9)47 390065

Management: Emeterio Martín García

Right on the main square of Santo Domingo, Tres Coronas used to be referred to simply as 'la casa grande' by local folk. It is indeed a solid old building of elegant proportions and well suited to its latter-day role of hotel — it was once a chemist's. Once you have entered under the original coat of arms you see that much remains of its mid-18th-century origins. Throughout the building there are terracotta floors, heavy Castilian furniture and massive beams. Exposed stone alternates with plaster to give every bedroom an authentically 'country' feel. They are medium sized, have all the extras, but what we liked most were the tiled floors and the views onto the square. No.9 (beneath the coat of arms) has its own balcony; perhaps the place to practise your crowd-stopping speeches. The restaurant is very popular, especially at weekends; it won its colours many years back and continues to win praise for its roast meats from a wood-fired oven. Big breakfasts, more interesting than most.

Rooms: 15 with bath & wc + 1 grander with balcony.
Price: S 5500-5900 Pts; D/Tw 8700-9200 Pts; Balcony room 9300-9800 Pts.
Breakfast: 850 Pts.
Meals: Lunch/Dinner 2500-3000 Pts (C).
Closed: Never.

How to get there: From Burgos N1 towards Madrid then N234 towards Soria. Right in Hacinas on BU903 to Santo Domingo de Silos. On right in centre of village.

Hostal Santo Domingo de Silos

Calle Santo Domingo
09610
Santo Domingo de Silos
Burgos

Tel: (9)47 390053
Fax: (9)47 390052

Management: Eleuterio del Alamo Castrillo

The highlight of a stay in Santo Domingo de Silos is the Gregorian chant in the monastery chapel; you can hear it every day of the year and it is well worth a detour as you travel north or south. You may consider overnighting at this simple little family hotel. Its real raison d'être is its busy dining room; at weekends visitors come from far and near to eat roast lunch or dinner prepared by Eleuterio in a wood-fired oven. His portions of lamb, goat and pork are worthy of a medieval banquet — and the prices are almost medieval too. The bedrooms on the attic floor have very low ceilings; those on the first floor are roomier. Some have tiled floors and animal-skin rugs; there are carved headboards and small night tables. The trimmings at this hostal come with the food rather than the rooms, but these are simple and perfectly clean and comfortable (an extension to create more rooms was being built when we visited; please let us know what you think). A friendly, unpretentious place. Come for the food, the value and the Gregorian chant.

Rooms: 35 (10D, 25Tw) with bath & wc.
Price: S 3200-3500 Pts; D/Tw 4500-4800 Pts.
Breakfast: 275-425 Pts.
Meals: Lunch/Dinner 1000 Pts (M), 2500 Pts (C).
Closed: Never.

How to get there: From Burgos N1 towards Madrid then N234 towards Soria.
Left in Hacinas on BU903 to Santo Domingo de Silos. On right as you go through village.

Molino del Rio Viejo

Carretera N110, Km 172
40170
Collado Hermoso
Segovia

Tel: (9)21 403063
Fax: (9)21 403051

Management: Antonio Armero

Tucked away among poplars, between the Guadarrama mountains to the south and the flatlands of northern Castille to the north, this old water mill lies to one side of the old transhumance route leading to Estremadura. The congenial owners declare that this is neither hotel nor restaurant but 'your own home'. Its timbered lounge is as intimate as they come; breakfast in front of a roaring log fire in winter and dine on trusty, family cooking in the evening — lamb and thick soups are among the favourites. In the warmer months, move outside to a terrace overlooking the gardens cut through by the Rio Viejo. The rooms are as cosy as the rest of the millhouse; pastel-painted, beamed with antique wooden or brass beds, they have flowered fabrics, pretty lamps and books — very 'English-country'. Upstairs is a quiet lounge-cum-library or, if you prefer more active pursuits, there are horses to saddle and ride out into the wonderful surrounding countryside. And Segovia and Pedraza are on your doorstep.

Rooms: 6 with bath & wc.
Price: D/Tw 9000 Pts inc. VAT.
Breakfast: 700.
Meals: Lunch/Dinner 3000-4000(C).
Closed: Never.

How to get there: From Segovia N110 towards Soria. After 20km at km172, 400m from Collado Hermoso the hotel is beside road next to bridge.

Map No: 12

124

La Tejera de Fausto

Carretera La Salceda-Sepúlveda Km 7
40173
Requijada (Por la Velilla)
Segovia

Tel: (9)21 127087
Fax: (9)1 5641519

Management: Jaime Armero Buchet

The two old stone buildings of the Tejera de Fausto stand gloriously alone more than a mile from the nearest village by the banks of the Cega river. It is no coincidence that the roofs are terracotta: tiles (tejas) used to be manufactured right here. Close by are the Guadarrama mountains, sentinels guarding Madrid and the Meseta; the setting is as Castilian as you could hope to find. The decoration is in perfect keeping; rooms have simple and attractive rustic furniture, central heating in winter, good bathrooms and neither telephone nor television to distract you from the views. There are books and local information in the lounge. The restaurant — a series of small adjoining rooms with blazing fires in the colder months — is pure Castile again; specialities are roast lamb, sucking pig and excellent game dishes (often wild boar). Owner Jaime loves communicating his knowledge of the area. Next door is a Romanesque chapel built with foundation stones from a Roman villa and you can walk out from the Tejera on the old transhumance routes that criss-cross the region.

Rooms: 7 with bath & wc + 1 suite.
Price: S 8000 Pts; D/Tw 9000 Pts; Tr 12000 Pts; Ste 16000 Pts.
Breakfast: 750 Pts.
Meals: Lunch/Dinner 3000-3500 Pts (C).
Closed: Mon-Thur exc. festivals.

How to get there: From Segovia, N110 towards Soria to La Salceda. There, left towards Pedraza. Hotel on left after Torre Val de San Pedro.

125

La Posada de los Vientos

Calle Encerradero 2
28755
La Acebeda
Madrid

Tel: (9)1 8699195
Fax: (9)1 8699195

Management: Josefina Maestre and Pedro Retamar

The small village of La Acebeda stands proudly 4000 feet up on the flank of the Sierra del Norte. It is within easy driving distance of Madrid but is still an utterly peaceful rural spot. Pedro and Josefa are young, cultured hosts; they set out to convert this 200-year-old village house into a country inn with a difference, somewhere guests could come not just to sleep off the stress of the city but also to immerse themselves completely in the country. It would be hard to choose a favourite room here; throughout the house the emphasis is on the 'natural', the homespun, the handmade. There are old chests and beds, wood floors, bright Indian bedcovers, good cotton sheets. Each room is named after a different wind (viento) — whence the name of the inn. The dining and sitting rooms couldn't be nicer; here again the base elements are stone, antiques and beams. On the menu? — whatever is in season, local if possible, much of it organic. And then there are the horses, eight of them, waiting to be saddled; and mountain bikes, too. ¡Magnífico!

Rooms: 9 with bath & wc.
Price: D/Tw 8000 (for 2) inc. breakfast Pts; Half board 11600 Pts (for 2); Full board 15200 Pts (for 2).
Breakfast: Included.
Meals: Lunch/Dinner 1800 Pts if not on half or full board.
Closed: Never.

How to get there: From Madrid N1
north; at km83 take exit to La Acebeda. In village first right to La Posada.

Map No: 12

126

Casón de la Pinilla

40592
Cerezo de Arriba
Segovia

Tel: (9)21 557201
Fax: (9)21 557209

Management: Juncal Chaves & Carmen de Frías

The few lucky Madrileños who are in on the secret flee the madness and pollution of the capital and drive over the mountains to be guests of Carmen Frías and Juncal Chaves. Both left successful careers to create a backdrop for their 'tertulias' in the peaceful outskirts of Cerezo de Arriba. They wanted it to be more than simply a good stopover for the skiers who head for the lifts at nearby Pinilla (snow normally from the end of December to March). They really do treat you as friends. Conversation at dinner is as important here as silence at bedtime. The building is long and modern, with books, comfy chairs and a dining room of human proportions to provide timeless warmth. The guestrooms are large and simply furnished. But our memories are more of food. Expect only the best cuts of meat, fresh veg and home-made puddings. When dining on the terrace as the mountains turn purple you'll be glad you stopped an hour short of the metropolis as guests of these two charming ladies. Medieval villages and spectacular mountain gorges are close by; cookery courses also take place regularly — write or phone for details.

Rooms: 9 with bath & wc.
Price: S 5600-6700 Pts; D/Tw 7500-8600 Pts.
Breakfast: Buffet included.
Meals: Lunch/Dinner 1850 Pts (M); 2500 Pts (C).
Closed: Never.

How to get there: From Madrid N1 towards Burgos. Leave at exit 104 onto N110 towards Soria. After 1.5km, right towards Cerezo de Arriba. Hotel on right shortly before entering village.

127

La Posada de Sigueruelo

Concepción Alarcos Rodriguez
Calle Badén 40
40590
Sigueruelo, Segovia

Tel: (9)21 508135
Fax: (9)21 508135

Management: Concha Alarcos

Concha Alarcos bravely left her social work to open this tiny country inn. As you approach down the old cobbled streets of the little hamlet something special awaits you; the outside gives little away but inside her 120-year-old farm-house is all homely comfort and warmth — above all, Concha's gentle welcome. After a day's walking, enjoy the comfy chairs, dark beams and open fire in the sitting room. A delicious smell of wood pervades the house; when renovating they only used 100% natural oils to treat rafters, doors and lintels. There are dried flowers, antique trunks and old wooden harvesting tools... and six attractive bedrooms. One room has Art Deco beds, others wrought-iron; Concha has gradually collected pieces from Madrid markets. The rooms have showers (a water-saving measure). Dinner is good regional cooking with vegetarian dishes if requested. Riding in the hills or canoeing (with the owner's son) in the unforgettable Duratón gorge can be arranged. Plus free use of mountain bikes. A very special place.

Rooms: 6 with shower & wc.
Price: Half-board only: D/Tw 12000 Pts.
Breakfast: Included.
Meals: Lunch 1100 Pts (M); 3500 Pts (C). Dinner included.
Closed: Never.

How to get there: From Madrid N1 towards Burgos. At km99, exit towards Santo Tomé del Puerto onto N110 towards Segovia. After 3km left to Sigueruelo. Ask for Posada in village.

El Parador de la Puebla

Plaza de Carlos Ruiz 2
28190
Puebla de la Sierra
Madrid

Tel: (9)1 8697256
Fax: (9)1 8697256

Management: Severiano Sánchez

Madrid may only be a couple of hour's drive yet it feels as if it were a million miles away. Puebla is a tiny village high up in the Sierra that shelters Madrid's northern flank. Until recently there was nowhere to stay here; now, thanks to the efforts of a local co-operative venture, there is a cosy little inn. Right on the main square of the village you might not recognise; it stands on the spot where the priest's house once stood. It is very new but its stone walls, wooden porch and tiled roof allow it to sit harmoniously among the older village buildings. You enter through a lively little bar; above it are the dining and sitting rooms whose tiled floors and wooden ceilings are immediately appealing. The food is incredibly inexpensive, the emphasis always on what's local and in season. Try the 'patatas resecas'; if you're lucky there will be freshly-picked mushrooms. The attic rooms are smallish, low-ceilinged and with sky-light windows; at night the silence is all-enveloping, a joy to those aching from the din of Madrid.

Rooms: 5 with bath & wc.
Price: S 3500 Pts; D/Tw 7000 Pts inc VAT.
Breakfast: Included.
Meals: Lunch/Dinner 1000 Pts (M), 3000 Pts (C).
Closed: Never.

How to get there: From Madrid N1 north. After Buitrago de Lozoya right on M127, through Gandullas to Pradena then M130 to Puebla de la Sierra.

Map No: 12

Hotel Infanta Isabel

Plaza Mayor
40001
Segovia

Tel: (9)21 461300
Fax: (9)21 462217

Management: Miguel de la Fuente

Segovia's cathedral is one of the great sights of Castile, especially when glimpsed for the first time as you approach from Madrid. Where better to stay than on the main square beside the great Gothic masterpiece in a room reaching out to the pinnacles, flying buttresses and gargoyles? The hotel is a fine old 19th-century townhouse and the decoration is in keeping — carved mirrors, elegant armchairs, a lovely staircase leading up and up — with a liberal dash of more modern furnishing. The rooms are most dapper; each has a different (pastel) colour scheme; headboards are handpainted, there are carefully-chosen rugs on the parquet floors with curtains to match, chandeliers — all slightly wedding-cakey but very welcoming and fairly priced given the level of comfort. We enjoyed having a room giving onto the square; the double glazing means you get a good night's sleep to go with the view. There is a small breakfast room downstairs or treat yourself to breakfast in bed. Come to Segovia for the cathedral, the aqueduct and this charming hotel.

Rooms: 29 rooms with bath & wc + 4 suites.
Price: S 7000 Pts; D/Tw 10300-10900 Pts; Ste 12500 Pts.
Breakfast: Buffet 850 Pts.
Meals: None.
Closed: Never.

How to get there: In Segovia, follow signs for hotels to Plaza Mayor. Hotel in main square.

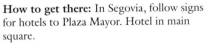

Hostal Andorra

Gran Vía 33, 7º
28013
Madrid

Tel: (9)1 5323116/5316603
Fax: (9)1 5217931

Management: Angel Bertero

The Gran Vía is the broad avenue that cuts a path through the heart of the Spanish capital, a place where night or day the street is alive, a place to wander or to people-watch from one of the many bars or restaurants. Why not stay here, up above it all, at the Hostal Andorra, run by the same family for more than 40 years? It is 100% Spanish, the furnishing nearly all modern but as you sit in its rounded dining room (see photo) or lie looking up at the high ceilings you still get some feel for how the building must have looked when completed in 1922. Rooms here are remarkably inexpensive considering their size and the address and they have gadgets and trimmings that you might not expect to find in a hostal. Simply furnished and impeccably clean, about half of them have balconies that look out to the street; there are quiet interior rooms, too. Their ceiling fans are a lovely alternative to noisy air conditioning. We feel this place is a real 'find' and hope you'll agree. Almost all the sights are within walking distance too.

Rooms: 20 with bath & wc.
Price: S 4500 Pts; D/Tw 6300 Pts;
Tr 7800 Pts inc. VAT.
Breakfast: 350 Pts
Meals: None.
Closed: Never.

How to get there: On Gran Vía very close to 'Palacio de la Música' cinema. For the car: Parking Tudescos in Calle Tudescos.

Map No: 12

Hotel Carlos V
Maestro Victoria 5
28013
Madrid

Tel: (9)1 5314100
Fax: (9)1 5313761

Management: José Gutiérrez

The Puerta del Sol is to Madrid what Trafalgar Square is to London; this is where the revellers meet to see the New Year in and all distances measured from the Spanish capital start here. Just yards away from it the recently renovated Carlos V is one of the city's older hotels; it was built in the 1920s and was called the Barcelona. Three generations of the Gutiérrez family have poured their energies into the hotel; for them 3 stars does not have to imply impersonality and the present young owner delights in meeting his guests. It has a lovely Art Nouveau doorway. Inside, classic elements (chandeliers, tapestries and cornices) are combined with modern (furniture, rugs and carpets). Welcoming enough to feel human, smart enough for business people as well as tourists. The staff are fun and they too are treated like family; most have been here for years. We could see why the owners are so proud of their rooms; they have every mod con and are attractively fitted. We'd take one with a balcony or with its own private terrace. Good value.

Rooms: 67 with bath & wc.
Price: S 11020 Pts; D/Tw 13870 Pts; Tr 18720 Pts.
Breakfast: Included.
Meals: Snacks available.
Closed: Never.

How to get there: From Puerta del Sol take Calle Arenal then 2nd right into Calle de San Martín. At Plaza right, to end, and left into Maestro Victoria.

Hotel Monaco

Calle Barbieri 5
28004
Madrid

Tel: (9)1 5224630
Fax: (9)1 5211601

Management: Guy Moreno

In a quiet street off the Gran Vía, the Monaco is one of the most unusual and fun places to stay in Madrid. The sumptuous, rather theatrical, interior has an air of delicious decadence more in keeping with a Parisian than a Madrileño hotel; it comes as no great surprise to learn that a Frenchman decorated its interior and this grand old '20s building was once one of the city's classier brothels! That ended in the fifties when it became the Hotel Monaco. What remains is the exuberant rampant kitsch of the reception, the bar and the rooms themselves. The queen of them is number 20 which comes complete with wall mirrors behind the bed and a raised central bath tub. Others are a little more subdued; nearly all have original mouldings, tiled or marble bathrooms and most at least one strategically-placed mirror or old antiquey piece of furniture. The whole place has frayed edges, the breakfast room with its original leather booths feels more the place for champagne than for coffee but visit the Monaco and its tongue-in-cheek 'grandeur'!

Rooms: 32 with bath or shower & wc.
Price: S 7000 Pts; D/Tw 10000 Pts.
Breakfast: 500-600.
Meals: None. Huge choice of restaurants nearby.
Closed: Never.

How to get there: From Plaza Cibeles take Calle de Alcalá and almost immediately right into Gran Vía. Left into Calle de las Infantas; park in Parking Plaza Vázquez de Mella. Hotel just up street on right.

133

Hostal del Cardenal

Paseo de Recaredo 24
45004
Toledo

Tel: (9)25 224900
Fax: (9)25 222991

Management: Luis González

Bartolomé Cossio wrote of Toledo that 'it is the city which offers the most complete and characteristic evidence of what was genuinely Spanish soil and civilisation'. Quintessentially Spanish it is and it is tempting to stay at the Cardenal; like Cossio's city it seems to have absorbed the richest elements of Moorish and Christian Spain. It was built as a mansion house by the Archbishop of Toledo, Cardenal Lorenzana, in the 13th century. The gardens are unforgettable — fountains and ponds and geraniums and climbing plants set against the rich ochres of the brick. Within there are patios, screens, arches and columns. There are lounges with oil paintings and mudéjar brickwork. A peaceful mantle lies softly over it all; you hear the tock-tock of the grandfather clock. Wide estera-matted corridors and a domed staircase lead up to the rooms; they have latticed cupboards, tiled floors, sensitive lighting and heavy wooden furniture. You can choose between several small dining rooms to feast on roast lamb, sucking pig or stewed partridge. Vintage stuff.

Rooms: 25 with bath & wc + 2 suites.
Price: S 6675 Pts; D/Tw 10800 Pts; Ste 15000 Pts.
Breakfast: 775 Pts.
Meals: Lunch/Dinner 4000-5000 Pts(C).
Closed: Never.

How to get there: From Madrid N401 to Toledo. As you arrive at old town walls and Puerta de la Bisagra turn right; hotel 25m on left beside ramparts.

Map No: 12

134

Hostal Descalzos

Calle de los Descalzos 30
45002
Toledo

Tel: (9)25 222888
Fax: (9)25 222888

Management: Julio Luis García

Hostal Descalzos is certainly different from our two rather grander hotels here but having spent two happy nights there we feel that it, too, is 'special' enough to be included — providing you get that room with a view. For it sits high up by the old city wall, just yards from El Greco's house. There is nothing fancy; the fittings are modern and the combination of pine furniture and satiny curtains will win no prizes for (conventional) good taste. But the view from those special rooms — especially at night when the old bridge down below is illuminated — is what we will remember. When you book choose one of the doubles at the front (like 31, 32, 41 or 42). The singles we saw were very small. The family who run the hostal are quiet, unassuming folk. They serve you breakfast in a tiny downstairs room; there is a photo-menu with 13 different breakfasts(!) and snacks are available in the recently opened cafeteria. At the foot of the hostal is a pretty walled garden with a fountain and flowers, a place to sit out and watch the sun set over the meseta after a day exploring the city.

Rooms: 12 with bath & wc; 2 sharing bath & wc.
Price: S 2000-2500 Pts; D/Tw 5000-5600 Pts. 500 Pts extra for 2 'best' rooms.
Breakfast: 175-600 Pts (photo-menu!).
Meals: None.
Closed: Feb.

How to get there: From Madrid N401 to Toledo then signs to old town. At town walls (Puerta de la Bisagra) right; continue with wall on left until you see signs for Casa del Greco to left; hostal signposted off to right in front of Hotel Pintor El Greco.

Hotel Pintor El Greco

Alamillos del Tránsito 13
45002
Toledo

Tel: (9)25 214250
Fax: (9)25 215819

Management: Mariano Sánchez Torregrosa

At the heart of Toledo's old Jewish quarter, just yards from the El Greco house and synagogue museum, this small hotel, which was once a bakery, has had much praise heaped upon it — and rightly so. Restoration was completed ten years ago and both façade and patio have been handsomely returned to their former glory. Although the main building is 17th-century, parts of the 'Pintor' were already standing when Toledo was the capital of the Moorish kingdom; there is even an escape tunnel, built when the Inquisition was at work. The interior is cool, quiet, plush; there is mainly modern furniture, lots of paintings and handicrafts by local artists, tiled floors and plants. The rooms are on three floors around the patio; some have balconies looking out to the front. There are armchairs, thick Zamora blankets and more paintings; the colours are warm and the beds have very good mattresses. At breakfast there is fresh fruit juice, cheese and cold sausage as well as fresh bread — alas, no longer baked here.

Rooms: 33 with bath & wc.
Price: S 9200-11200 Pts; D/Tw 11500-14000 Pts; Tr 14000-16500 Pts.
Breakfast: Buffet 750 Pts.
Meals: None.
Closed: Never.

How to get there: From Madrid N401 to Toledo then signs to old town. At town walls (Puerta de la Bisagra) right; continue with wall on left until you see signs for Casa del Greco to left; hotel on left.

Hotel Los Tilos

Extraradio s/n
16870
Beteta
Cuenca

Tel: (9)69 318097/98
Fax: (9)69 318299

Management: Pedro Fernández Guillamon

Beteta is a small village 4000 feet up in the spectacular limestone mountains that lie to the north of Cuenca, an area of lakes and gorges, a walker's dream. On the outskirts of the village, with long views across the valley, Los Tilos is a wonderful place to base oneself for exploring the area (one English walking company has done just that). The building is unexciting, a rather monolithic structure from the 70s. But the kind, caring manners of the owners dispel any doubts. In the enormous tiled dining room, screens help to dissipate a slightly stark feel as does the fireplace at one end. You eat well here; roasts are the speciality, particularly venison and lamb. There is locally-farmed trout, too. The bedrooms have the same sober feel as the rest of the hotel but we rather liked them for that. They are large with wooden beds and writing desks, nice cotton bedcovers and curtains, terracotta floors and views from their French windows. The peacefulness of the setting gives them an almost monastic air. Riding, walking and caving close by.

Rooms: 24 with bath & wc.
Price: S 3600-4000 Pts; D/Tw 6000-7000 Pts; Tr 6500-7500 Pts.
Breakfast: 450 Pts.
Meals: Lunch/Dinner 1600 Pts (M), 3000 Pts (C).
Closed: 24-25 Dec.

How to get there: From Madrid N111-E901 to Tarancón. Left on N400 towards Cuenca. 5km before Cuenca left on N320 towards Guadalajara. Just after Villar de Domingo right on CU904 then CU902 and CU202 to Beteta.

137

Posada de San José

Calle Julián Romero 4
16001
Cuenca

Tel: (9)69 211300
Fax: (9)69 230365

Management: Antonio Cortinas
Vegas & Jennifer Morter

Cuenca is unique, a town that astonishes, delights and engraves itself on the memory. Sitting on the rim of the town's unforgettable gorge, the Posada de San José is an inn to match the town. A sculpted portal beckons you to enter but gives little away. For this is a labyrinthine house and only from inside do you realise that it is multi-levelled. Staircases lead up and down, twisting and turning... the perfect antidote to the mass-produced hotels that we so dislike. Every room is different, some small, some large, some with balconies, some without; most have bathrooms, a few share. Nearly all have old furniture, perhaps a canopy bed or a little terrace. We would all ask for one that looks out to the gorge but all of them, view or no view, are lovely and are witness to Antonio and Jennifer's decorative flair; they know that a vase of fresh flowers is a match for ANY number of satellite channels. In their welcoming little restaurant, with that heart-stopping view and a good meal to come, few could fail to feel content with their lot!

Rooms: 22 with bath or shower & wc; 9 sharing.
Price: D/Tw 6600-8900 Pts; D/Tw sharing 3800-4600 Pts; S 3800-4600 Pts; S sharing 2200-2500 Pts.
Breakfast: 450 Pts.
Meals: Lunch/Dinner 1700 Pts.
Closed: Never.

How to get there: From Madrid N111-E901 to Tarancón. Left here on N400 to Cuenca. Follow signs to Casco Antiguo. Hostal is just 50m from main entrance to Cathedral. Best to park in Plaza Mayor by cathedral.

Map No: 13

Hotel Leonor de Aquitania

Calle San Pedro 60
16001
Cuenca

Tel: (9)69 231000
Fax: (9)69 231004

Management: Francisco de Borja García

A grand 18th-century townhouse is now home to Cuenca's smartest small hotel. Its position could hardly be more magnificent — a perch right at the edge of the deep gorge, next to the church of San Pedro and a few hundred yards from the main square and cathedral. The well-known Spanish interior designer Gerardo Rueda has decorated the hotel, cleverly weaving innovation in and out of tradition. You see this immediately as you enter: first the heavy old wooden door, then a heavy modern glass door. In reception and bar, furniture that is unmistakably '90s goes well with terracotta floors and estera matting. In the dining room and bar, the lighting is subtle, diffuse and there are old tapestries and photographs — a lovely spot to breakfast. The rooms are equally enticing, with hand-painted tiles, wooden beds, matching fabrics on bedcovers and curtains and exposed beams (rafters on the top floor). Some have a terrace, many a balcony; the view has to be seen to be believed. And the suite is one of the most enchanting in Spain.

Rooms: 48 with bath & wc + 1 suite.
Price: S 5000-6000 Pts; D/Tw 8500 Pts; D/Tw with view 10000 Pts; Ste 25000 Pts.
Breakfast: Buffet included.
Meals: None.
Closed: Never.

How to get there: From Madrid N111-E901 to Tarancón. Left on N400 to Cuenca. Follow signs to Casco Antiguo. Cross Plaza Mayor, continue up Calle San Pedro. Hotel on right after 200m.

Hosteria del Monasterio de S. Millán

Monasterio de Yuso s/n
26226
San Millán de la Cogolla
La Rioja

Tel: (9)41 373277
Fax: (9)41 373266

Management: Sonia Bartolomé Nájera

Whether you make a long or short detour, don't miss the monastery of San Millán at the heart of the Rioja, just to one side of the Pilgrim's Way to Santiago and in a heart-filling arena of valley and mountain. The Spanish know it as being the 'cradle of Castillian'; here one of the brothers first wrote the language as he jotted notes beside a religious text. The prize-winning restoration of one of the building's wings has ushered in one of Spain's most remarkable hostelries, a successful fusion of 16th-century building with 20th-century creature comforts. Downstairs are sitting room, billiards room, large dining room and vaulted bar. Pink is the leitmotif; marble-floored throughout, there are rugs, designer sofas, potted plants and taped classical music. Long, carpeted corridors lead to your very smart rooms. Wooden floors add a gentle note, marble-floored bathrooms and big beds remind you of 4-star status. The view is either to the cloister or out to the Rioja mountains; and it's all properly insulated against cold and noise. (Avoid weekends when coaches of visitors arrive en masse.) Eat well — buffet breakfast, Rioja cuisine at lunch or dinner — and walk at least a part of the Camino de Santiago.

Rooms: 22 with bath & wc + 3 suites.
Price: S 7500-8000 Pts; D/Tw 9850-12000 Pts; Ste 12500-19000 Pts inc. VAT.
Breakfast: 800 Pts.
Meals: Lunch/Dinner 1800 Pts (M); 3000 Pts (C).
Closed: Christmas.

How to get there: From Burgos N120 east to Santo Domingo de la Calzada. Through centre of village then right at sign for San Millán de la Cogolla.

Casa Bermeja

Plaza del Piloncillo s/n
45572
Valdeverdeja
Toledo

Tel: (9)25 454586
Fax: (9)25 454595
E-mail: zabzab@arrakis.es

Management: Jorge Velasco Merchán

Angela González happened upon an old village house in this unknown village and knew she'd found the place where an old dream could be fulfilled: a house where her many friends could get together, far from the noise and pollution of Madrid, to share food, conversation — and fun. Luckily for us, she later decided to share her home with paying guests too. Architect brother, Luis, took renovation in hand, while the decoration was Angela's creation; she is an interior designer. Beyond the red and cream façade, a coquettish home awaits you; the sun and red earth of Castille are reflected in the warm colours of paint and fabrics, there are old pieces side-by-side with '90s 'design', lofty lounge and dining room with beam above and terracotta beneath. The apartments look onto the inner patio; the rooms are in the main house. The same eye for detail has ensured that they are as attractive as they are comfortable. Blissfully quiet, and the capable young manager Jorge bends over backwards to make you welcome. With such wild countryside on your doorstep this is an ornithological dream-land.

Rooms: 5 with bath & wc, 1 suite + 6 apartments.
Price: D/Tw 15200 Pts; Ste 22000 Pts; Apt 14000-22000 Pts.
Breakfast: Included.
Meals: Lunch/Dinner 3500 Pts.
Closed: Never.

How to get there: From Madrid NV/E90 towards Badajoz. Exit at km148 for Oropesa. From there to Puente del Arzobispo and here, right to Valdeverdeja. In main square, opposite 'ayuntamiento', turn left to Casa Bermeja.

141

Map No: 18

Palacio de la Serna

Calle Cervantes 18
13432
Ballesteros de Calatrava
Ciudad Real

Tel: (9)26 842208
Fax: (9)26 842224/08

Management: Eugenio Bermejo

In the wide landscapes of Castilla-La Mancha the divide between vision and reality seems to blur — not just for hapless Quijotes tilting at windmills. In a forgotten village of the province of Ciudad Real, this neo-classical palace may have you wondering if the sun hasn't got to you! Its unexpected opulence will remind you of a time when mining made many a fortune in the area. It was all abandoned to the Meseta, until designer Eugenio Bermejo saw in Serna a perfect outlet for his creative impulse. Two and a half years later nearly every corner of the Palace is embellished with his sculptures, paintings and eclectic taste in interior design. Each guest room is different, all are huge fun, with colour schemes to match paintings — or sometimes vice versa. Post-modern to the core. There are red roses in the gardens, music is ever-present — from Nyman to Bach — as are intriguing objects at every turn. Dinners are by torchlight; you might expect a Knight of the Calatrava Order to wander in. Fun, whacky, and very different; well worth a detour as you drive north or south.

Rooms: 12 with bath & wc, 3 suites + 2 apartments.
Price: S 8000; D/Tw 10000-12000 Pts; Ste 14000-15000 Pts; Apt 16000 Pts.
Breakfast: 1000 Pts.
Meals: Lunch/Dinner 2000 Pts (M); 3500 Pts (C).
Closed: Never.

How to get there: From Ciudad Real south on N420 towards Puertollano. After aprox.18km left to Cañada de Calatrava, on to Villar del Pozo and then to Ballesteros de Calatrava. Palacio to right as you drive past village.

Map No: 19

142

"Dale limosna mujer
Que no hay en la Vida nada
Como la pena de ser
Ciego en Granada."

Alms, lady, Alms!
For there is nothing crueller in life
Than to be blind in Granada

JAN MORRIS - *Spain*

Andalusia

Finca Buen Vino

Los Marines
21293
Huelva

Tel: (9)59 124034
Fax: (9)59 501029
E-mail: buenvino@facilnet.es

Management: Sam and Jeannie Chesterton

After running shooting lodges in the Scottish Highlands, Sam and Jeannie knew that to settle happily in Spain they would need to find a place of wild natural beauty — whence this divinely isolated spot amid the thick oak and chestnut woods of the Aracena mountains. It is hard to believe that the Finca Buen Vino was only built 14 years ago. Indeed, many of the building materials are old; we especially liked the panelled dining room, the arched doors and the very fine wooden staircase leading up to the guestrooms. The Chestertons' sense of hospitality is Scottish and after one night there we had made new friends. It is supremely elegant, Jeannie is a Cordon Bleu cook and the candlelit dinner with quail and Cerdo Ibérico (Iberian pork with woodland 'setas') was unforgettable (starlit on the terrace in summer). The guestrooms are all different: the Pink room has a bathtub with a view, the Yellow room a sitting-cum-dressing room, the Bird room its own hearth. There's also an independent cottage that can be rented — no better place to pen that novel.

Rooms: 5 with bath & wc + 1 cottage.
Price: S 14000 Pts; D/Tw 22000-26000 Pts inc. breakfast and dinner. Cottage: ring/fax for details.
Breakfast: Included.
Meals: Lunch (summer only on request) 3000 (M) Pts Dinner included.
Closed: Varies — please consult.

How to get there: From Seville N630 north for 37km then N433 towards Portugal/Aracena. Los Marines is 6km west of Aracena; Finca Buen Vino is 1.5km west of Los Marines off to the right at km95. More details on booking.

143

Map No: 17

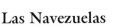

Las Navezuelas

Apartado 14
41370
Cazalla de la Sierra
Sevilla

Tel: (9)5 4884764
Fax: (9)5 4884764

Management: Luca and Mariló Cicorella

A place of peace and great natural beauty, Las Navezuelas is a 16th-century olive mill on a farm set in 136 hectares of green meadows, oak forest and olive groves. Water streams down from the Sierra, often along Moorish-built channels. Boar and deer roam the Aracena range to the north and pretty Cazalla is two miles away. The house is pure Andalusia with beams and tiles while the garden has palms and orange trees. The rooms are fresh, light and simple with old bits of furniture and nothing fussy to distract you from the main pleasure of simply being here. There are two sitting rooms and a welcoming restaurant with log fires in winter. The menu offers delicious local dishes made almost exclusively with ingredients from the farm — from veg to chicken, lamb and ham. There is home-made jam for breakfast too. The friendly young owners will go out of their way to help and give advice on expeditions on foot, horse or bicycle and where to watch birds.

Rooms: 5 with shower & wc; 2 sharing shower & wc + 1 suite.
Price: D/Tw 7500-8500 Pts; Tr 9000-10000 Pts; Ste 8500-9500 Pts, inc VAT.
Breakfast: Included.
Meals: Lunch/Dinner 1750 Pts (M).
Closed: 2 weeks in Jan and 2 weeks in May.

How to get there: E5 from Sevilla and exit on SE111 to Brenes then Cantillana. Here towards El Pedroso/Cazalla. Through El Pedroso on C433; shortly before Cazalla de la Sierra at km42 right at sign.

Map No: 18

Hotel Restaurante Posada del Moro

Paseo del Moro s/n   **Tel:** (9)5 4884858
41370   **Fax:** (9)5 4884858
Cazalla de la Sierra
Sevilla

Management: Julia and Lucía Piñeiro Marrón

Cazalla is a summer refuge for Sevillians gasping for clean cool air. The well-advised stay with Julia and Lucía Piñeiro Marrón, the charming and gregarious sisters who have devoted themselves to this hotel with much warmth and enthusiasm for the past decade. If it looks rather like a wedding cake, maybe it's because staying here IS something of an occasion, especially so for lovers of good food. The roast game is superb — try the rabbit or hare — as is the mountain ham. In summer, expect poolside barbecues and an occasional flamenco evening. The restaurant is decorated in 1920s style. The guestrooms look out over the garden at the back. They are smart, comfortable and very southern with lots of marble and original paintings, many of them by Julia. It is all delectably Andalusian with an amusing hint of kitsch. Base yourselves here and explore the narrow streets of Cazalla and the lovely mountains just beyond. Rooms and food are both good value. The owners, too, clearly enjoy their hotel; we felt they would like to be their own guests!

Rooms: 15 with bath or shower & wc.
Price: S 5000 Pts; D/Tw 7500 Pts; Tr 9000 Pts inc. VAT.
Breakfast: 500 Pts.
Meals: Lunch/Dinner 2000 Pts (M); 3000 Pts (C).
Closed: Never.

How to get there: From Sevilla N630 towards Mérida. Shortly after Santiponce, right onto C431 to Alcalá del Río. Round Alcalá onto C433 to Cazalla. At roundabout entering Cazalla, right at sign for hotel — 200m on left.

La Cartuja de Cazalla

Ctra Cazalla — Constantina Km 55.2
Finca La Cartuja
41370
Cazalla de la Sierra, Sevilla

Tel: (9)5 4884516
Fax: (9)5 4883515

Management: Carmen Ladrón de Guevara Bracho

An exceptional place, an exceptional owner. The 15th-century monastery lay empty for 150 years until Carmen Ladrón, visiting in the 1970s, knew she had found her mission. She founded a Centre for Contemporary Culture with an art gallery (paintings by resident artist Amaya Espinoza). The rooms are decorated with works by artist guests; painters, sculptors or musicians can sometimes give of their art in exchange for their stay. The guestrooms (they finance the centre) are in the old monastery gate-house. It has been daringly restored, marrying 90s designer chic with a sense of the past. Light streams in through a huge skylight — Carmen calls it a 21st-century building! The rooms have modern furniture and bathrooms, no telephone or television to spoil the peace; some have views of the chapel. Dine with Carmen in her home next door (local dishes often made with home-grown ingredients) but give most importance to the tertulia afterwards, a forum for sharing knowledge and ideas. One of the most remarkable places to stay in Spain.

Rooms: 9 with bath or shower & wc.
Price: 6000 Pts p.p. inc VAT.
Breakfast: Included.
Meals: Lunch/Dinner 2500 Pts (M).
Closed: Never.

How to get there: From Sevilla C431 to Cantillana then C433 to El Pedroso & Cazalla. There, right onto C432 towards Constantina. La Cartuja is at km55.2.

Hospedería Fuentenueva

Paseo Arca del Agua s/n
23440
Baeza
Jaén

Tel: (9)53 743100
Fax: (9)53 743200

Management: Victor Rodríguez

The Fuentenueva, behind a rather forbidding façade, was once a women's prison. Under the aegis of the town council it is now an open, airy, friendly hotel run by a cooperative of five delightfully enthusiastic and professional young people. Inside, the arches and vistas, the marble floors, the tinkling fountain and the neo-Moorish cupola create impressions of space and gentle cool. Exhibitions of works by local artists and craftsmen are held in the salons. The bedrooms are mostly large and light with modern locally-built furniture and fittings, bright bedcovers and plush bathrooms. On summer evenings drink in the outside bar in the shadow of the old prison tower then dine in the patio on local fish specialities. When all the windows are opened in the morning, the characteristic scent of high-quality olive oil will drift in and envelop you. Visit unsung Baeza, revel in her exuberant Renaissance palaces and richly-endowed churches and don't miss the cathedral's silver monstrance (hidden behind St Peter...).

Rooms: 12 with bath & wc.
Price: S 5700 Pts; D/TW 8000 Pts; TR 9700 Pts.
Breakfast: Included.
Meals: Lunch/Dinner 2000 Pts (M), 2300 Pts (C).
Closed: Never.

How to get there: From Granada N323 to just before Jaén and then N321 to Baeza.
On far side of Baeza on left as you leave in direction of Ubeda.

147

Palacio de la Rambla

Plaza del Marqués 1
23400
Ubeda
Jaen

Tel: (9)53 750196
Fax: (9)53 750267

Management: Elena and Cristina Meneses de Orozco

The old towns of Ubeda and nearby Baeza are often missed as travellers hurry between Madrid and the Costa. They are two of the brightest jewels in the crown of Spanish Renaissance architecture. At the heart of old Ubeda, exquisite Palacio de la Rambla dates from this period and has never left the Orozco family; bless the day the family decided to share it all with you and me! A frisson of excitement passes through you as you go through the ornate Corinthian-columned portal into the main patio; colonnaded on two levels, ivy-covered and with delicately carved lozenges and heraldry, its opulence takes you by surprise. Sitting, dining and bedrooms are a match for their setting; there are antique beds, chests, lamps, claw-footed bath tubs, oil paintings of religious themes and — as you might expect — the family portraits. Native terracotta is softened by estera matting. Anita the maid is here to fuss over you, and in the morning, serves a full Andalusian breakfast: eggs, toast with olive oil, fresh orange juice — have it in your room if you like. A home with a tradition of regal welcoming; King Alfonso XIII stayed here when he was in town.

Rooms: 7 with bath & wc + 1 suite.
Price: D/Tw 14000 Pts; Ste 16000 Pts.
Breakfast: Included.
Meals: None.
Closed: Never.

How to get there: From Madrid south on NVI. At km292 take N322 to Ubeda. There, follow 'Centro Ciudad' until Palace in front of you between c/Caja and c/Rastro.

Map No: 24

148

Hotel Cortijo Aguila Real

Carretera Guillena-Burguillos, Km 4
41210
Guillena
Sevilla

Tel: (9)5 5785006
Fax: (9)5 5784330

Management: Isabel Martínez

If you are seeking a taste of refined aristocratic Andalusia... this could be for you. Aguila Real is every inch the classic 'cortijo' and just a dozen miles from the narcotic charms of Sevilla (you can just see the Giralda tower from the gardens). Passing under the main gate you enter the huge inner courtyard where there is bougainvillea in profusion; the old dovecote and a water trough remind you that this was once a working farm. The public rooms are an exercise in controlled elegance, decorated in pastel colours with heavy old tables, paintings and lots of books — and beautiful barrel-vaulted ceilings. Silver cutlery and classical music in the dining room seem perfectly in keeping with the food, which is fairly haute cuisine. Most vegetables are home-grown, portions are generous, the wine list extensive. The rooms are plush with hand-painted furniture, huge double beds and attractive bathrooms; some have their own terrace. But what makes it unforgettable is the palm-filled garden, carefully lit at night — an irresistibly romantic spot.

Rooms: 9 with bath & wc + 3 suites.
Price: D/Tw 15000-18000 Pts; Tr 20000-23000 Pts; Ste 20000-25000 Pts.
Breakfast: Buffet 1500 Pts.
Meals: Lunch/Dinner 3500 Pts.
Closed: Never.

How to get there: From Sevilla N630 towards Mérida. After approx 9km right on SE180 to Guillena. Through village and SE181 towards Burguillos. After 4km on right.

149

Cortijo Torre de la Reina

Paseo de la Alameda s/n
41209
Torre de la Reina (Guillena)
Sevilla

Tel: (9)5 5780136/
907 531227
Fax: (9)5 5780122

Management: Paz Medina and José María Medina

We were instantly won over by the SILENCE of the cortijo, enhanced at night when the beautiful courtyard, gardens and old watchtower are delicately lit. Originally a medieval house-fortress, later converted into a true Renaissance hacienda, it is now a national monument. The gardens are indisputably southern with huge palm trees, bougainvillea and scented jasmine. The house is just as peaceful and elegant inside. In what used to be the granary is a vast guest lounge with antique furniture, lovely estera woven matting, chess games and plenty of books. Yellow, ochre and white combine to give warmth to this light airy building and in winter a log fire burns in the great old hearth. Despite the minibars, satellite television and super-plush bathrooms in the comfortable guestrooms (presumably for business conventions), humanity is again preserved thanks to warm earthy colours, old prints, bright rugs and even fireplaces (in suites). An elegant hotel with, it should be added, elegant prices to match.

Rooms: 14 inc. 8 suites, with bath & wc.
Price: D/Tw 16500-21500 Pts; Ste 20500-26000 Pts.
Breakfast: 1300 Pts.
Meals: Lunch/Dinner 3500 Pts (M).
Closed: Never.

How to get there: From Sevilla N630 towards Mérida. After Itálica ruins, right towards Córdoba/La Alcaba. At roundabout in La Alcaba, road towards Alcalá del Río. After about 1.5km left to Torre de la Reina. On left as you enter village: white and yellow gate.

El Esparragal

Carretera Sevilla-Mérida, Km 21
41860
Gerena
Sevilla

Tel: (9)5 5782702
Fax: (9)5 5782783

Management: Enrique Soto

Monks of the order of San Jerónimo built a monastery here in the 15th century in an setting of isolated beauty; later, a cortijo was carefully grafted onto the religious edifice when Disestablishment sent the Brothers packing. At the end of the 19th century came extensive reform and embellishment; thus was created one of the most beguiling buildings of southern Spain. The main façade raises a sigh with its ceramic-tiled tower, Roman-arched windows and bougainvillea; its left flank takes in the 17th-century chapel. Beyond are two main patios (one of them the original cloister) and, surrounding them, the matchless guest rooms and suites. Approach them past fountains and arches; some of Spain's best-known designers have created a southern miracle in salons, dining room and guest suites; the whole hotel is a 'Who's Who' of fabric, tile, and furniture 'names'. We can only suggest the oil paintings, the mudejar doors, the gilt mirrors, the tapestries and the elegance that permeates every corner. Ride out into Esparragal's 3000 hectares on Andalusian thoroughbreds, dine on game or estate-raised beef; treat yourself to an Arabian night that you'll never forget.

Rooms: 10 with bath & wc + 7 suites.
Price: S 15000 Pts; D/Tw 18800 Pts; Ste 20000 Pts inc VAT.
Breakfast: Included.
Meals: Lunch/Dinner 3200 Pts (M).
Closed: Never.

How to get there: From Seville N630 north towards Mérida. After 21km left towards Gerena. Continue on for approx. 2km passing under bridge; signposted.

151

Map No: 24

Posada de Palacio
Calle Caballeros 11
11540
Sanlúcar de Barrameda
Cádiz

Tel: (9)56 364840
Fax: (9)56 365060

Management: Renata Strobel
and Antonio Naverrete

A sleepy town at the mouth of the Guadalquivir, Sanlúcar has one great claim to fame — it is home to delectable pale dry Manzanilla. Among the bodegas and palaces of the old town this 18th-century palace/convent is a lovely place to stay. Every corner has a flavour of its own; the house has grown organically, decorated with things collected piecemeal by its young owners. You enter a slightly magical world as you take the grand old entrance into the courtyard. Some rooms have sitting-rooms, others have terraces, many have beautiful period tiled floors. There are geraniums, fans and mementos from South American travels; fern and jasmine-shaded corners in which to sit and read. There is a small bar; the restaurant, open only to posada guests, is in the old stables. Antonio is the chef, specialising in local dishes with lots of vegetables and salads, all fresh from the market. The house and owners are utterly charming and will even arrange boat tours of the nearby Doñana Park wetlands. One of our very favourites.

Rooms: 13 with shower or bath & wc.
Price: S 5000 Pts; D/Tw 6000-8000 Pts; Tr/Q 12000 Pts; Ste 10000 Pts.
Breakfast: 800 Pts.
Meals: Dinner 2000 Pts (M).
Closed: Jan-Feb.

How to get there: From Sevilla, A4 motorway. Leave at Las Cabezas exit onto C441 to Sanlúcar (via Lebrija and Trebujena). In town, follow signs to Casco Antiguo then Palacio Municipal. Hostal is opposite Palacio.

Map No: 24

Casa Montehuéznar

Avenida de la Estación 15
41360
El Pedroso
Sevilla

Tel: (9)5 4889000/4889015
Fax: (9)5 4889062/4889304

Management: Pablo García Rios

This could be a perfect place to stay if you want to combine walks in the Sierra Morena with day trips to Seville; from El Pedroso you can take a train to the city mid-morning and then back early in the evening — and it is a lovely ride. This grand town house was built at the end of the last century, when mineral extraction briefly brought wealth and fame to the area. Last year two young brothers joined a growing number of hoteliers who believe that 'Small' can be just as 'Beautiful'. It is all utterly Andaluz: a sober façade with the original wrought-iron balconies and window grilles, a weighty door leading through to the central patio, where ferns, aspidistra, geraniums, palm tree and fountain make it the spot to breakfast or dine when the weather is right. The original tiled and bannistered staircase leads to the rooms; they have attractively carved wooden furniture and each is named after one of Andalusia's provinces — Seville being the biggest. Food is regional/family with deer, boar and rabbit the specialities; Riojas and Ribera del Duero are the right accompaniment. Kind staff and very kind prices, too.

Rooms: 8 with bath & wc.
Price: S 4000 Pts; D/Tw 7500 Pts.
Breakfast: Included.
Meals: Lunch/Dinner 1500(M), 2500(C).
Closed: Never.

How to get there: Arriving in Seville from Madrid take SE30 ringroad towards Mérida. Exit off this ring road at signs for C433 La Rinconada. Follow C443 towards Cazalla to Pedroso, where hotel is opposite the railway station.

Hotel Los Abetos del Maestre Escuela

Calle Santo Domingo Km 2.8
14012
Córdoba

Tel: (9)57 282132/282105
Fax: (9)57 282175

Management: Rafael Jurado Díaz

'Los Abetos' (a type of yew) is in a quiet residential area to the north of the city, just at the foot of the Sierra Morena and a ten-minute drive from the centre. The 200-year-old colonial-style hotel stands among lovely palm trees; these and the hotel's pink and white façade give it a most beguiling look. There is a peaceful pebbled courtyard with wicker chairs for sitting out and other equally attractive spots beneath the palms. The restaurant and lounge have much less of a period feel; the hotel was very considerably renovated in 1992, perhaps for the business folk who often come to stay or to dine; this too explains why the dining room is so cavernous — banquets are often held here. The guestrooms have all the fineries you need. We certainly preferred those with views across the estate towards Córdoba; they have Provençal furniture and modern tiled floors. In spite of the muzak and a definite 'hotelly' feel, this is a good place if you want to be just out of town.

Rooms: 34 with bath & wc + 2 suites.
Price: S 6500-8500 Pts; D/Tw 9000-11000 Pts; Ste 11000-13000 Pts.
Breakfast: 650 Pts.
Meals: Lunch/Dinner 2000 Pts (M); 3000 Pts (C).
Closed: Never.

How to get there: From centre of Córdoba, Avenida del Brillante northwards; as you arrive in more residential area, right onto Avenida San José de Calasanz (formerly called Santo Domingo if asking way!). Continue to hotel.

Los Omeyas

Calle Encarnación 17
14003
Córdoba

Tel: (9)57 492267
Fax: (9)57 491659

Management: Juan de la Rubia
Villalba

This, one of the latest small hotels to open in Córdoba, is a real gem. Juan de la Rubia Villalba's many years of experience in hostelry were put to good use when he came to build and decorate Los Omeyas. The position is a delight, just a few yards from the Mezquita yet in a quiet narrow street of the old Jewish quarter (a plexus of mystic alleys). The building is in harmony with much older neighbours; the whitewashed façade with its wrought-iron balconies and wooden shutters is classic Córdoban architecture. And so too within, where a small patio gives access to rooms on two levels. The design may seem a bit theatrical to some — the mezquita-style arches in reception, the marble staircase — but we ARE in the larger-than-life south and the whole hotel is as clean as the newest pin. Everything is young and fresh from curtains to mattresses to bedcovers. Marble floors throughout the building and whitewashed walls are the perfect foil for the summer heat; and there's air conditioning, too. Kind and helpful staff and a reliable little inn.

Rooms: 27 with bath & wc.
Price: S 4000 Pts; D/Tw 7000 Pts; Tr 8500 Pts.
Breakfast: 500 Pts.
Meals: None.
Closed: Never.

How to get there: Entering Córdoba follow signs for centre then Mezquita. In a street just off north-east corner of the Mezquita. Nearest parking by Alcázar de los Reyes Católicos.

Hotel Simón

Calle García de Vinuesa 19
41001
Sevilla

Tel: (9)5 4226660
Fax: (9)5 4562241

Management: Francisco Aguayo
García and Manuel Lissen

A stone's throw from the cathedral in a quiet street leading down towards the Guadalquivir river, the Simón is a friendly, unpretentious little hotel that is ideal for those travelling on a tighter budget. The gentle-mannered owner, Francisco ('Frank') Aguayo García enjoys receiving English guests and practising his (excellent) English. The hotel is utterly Sevillian; you pass through the main portal, then a second wrought-iron door and on into a cool inner patio. There are tables here to sit amidst aspidistras and ferns, the perfect escape from the throbbing heat. The dining room has mirrors and ceramic-tiled walls, period tables and chandeliers to remind you that this was once a bourgeois residence. The guestrooms are set around the patio and reached by a marble staircase. They are clean, bright, simply decorated, come in varying sizes and have that blissful summer luxury — air conditioning. There are plenty of restaurants and bars nearby and advice from the young, friendly staff on where to find the best 'tapas'.

Rooms: 25 with bath & wc + 4 suites.
Price: S 5000-6000 Pts; D/Tw 7000-9800 Pts; Ste 10000-13500 Pts.
Breakfast: 450 Pts.
Meals: None.
Closed: Never.

How to get there: From Plaza Nueva in centre of Seville take Avenida de la Constitución (if closed to traffic tell police

you are going to hotel) then right onto Calle Vinuesa (one way).

Hostería del Laurel

Plaza de los Venerables 5
41004
Sevilla

Tel: (9)5 4220295/4210759
Fax: (9)5 4210450

Management: David Márquez
López

The Laurel stands in an attractively authentic setting at the heart of Santa Cruz (the old Jewish quarter); you knew it must exist somewhere in the delicious anarchy of this labyrinthine quarter but it didn't until the Márquez family converted the building above their successful restaurant to install 21 guestrooms. The bodega has been here for a very long time — it is mentioned in Zorilla's 'Don Juan Tenorio'. You enter by way of a classic Sevillian bar with its hams and beautiful old tiles. Its reputation with the locals is clearly well-established if a head count is anything to go by! We have to agree with the hotel's young owner, David Márquez Lopez, who describes the home cooking here as "simply buenísima". If you're in carnivorous mood try the oxtail — 'rabo de toro' — if not, the 'merluza Doña Inés'. The setting alone would make it memorable. Oh, and the rooms? Refreshingly simple (well-equipped nonetheless), spotlessly clean and worth every peseta, they are all named after one of Zorilla's characters.

Rooms: 21 with bath or shower & wc.
Price: S 5000-9000 Pts; D/Tw 7000-12000 Pts; Tr 9000-15000 Pts.
Breakfast: 600 Pts.
Meals: Lunch/Dinner 2200 Pts (M); 4000 Pts(C).
Closed: Never.

How to get there: On foot: From the Giralda, take Calle Mateos Gago. Take first right at bar Las Columnas and ask for Plaza de los Venerables. Nearest parking next to Hotel Alfonso XIII.

Patio de La Cartuja

Calle Lumbreras 8-10
41002
Sevilla

Tel: (9)5 4900200
Fax: (9)5 4902056

Management: Sebastián Martín González

The Patio de la Cartuja is a peculiarly original hotel. At the eastern end of the Alameda de Hércules, one of the city's more bohemian districts, it was formerly a classic 'patio' — several flats laid out around a central court. Although the present building was completed in 1992 it is an almost exact replica of the old building. Each apartment — on three levels around the patio — varies slightly in colour scheme and furnishing. Each has a roomy sitting-room with a sofa-bed, a small kitchen (crockery and cutlery provided at reception against a small, returnable deposit) and a double bedroom. Marble floors were the right choice for the Sevillian heat. Curtains and bedcovers are bright geometric prints. There is a small room for breakfast — or you can make your own. A big plus is the large car park in the basement; everything is within walking distance in Seville. From here the river Guadalquivir and the Expo site are five minutes away, the cathedral twenty. There is a 'sister' patio on the other side of the Alameda with similar architecture and furnishing.

Rooms: 34 with bath & wc.
Price: D 7700-12000 Pts.
Breakfast: 600 Pts.
Meals: None.
Closed: Never.

How to get there: From Puente de la Barqueta, turn left and then right into Calle Calatrava to Alameda de Hércules then immediately right into Calle Lumbreras. Leave car at parking sign and advise reception!

Map No: 25

158

El Convento

Calle Maldonado 2
11630
Arcos de la Frontera
Cádiz

Tel: (9)56 702333
Fax: (9)56 702333

Management: Maria Moreno Moreno and José Antonio Roldán Caro

Arcos is spread like icing along the top of a craggy limestone outcrop. It was a great stronghold when Moors and Christians fought over the ever-shifting 'frontera'. The Convento, a former cloister, is perched right at the edge of the cliff in the heart of the old town. Behind the plain white façade is a deliciously labyrinthine hotel and rooms with views to die for. The best have terraces over the cliff where watching the sun set will make your heart soar. José Roldán Caros knows and loves his 'patria chica' and he and his wife have filled their hotel with works by local artists. The decoration varies and, like the paintings, is sometimes a little dated; but all rooms are perfectly comfortable. The small dining room — with rather inappropriate plastic furniture — is in the old sacristy but on warm days you can eat in the patio. The Roldán Caros also own a restaurant in the covered colonnaded patio of a 16th-century palace just up the road (see photo) which has a reputation for serving some of the best Andalusian food in the Province of Cadiz.

Rooms: 10 with bath & wc.
Price: S 4000-5000 Pts; D/Tw 6000-7500 Pts; Tr 8000-9500 Pts.
Breakfast: 700 Pts.
Meals: Sister restaurant — Lunch/Dinner 2500 Pts (M); 3500 Pts (C).
Closed: Never.

How to get there: In Arcos, follow signs to Parador. Park in front of Santa María church; hotel is behind Parador at 100m.

159

Hotel Los Olivos del Convento

Paseo de Boliches, 30
11630
Arcos de la Frontera
Cádiz

Tel: (9)56 700811
Fax: (9)56 702018

Management: José Antonio Roldán Caro

Just off a street leading to the old quarter of Arcos, Los Olivos is an unmistakably Andalusian townhouse with arches, geraniums and palms, terracotta floors, white walls and a huge oak door into a cool wicker-furnished lounge. Beyond is the courtyard bringing light and air. The bedrooms all give onto it and those at the front also have fine views across the gentle hills and olive groves down towards the Atlantic. Those at the back are very quiet. They all have high ceilings and a pleasant mix of old and modern furniture. You can have breakfast in the patio until the hotter summer days chase you indoors to breathe conditioned air. The staff clearly enjoy working here and their eagerness to please is reflected in the hotel's participation in the scheme offering visitors free guided tours of Arcos (twice daily in season). The old town with its arches ('arcos') and narrow winding streets is a short walk from Los Olivos whose owner also runs El Convento in another part of town.

Rooms: 19 with bath & wc.
Price: S 4000-5000 Pts; D/Tw 7000-9000 Pts; Tr 9000-11000 Pts.
Breakfast: 600 Pts.
Meals: Sister restaurant — Lunch/Dinner 2500 Pts (M); 3000-3500 Pts (C).
Closed: Never.

How to get there: In Arcos, follow signs for Centro Ciudad towards Parador. As you climb up into town following one-way system, hotel is on left in road parallel to main street.

Map No: 25

160

Hacienda El Santiscal

Avenida El Santiscal 129 (Lago de Arcos)
11630
Arcos de la Frontera
Cádiz

Tel: (9)56 708313
Fax: (9)56 708268

Management: Paqui Gallardo

After many years of working with tourists Paqui and Rocío Gallardo, the dynamic managers of El Santiscal, had a very clear idea of what a small hotel should be. Much the sort of thing that we would look for, too. This grand old cortijo is a short drive from Arcos yet in a place of perfect quiet. The building has been sensitively converted from a forgotten family home into an elegant but simple hotel. The building is classical Andalusian: an austere whitewashed façade, a grander portal and then the blissful peace and cool of the central courtyard. Each of the rooms that surround the patio (and nearly all have views out across the estate too) is decorated differently but with the same attention to detail: carefully-chosen matching fabrics, lovely old beds, terracotta floors and good bathrooms. The suite was really special, we thought, and very good value. It was refreshing to find rooms of 'single' dimensions that were kept as single rooms rather than forced into double status by cramming in an extra bed. Very professional, very good value.

Rooms: 11 with bath & wc + 1 suite.
Price: Tw 8500-10000 Pts; Tw with view 10200-12000 Pts; Ste 12000-15000 Pts.
Breakfast: Included.
Meals: Lunch/Dinner 2500-3000 Pts (M).
Closed: Never.

How to get there: From Arcos C334 towards El Bosque. 1km after crossing bridge turn left and follow signs to El Santiscal.

Cortijo Barranco

Carretera Arcos — El Bosque Km 8.2
11630
Arcos de la Frontera
Cádiz

Tel: (9)56 231402
Fax: (9)56 231402

Management: María José Gil Amián

Barranco offers as authentic an insight into Andalusian country life as you could hope for. Leave the main road, drive up through the olive groves and you will know you are leaving the 'real' world behind. The sensation heightens on arrival at this magnificent isolated place. It is a classic cortijo — private living quarters and (former) stables giving onto the inner sanctum. The guestrooms are perfect: terracotta floors, old wrought-iron bedsteads, lovely heavy linen curtains and hand-crocheted and knitted bedspreads. The big bathrooms have the same tiles and generous baths. The whole place is uncannily quiet: prick back your ears for the owl's hoot or the bird's first hymn at dawn. The sitting room is enormous with space for a billiard table; most memorable of all is the dining room with a gallery, a lofty beamed ceiling and a handsome open hearth. The food is good solid Andalusian fare served with panache.

Rooms: 8 with bath & wc.
Price: D/Tw 7000-8000 Pts inc VAT.
Breakfast: 500 Pts.
Meals: Lunch/Dinner 2500-3000 Pts (M). Book ahead.
Closed: 24-31 Dec.

How to get there: From Arcos de la Frontera, C344 towards El Bosque. After 8km, at end of long straight section, left at sign onto track for 2km.

Map No: 25

162

Cortijo Huerta Dorotea

Carretera Villamartín — Ubrique Km 12
11660
Prado del Rey
Cádiz

Tel: (9)56 724291
Fax: (9)56 724289

Management: Antonio Fernández Barrera

An old Andalusian farmstead in an olive grove beneath the Grazalema Sierra near the Roman and Moorish sites of Prado del Rey — pure southern Spain. Strange to build Finnish log cabins here... but they are well-concealed among the trees and very welcoming; each has two bedrooms, a small shower-room, a sitting room with an open fire and even air-conditioning. The old cortijo also has eight simply-furnished guestrooms, some with mountain views, and there are 18 horses for hire for exhilarating rides in this spectacular countryside. With its heavy old beams, pink table cloths and, for once, subtle lighting (a real relief after the ugly fluorescent strips of so many Andalusian restaurants), the dining room is warm and intimate. Good traditional fare is the norm — thick country soups, roasts and locally-farmed trout. It is a favourite with local Spaniards for weekend meals so try to stay midweek. Exceptionally kind staff.

Rooms: 8 with bath or shower & wc; 14 log cabins.
Price: S 3000 Pts; D/Tw 6000 Pts; cabins (for 4) 11000 Pts.
Breakfast: 250 Pts; Full 1000 Pts.
Meals: Lunch/Dinner 1200 Pts (M); 2000 Pts (C).
Closed: Never.

How to get there: From Jerez, N342 through Arcos to Villamartín. Go through town then right towards Ubrique. After 12km pass Prado Del Rey on right then left to Zahara and immediately left on dirt road to Dorotea.

Map No: 25

Hacienda Buena Suerte

Apartado 60
11650
Villamartín
Cádiz

Tel: (9)56 231286
Fax: (9)56 231286

Management: Magda and Jean-Claude Dysli

What a grand arrival! As you pass under the great portal and up the drive you feel the marriage of Andalusia's past (the great estates or 'latifundia') and its present (Judas trees, bougainvillea, palm trees, whitewash and terracotta tiles). All this in the loveliest of settings — the gently rolling olive groves and wheatfields of the foothills of the Grazalema mountains. But the star here is the horse. Groups of riders come to learn with owners Jean-Claude and Magda Dysli. They are rarely out of the saddle, either teaching in the riding school or trekking in the hills with their guests. Non-riders are also very welcome and there are lovely walks from the farm. The rooms, most of them in the converted granary, are large and simply furnished, decorated — naturally — with prints of horses and riders and animal skins on the floors. You may find sweets on pillows or a candle in the corner. Meals, taken round the huge dining table, are 'international' — everything from goulash to bouillabaisse to couscous, all with organic ingredients. A paradise for children, too.

Rooms: 11 with bath & wc.
Price: S 7500; D/Tw 15000 Pts.
Breakfast: Included.
Meals: Lunch 2000 Pts (M); Dinner 3000 Pts (M).
Closed: July-Aug.

How to get there: From Ronda, C339 towards Sevilla. At junction with N342, left towards Jerez. 7km before Villamartín, left at sign for El Bosque & Ubrique. Buena Suerte is about 1.5km along on the left.

Map No: 25

164

Hostal Marqués de Zahara

Parque Natural "Sierra de Grazalema"
San Juan 3
11688
Zahara de la Sierra, Cádiz

Tel: (9)56 123061
Fax: (9)56 123061

Management: Santiago Javier Tardío Pico

Zahara was sentinel to the Sierra in the days when it stood on the 'frontera' between Christian and Muslim Spain. Climb up to the old Moorish fortress to appreciate just how hard a nut it was for Ponce de León — later Marqués of Zahara — to crack. At the heart of this prettiest of white villages, this little family hotel is one of our favourites. José-Mari and brother Santiago officiate (rather seriously) in vaulted bar and reception, while mother rules the kitchen. Rooms are on two floors around a central, covered patio. They vary considerably in size and are simply furnished, with bright curtains and bedspreads; the prettiest of them have old hexagonal floor tiles. We would choose one of the larger rooms looking out to the main square; light sleepers might prefer one to the rear. Dine in at the Marqués; the cooking is properly Andalusian, with thick soups and game the mainstays. Just outside are a number of bars to choose from if you prefer a tapas meal, and along the street the tourist office can help you plan your walks in the nearby Grazalema National Park. Book well ahead in season, and very early if you plan to take part in the unforgettable Corpus Christi festivities.

Rooms: 10 with bath & wc.
Price: D/Tw 4950-5650 Pts inc. VAT.
Breakfast: 450 Pts.
Meals: 1450 Pts (M), 2000 Pts (C).
Closed: Never.

How to get there: From San Pedro C339 to Ronda. Round town on ring road and on towards Sevilla. After approx. 15km left towards Grazalema. Don't take next left to Grazalema but continue straight on to Zahara. Hotel in main square.

Map No: 25

Casa de las Piedras

Calle las Piedras 32
11610
Grazalema
Cádiz

Tel: (9)56 132014/132323

Management: Rafael and Katy
Lirio Sánchez

Grazalema is one of the most dazzling of Andalusia's mountain villages, clinging to grey and ochre cliffs and dominated by craggy peaks that are home to eagles and mountain goats. A special place with a special hostal, half of which is in a grand 300-year-old house (witness to the days when a thriving weaving industry made many a Grazalema fortune) where rooms vary in size, are full of family antiques and loaded with charm. The new half, built and decorated in traditional style, has 16 simple and attractive rooms with their own bathrooms and central heating (temperatures can drop sharply during winter nights). Some have views across the terracotta roofs to the mountains beyond. Rafael and Katy are enthusiastic young hosts and serve much-appreciated local dishes in their lively restaurant. Don't miss the wild thistle or asparagus omelettes (in the right season), roast partridge or quail, or trout baked with a slice of mountain ham. This is a walkers' and eaters' base and breakfast is appropriately hearty. An unassuming and charming place.

Rooms: 16 with bath or shower & wc; 16 sharing.
Price: S 1500 Pts sharing; S 3600 Pts ; D/Tw sharing 3000 Pts; D/TW 4800 Pts inc VAT.
Breakfast: 225 Pts.
Meals: Lunch/Dinner 1100 Pts (M); 2000 Pts (C).
Closed: Never.

How to get there: From Ronda, C339 towards Sevilla. After about 14km left to Grazalema. Enter main square & turn directly right up street beside Unicaja. Hotel is 100m up on right.

Map No: 25

Molino del Santo

Bda. Estación s/n
29370
Benaoján
Málaga

Tel: (9)5 2167151
Fax: (9)5 2167327
E-mail: molino@logiccontrol.es

Management: Pauline Elkin and Andy Chapell

Pauline Elkin and Andy Chapell moved south in search of a better life. They have restored a century-old mill in a spectacular area of the Grazalema National Park and are now thoroughly part of local life. Water rushes past flower-filled terraces, under willows and fig trees, into the pool (heated for the cooler months). Rooms and restaurant all wear local garb — terracotta tiles, beams and rustic chairs. Some rooms have private terraces. Fresh flowers are ever present and the Molino's reputation for good Spanish food is made; many hotel guests are British but the Spanish flock in at weekends to enjoy local hams and sausages, rabbit and fresh fish as well as imaginative vegetarian cooking. Staff and owners are generous with advice on walks or bike rides straight from the hotel or will direct you to the delightfully sleepy station for trains to Ronda or in the other direction past some of the loveliest 'white villages' of Andalusia. Fly to Gibraltar and then come by train! The Molino is deservedly one of the Sierra's most popular small hotels — book well ahead to guarantee a room.

Rooms: 15 with bath or shower & wc; some with terrace.
Price: S 5550-6600 Pts; D/Tw 7100-9300 Pts inc. VAT. Add 800 Pts for bath or terrace/1350 Pts for both.
Breakfast: 900 Pts.
Meals: Lunch/Dinner 2000 Pts (M); 2750 Pts (C).
Closed: Beg. Dec-end Feb.

How to get there: From Ronda, C339/A473 towards Seville; just after km118, left towards Benaoján. After 10km, having crossed railway and river bridges, left to station and follow signs.

167

Map No: 25

Hotel Polo

Mariano Soubirón 8
29400
Ronda
Málaga

Tel: (9)5 2872447
Fax: (9)5 2872449

Management: Rafael, Javier and Blanca Puya García de Leaniz

What a privilege to stay in one of Ronda's oldest hotels, its sober, almost austere façade softened with simple mouldings, tall stone-framed windows and authentic cierros (the mudejar-inspired observation window jutting over the pavement and enclosed in a decorative wrought-iron grille). The aristocratic elegance is echoed inside where the marble hall, columns, antiques and deep sofas promise cool comfort and attentive service. Brothers Javier and Rafael and sister Blanca have taken over the family business; they are warm, generous and welcoming — another touch of class. The bedrooms are large and light with a blue-and-white theme. On the top floor you may have views across rooftops to the Serranía. One of the nicest even has a bathroom with a view. The decoration is basically classic Spanish with wrought-iron bedheads, Majorca weave curtains; it is all carpeted and mattresses are brand new. In the lively and animated centre of Ronda, with a congenial bar and excellent restaurant under the caring and expert eye of sister Marta, this is real Andalusian hospitality.

Rooms: 30 with bath & wc + 3 suites.
Price: S 4500 Pts; D 6750-9000 Pts.
Breakfast: 490 Pts.
Meals: Lunch/Dinner 1100 Pts (M); 2500 Pts (C).
Closed: Never.

How to get there: In centre of Ronda, very near Plaza del Socorro (best place to park in underground car park; 1000 Pts daily for hotel guests).

Map No: 25

168

Hotel Posada del Canónigo

Calle Mesones 24   **Tel:** (9)5 2160185
29420
El Burgo
Málaga

Management: María Reyes

Your arrival in the mountain village of El Burgo will be memorable: it is a splash of brilliant white amidst the ochres and greys of the surrounding limestone massif. Little visited, it will give you as essential a taste of Andalusian mountain life as can be found anywhere. This grand old village house, a perfect example of what 'rural tourism' should be about, is another good reason for coming. It is a family affair; 13 (!) brothers and sisters helped restore and decorate the house. The bedrooms are simply furnished in local style with tiled floors, old bedsteads and lots of family things. The old prints, paintings and dried flowers are lovingly arranged by María Reyes. It is all spotless — the owners are visibly proud of their creation. There is a small dining-room leading to a little patio for breakfast. The two sitting-rooms have open hearths and exposed stonework and the whole place is uncannily quiet by Andalusian standards. Stay two nights to walk or ride in the virtually unknown National Park of the Sierra de la Nieves above Ronda. Pure unadulterated Andalusia!

Rooms: 12 with bath & wc.
Price: S 3000-4000 Pts; D/Tw 5000-6000 Pts.
Breakfast: Included.
Meals: None.
Closed: July.

How to get there: From Torremolinos to Cártama then continue to Calea, Alozaina, Yunquera and El Burgo. Turn right into village and ask — hotel is next to church of San Agustín.

169   **Map No:** 25

La Posada del Torcal

29230
Villanueva de la Concepción
Málaga

Tel: (9)5 2111983
Fax: (9)5 2031006
E-mail: http://www.andalucia.
com/posada-torcal

Management: Jan Rautavuori and Karen Ducker

Jan and Karen lived and worked on the nearby Costa until, one happy day, they ventured up into the magnificent Torcal National Park and saw the light! The fruit of their conversion is one of the South's most luxurious small hotels. The posada's base elements — tile, beam and woodwork — are true to local tradition; it feels first and foremost Andaluz. Each bedroom is dedicated to a different Spanish artist; oils are copies of the originals by Karen's brother Greg. Trimmings come from further afield — most remarkable are the king-size beds, some brass, some Gothic, some four-poster; they were shipped out from England. No expense nor care has been spared for your comfort; we liked the open-plan rooms which allow you to sip your welcoming bottle of cava from a corner tub yet not miss a second of the amazing views beyond. The menu is local/Spanish; the staff are delightfully friendly; underfloor heating in winter, Casablanca fans in summer, saunas at all times make this a place for those who like mixing comfort and beauty as well as for keen hunters and fishermen.

Rooms: 8 with bath & wc.
Price: S 10000 Pts; S use D/Tw 12000 Pts; D/Tw 14000 Pts.
Breakfast: 1100 Pts.
Meals: Lunch/Dinner 3500 Pts (M).
Closed: Nov.

How to get there: From Málaga N331 towards Antequera; take exit 148 for Casabermeja/Colmenar. In Casabermeja right to Villanueva de la C. At top of village, left at junction; after 1.5km right for La Joya/La Higuera. 3km to Hotel; on left.

Map No: 25

170

Finca La Mota

Carretera de Mijas s/n
29120
Alhaurín El Grande
Málaga

Tel: (9)5 2490901/2594120
Fax: (9)5 2594120

Management: Jean and Arun Narang

The Narangs abandoned their successful bar on the coast for a quieter life in the rolling hills near Alhaurín. With two young children of their own, they clearly enjoy having families at La Mota, a 300-year-old farm-house surrounded by citrus groves. We immediately warmed to Jean's gentle manner with her guests. The general style in the guestrooms is 'Spanish rustic with a hint of the east' and the public areas are a delight — a large sitting room with log fires in winter, a flower-filled patio, a poolside bar — with fine views over the Guadalhorce valley to the mountains of the Ronda massif. The Narangs have four well-mannered horses and gladly organise riding trips (Spanish or English tack). They also breed chickens and ducks (eggs of the day at breakfast) and dinner is an interesting mix of Andalusian, Italian, even Indian food, often with home-grown ingredients. In summer there are barbecue suppers by the pool with legs of lamb from the farm grilled with rosemary. A wonderful place for a full and active family holiday. Let us know if you find it too casual.

Rooms: 9 with own bath & wc; 4 sharing.
Price: S 5000 Pts; D/Tw sharing 6000 Pts; D/Tw 9000 Pts; Ste 10000 Pts, inc VAT.
Breakfast: Included.
Meals: Lunch/Dinner 2000 Pts (M); 3000 Pts (C).
Closed: Never.

How to get there: From Málaga N340 towards Cádiz. 1km after airport, C344 to Alhaurín de la Torre. Then on to Alhaurín El Grande. Here follow signs to Mijas. 2 km out of town pass 'El Postillón'; Finca La Mota is after 500m on right.

171

Map No: 25

Santa Fe

Carretera de Monda Km3
Apartado 147
29100
Coín, Málaga

Tel: (9)5 2452916
Fax: (9)5 2453843

Management: Warden and Arjan van de Vrande

Two young and enthusiastic multi-lingual Dutch brothers have recently taken over the reins of Santa Fe. This old farm-house is tucked away in a lovely spot among the citrus groves of the Guadalhorce valley. The transition from farm to guest house has been scrupulously faithful to local tradition; you'll enjoy the bedrooms with their pretty ceramic basins, rustic furniture and terracotta floors (the tiles fired with a dog-paw print are for good luck). Ochre walls feel properly ethnic; kilims add a gay note. Guests here are Spanish and Costa-cosmopolitan; a Belgian chef does great local and international food for which devotees will drive for up to two hours. We tried delicious iced gazpacho when we visited on a hot June day; flambéed langoustines in brandy, sirloin of pork in cream, raisins, sherry and pine kernel are just a couple of the main courses — try the Dutch apple pie to follow! There is an attractive dining room of friendly proportions — log-fired in the winter — but most of the time you'll dine out beneath the old olive tree. Occasional, and imaginative, attractions include barbecues and live jazz. A casual and relaxed atmosphere but much attention to detail.

Rooms: 3 with bath & wc + 2 with basins sharing bathroom.
Price: S sharing 5000-6500 Pts; S 6000-7500 Pts; D/Tw sharing 6000-7500 Pts; D/Tw 7000-8500 Pts inc VAT.
Breakfast: Included.
Meals: Lunch/Dinner 1600 Pts (M); 2500 Pts (C).
Closed: 2 weeks in Jan/Feb and 2 weeks in Nov.

How to get there: From Málaga, N340 towards Cádiz. About 1km after airport, right to Coín. In Coín take Marbella road. After 3km Santa Fe is on right (signposted).

Hostal La Janda

Hermanos Machado s/n
11150
Vejer de la Frontera
Cádiz

Tel: (9)56 450142

Management: Juana María Carpinter Gómez

La Janda is authentic, unpretentious and comfortable. It sits at the top of Vejer de la Frontera, one of the original 'white villages' with its unmistakably North African look, winding streets, iron-grilled windows, monasteries, churches and whiffs of sea air from the ocean below, though, unhappily for eager tourists, happily for the women of Vejer, no more women in full nun-like black garb. If measured by purely North European yardsticks the hostel may appear rather basic. But Juani and her mother are gentle and charming and La Janda reflects these qualities, as well as being unassuming and quintessentially Spanish. The bedrooms in the new part are slightly larger than the others and some have terraces looking out over Vejer. Beds and tables are simple modern pine and the choice of tiles and paintings may seem a bit kitsch. However, the rooms are quiet and have comfortable beds. The bathrooms we saw were smallish. La Janda, cooled by sea breezes in summer, is very good value and Vejer is an absolute must when visiting this part of Spain.

Rooms: 24 with bath & wc.
Price: S 2000-4000 Pts; D/Tw 3500-4000 Pts.
Breakfast: None; café nearby.
Meals: None. Choice of restaurants.
Closed: Never.

How to get there: From Cádiz, N340 south for about 28km then right to Vejar and follow road up into village. Follow signs to Conjunto Histórico/Monumental to top of village. Ask for Ambulatorio — hotel just opposite.

173

Map No: 25

Hotel Restaurante Antonio

Bahia de la Plata
Atlantera
11393
Tarifa (Zahara de los Atunes) Cadiz

Tel: (9)56 439141/439346
Fax: (9)56 439135

Management: Antonio Mota

A short drive from the workaday little fishing village of Zahara de los Atunes, and with a garden that leads straight out to one of the best beaches on the Atlantic coast, Antonio Mota's hotel is in a very special position. Few foreigners seem to be in the know, but this family-run hotel is deservedly popular with the Spanish. It is an utterly southern hotel: repro prints of some rather sugary subjects (swans, etc) and others rather grisly (bull-fighting). Rooms and restaurant are light, clean and functional; expect the fish to be memorable and prices more than reasonable. It is unusual to come across so hearty a breakfast in Spain: eggs, fruit, cheeses and hams. Some rooms give onto an inner patio with fountain, palms and geraniums; pretty enough, but we'd prefer a room with a small terrace looking out over the palm-filled gardens to the sea. Some rooms have a lounge-cum-second bedroom, ideal for families. And there are horses for hire — try and stay at least two nights and ride (or walk) along the beach to Bolonia, where there are Roman ruins and more good restaurants. Old faithfuls return time and again.

Rooms: 30 with bath & wc + 3 suites.
Price: S 5000-8000 Pts; D/Tw 8500-11500 Pts; Ste 11000-14500 Pts inc VAT.
Breakfast: Included.
Meals: Lunch/Dinner 2000 Pts (M); 3500-4500 Pts (C).
Closed: Never.

How to get there: From Algeciras E5/N340 to Cádiz. 25km after Tarifa take left turning to Barbate and Zahara on left after 10 km. Hotel signposted in village.

Hurricane Hotel

Carretera de Málaga a Cádiz
11380
Tarifa
Cádiz

Tel: (9)56 684919
Fax: (9)56 684508

Management: James Whaley

You could be on a film set as you look through the Hurricane's high arches to the palm trees, the glinting ocean and beyond to the Rif rising on the African shore. But despite the echoes of Al Andalus, this place is anchored in the 1990s surf culture — here are the best waves in Europe and a definite whiff of California (fully-equipped gym, two pools, windsurfing school, horses and mountain bikes). The debt to the East is clear in the guestrooms. They are uncluttered, decorated with geometric designs and whirling fans, here a keyhole arch over the bath, there an oriental couch with cotton bolsters — some reminded us of palace hotels in Rajasthan. Sea-facing rooms are preferable: the busy N340 might disturb Arabian-night dreams on the other side. The food unashamedly mixes America, Spain and the East too. Ingredients are fresh (fish of the day, home-made pasta, herbs from the garden), there are Louisiana prawns with basmati rice, spicy chicken with Peruvian sauce and good vegetarian dishes. The quality, the views, the furnishings make it worth the price.

Rooms: 35 with bath & wc.
Price: S 6000-12100 Pts; D 8000-16500 Pts; Ste 14500-29500 Pts.
Breakfast: Included.
Meals: Lunch/Dinner 1500 Pts (M); 3500 Pts (C).
Closed: Never.

How to get there: From Cádiz, N340 south. Hurricane is 7km before Tarifa on the right.

175

Map No: 25

100% Fun

Carretera Cádiz — Málaga Km 76
11380
Tarifa
Cádiz

Tel: (9)56 680330/680013
Fax: (9)56 680013

Management: Ula Walters and Barry Pussell

With such a name you expect something out of the ordinary — and this young, distinctly whacky hotel caught our imagination. The busy N340 lies between it and that oh-so-desirable surf but in the exuberant greenery of the garden with thatched roofs overhead we felt we were in deepest Mexico... or an Amazonian lodge... or was it Polynesia? Amazing to have transformed a bog-standard road-side hostal into something quite as spicy as this. The decoration is like the nearby Hurricane's, only simpler with a pleasing combination of floor tiles, warm ochres and fans to beat the summer sizzlers. The rooms have a fresh if rather spartan feel, comfortable beds and terraces over the garden. There are gurgling fountains, a swimming pool and an airy restaurant serving Indian, Mexican, Moroccan and excellent far-eastern dishes — one of the owners studied Thai cookery in Chiang Mai. It also has the best-equipped surf shop on the Tarifa coast selling the owner's hand-crafted windsurfing boards. Especially good value out of (surf) season, this is a young, FUN hotel!

Rooms: 16 with bath & wc.
Price: D/Tw 4600-8900 Pts.
Breakfast: Included.
Meals: Lunch/Dinner 1800 Pts (M); 2500 Pts (C) only from May-Oct.
Closed: Nov-end Feb.

How to get there: From Cádiz N340 towards Algeciras. At beginning of Tarifa Beach, hotel flagged on left, next to La Ensenada (10km north of Tarifa).

Map No: 25

176

Monte de la Torre

Apartado 66
11370
Los Barrios
Cádiz

Tel: (9)56 660000
Fax: (9)56 634863

Management: Sue and Quentin
Agnew-Larios

Quentin Agnew's family has farmed this estate for generations. It is puzzling to come across this utterly Edwardian building in the very south of Spain; it was built by the British when they were pushing the railway through the mountains to Ronda. This commingling of northern architecture and southern vegetation and climate is every bit as seductive as it is unexpected. The house stands alone on a hill, surrounded by palm trees, with views across the Gibraltar hinterland towards Morocco. The drawing room is panelled, the dining room elegant; there are masses of books, family portraits, a grandfather clock and dogs... more like a home than a hotel. The bedrooms (reached by a grand staircase) are high-ceilinged, decorated with family heirlooms and have period bathrooms — a festival of tubs and taps. Each is different, all are lovely. The apartments are in the former servants' quarters; lucky servants if they could stay here now! Sue and Quentin are gracious hosts and it is wonderful to meet them and share the beauty of their home and estate. A VERY special place.

Rooms: 4 twins with bath or shower + 2 apartments in house.
Price: Tw 15000 Pts; Tw (adj bathroom)13000 Pts; Apmt for 4/5 45000-88000 Pts weekly inc VAT.
Breakfast: Included.
Meals: None.
Closed: 20 Dec-7 Jan.

How to get there: From Málaga N340 towards Algeciras. 8km after San Roque right on C440 towards Jerez; after 4km (in Los Barrios) at end of palm tree avenue turn left and continue 3km; at stone marker right into main drive. 1km to house.

177   Map No: 25

Casa Convento La Almoraima

11350
Castellar de la Frontera
Cádiz

Tel: (9)56 693002
Fax: (9)56 693214

Management: Inma Martín

Just inland from the Mediterranean, within reach of the big Atlantic breakers, La Almoraima is one of Spain's more remarkable 'historic' hotels. The convent (cum hunting lodge!), built nearly 400 years ago, has been expropriated twice during its troubled history: once from the religious order, more recently from maverick financier Ruiz Mateos. It remains one of the largest latifundia in Europe. At the end of the main drive that winds up through the forest you are greeted by palm trees, a Florentine tower and a belfry where storks nest — a bewitching sight. The ballustraded façade gives way to an inner patio; there are areas of shade beneath the citrus trees with tables for sitting out; it is irresistible. The bedrooms are faithful to the building's past; they are simply furnished and some have fireplaces for the colder months. They give onto the patio or onto the gardens. An almost colonial air is added by the billiards room, grand piano and tapestries. You can play tennis or explore the huge estate, or just listen to the silence.

Rooms: 17 with bath & wc.
Price: S 8000 Pts; D/Tw 13000 Pts.
Breakfast: 750 Pts.
Meals: Lunch/Dinner 3000 Pts (M); 4000 Pts (C).
Closed: Never.

How to get there: From Algeciras, N340 north then C3331 towards Jimena de la Frontera. Hotel is signposted on the left near the turning to Castellar.

Hotel Casa Señorial La Solana

Carretera Cádiz-Málaga
N340 km 116.5 North Side
11360
San Roque, Cádiz

Tel: (9)56 780236
Fax: (9)56 780236

Management: José Antonio Ceballos

An unmistakably Spanish house, La Solana was built for a noble family in the 18th century. It stands grandly in 14 hectares of lush gardens and parkland; brilliantly-flowered southern plants climb the façade. The beautifully-glazed door beckons you in. A decade ago, the present owner, an artist and sculptor, restored it with great sensitivity and the overhanging eaves outside and the covered patio inside give it a colonial air. The interior is finely furnished with 16th- and 17th-century antiques from Spain's 'alta época', a profusion of carved wood, rich rugs, velvets and brocades, crystal chandeliers and heavy wardrobes. The very comfortable bedrooms are furnished with a mixture of old and less old pieces and the bathrooms are thoroughly modern. The brilliant 'white villages' of the Grazalema Sierra and the lesser-known beaches of the Atlantic coast are magnificent in their rhythm and colour. After a day delighting in these hidden treasures of Andalusia it is an extra joy to return to the secluded comfort of your country mansion.

Rooms: 18 with bath & wc + 6 suites.
Price: S 7000 Pts; D/Tw 9000 Pts; Tr 12000 Pts; Ste 11000 Pts inc VAT.
Breakfast: 700 Pts.
Meals: Lunch/Dinner 2500 Pts (M); 4500 Pts (C).
Closed: Jan.

How to get there: From Málaga take N340 towards Algeciras. Leave road at km116.5 and follow signs to hotel for 0.8km. (Or coming from Cádiz leave at exit 117, then U-turn.)

Map No: 25

Hostal El Anón

Calle Consuelo 34-40
11330
Jimena de la Frontera
Cádiz

Tel: (9)56 640113/640416
Fax: (9)56 641110

Management: Suzana Odell and Gabriel Delgado

Five village houses and stables have been joined to make an organic whole of changing levels, interconnecting patios and intimate terraces. It is a delicious little piece of authentic Spain. Suzana is warm and relaxed and welcoming. She has lived in Jimena for years and knows the people and country like her own. She will disentangle the rich web of local history for you while organising horse-riding or advising on painting, bird-watching and flora-spotting expeditions. The countryside has treasures galore for nature-lovers. See it from the little rooftop swimming pool where the eye travels over the roofs of Jimena and across to Gibraltar. Dine on the geranium-lit terrace off spare ribs or tapas. Enjoy the cool peace of the arched main courtyard and the exotic banana and custard-fruit trees, rejoice in the rich furnishings collected over the years (wall-hangings, paintings, imaginative sculptural bits and pieces) and the heavy beams and low ceilings of the old buildings. Come and soak up quantities of Spanishness in a congenial cosmopolitan atmosphere.

Rooms: 11 with bath & wc + 1 apartment.
Price: S 3200 Pts; D/Tw 6000 Pts; Tr 7500 Pts; Apt 6500 Pts inc VAT.
Breakfast: Included.
Meals: Lunch/Dinner 2500-2750 Pts (C). Bar snacks. Rest. and bar closed Weds.
Closed: June.

How to get there: From Málaga N340 towards Algeciras. Just after Puerto de Sotogrande right towards San Martín del Tesorillo. Continue to Jimena; in village take first left; signposted.

Map No: 25

180

La Almuña

Apartado 20
29480
Gaucín
Málaga

Tel: (9)5 2151200
Fax: (9)5 2151200

Management: Diana Paget

The old farmstead of La Almuña sits high up on a mountainside beside ancient footpaths used in former days by smugglers and bandaleros; later, officers and their mounts would pass by en route from Gibraltar to Ronda. Views from the house's terrace are dream-like; the eye reaches across the last foothills of the Sierra, white hilltop villages, all the way down to the coast — and on to Africa. Diana's is a warm, relaxed home; she greets you with a smile and always the offer of tea or something stronger. Her cooking is legendary in the area; expect to be dining in company. Much of her food has come from the estate and what doesn't is carefully chosen locally; you may be treated to smoked salmon, lamb, partridge or quail. Veg is fresh, herbs straight from the garden and wine always à volonté. Diana and her mother busy to and fro from kitchen to table; four Staffordshire bull terriers look on. The drawing room (see photo) is utterly homely; bedrooms are a happy marriage of 'English-country' and 'Spanish rustic'. Come to La Almuña to walk, talk and dine in the most congenial company.

Rooms: 4 with bath & wc.
Price: S 6000 Pts; D/Tw 12000 Pts.
Breakfast: Included.
Meals: Dinner 3000 Pts (M); Lunch by prior arrangment.
Closed: Never.

How to get there: From Gaucín take C341 towards Algeciras. Between km stones 103 and 104 turn left onto estate's private drive; La Almuña to right.

181

Hotel Casablanca

Calle Teodoro de Molina 12
29480
Gaucín
Málaga

Tel: (9)5 2151019
Fax: (9)5 2151019

Management: Susan and Michael Dring

Gaucín is one of Andalusia's most spectacular mountain villages. Its labyrinthine, whitewashed streets huddle against a hillside beneath a Moorish castle; eagles wheel overhead, the views are glorious. But the town lacked anywhere decent to stay until Mike and Sue — they left another successful small hotel near the coast to move further inland — came across this grand old village house and set about creating the hotel of their dreams. You'll soon fall under its spell too; you pass through the enormous old doors to emerge into the bar; beyond it is a walled garden where palms, magnolia and jacaranda lend colour and shade — a fountain murmurs beside the pool. Terraces on different levels look out across terracotta rooftops to the castle and all the way to the distant Rif mountains of Morocco. Most rooms have their own private terrace; there are parquet or terracotta floors, good beds, and bright colours jazz up the bathrooms. Dine in at least once; the menu is spicy and cosmopolitan, following the dictates of what's in season, and is the fruit of many years of catering experience. And the included breakfast is properly generous. Don't miss the sunset!

Rooms: 5 with bath & wc.
Price: S 5000-6000 Pts; D/Tw 9000-10000 Pts.
Breakfast: Included.
Meals: Lunch/Dinner 2250 Pts (M-Sundays only); 3000 Pts (C).
Closed: 1 Nov-1 March.

How to get there: From Málaga N340 towards Algeciras. After Estepona right on MA539 via Manilva to Gaucín (don't take Casares turn!). Follow one way system (right towards Ronda) for centre; hotel is near San Sebastian church.

Casa Tanga Tanga

Apartado 349
29680
Estepona
Málaga

Tel: (9)5 2886590
Fax: (9)5 2886590

Management: Glenn & Caro Wallace-Davis

This is a fun place to stay — Glenn ran a safari lodge for 10 years in Kenya and "tanga tanga" means to enjoy oneself in Swahili. Guests become members of a lively family; join them and other guests at the 'Dog & Duck' (sic) poolhouse for the daily cocktail or weekly barbecue; improve your tennis (Glenn is a qualified tennis coach); laze in the guests' sitting/music room in its own casita, or on the verandah beside the pool. Although life is mostly lived out of doors, the old house is large, rambling and welcoming with its durries, bookshelves and generous dining table. Caro has a designer's touch and loves cooking, both Spanish and other food. She grows her own Mediterranean vegetables and makes her own marmalade. The lovely bedrooms are big and filled with light from the windows that gaze over the hills. There are books and bits of old furniture, soft materials and cool tiles as well as attractive well-fitted bathrooms. Glenn and Caro organise local visits, 10-day Moroccan trips and willingly help with requests for bird-watching, golf or bikes.

Rooms: 6 doubles (one with adjacent single room) with shower or bath & wc (one not en-suite).
Price: D/Tw 12000 Pts.
Breakfast: Included.
Meals: Dinner approx. 4000 Pts (M).
Closed: 1 Dec-1 March.

How to get there: From San Pedro de Alcántara N340 towards Estepona. After 4.5km right to Cancelada. Through village following signs to Clínica Dr Oliver. Follow unsurfaced road for 1km to Tanga Tanga on the right. (Details on booking.)

183

Map No: 25

Breakers Lodge

Avenida Las Mimosas 189
Linda Vista Baja
29678
San Pedro de Alcántara, Málaga

Tel: (9)5 2784780
Fax: (9)5 2784780

Management: Sharon and Mark Knight

If you want to spend a first or last night on the coast Breakers Inn would be a safe port of call. This modern villa is tucked away in a residential area of San Pedro on a quiet road that leads straight down to the beach. Mark and Sharon have been in Southern Spain for many years and, though widely travelled, would live nowhere else. You'll be greeted with a smile here; they are sociable, talkative types, but know that your intimacy is precious. An electronic gate pulls shut behind you, reminding you that things have moved on since Laurie Lee arrived, fiddle in hand. The style of the place is very 'Marbella': a bit ritzy with Doric columns, white cane furniture, a corner bar, padded headboards in the bedrooms. Some of the rooms give onto the pool at the back of the house; there is also a terrace area for sitting out with tea, or a beer. Give Sharon advance warning and her maid will come in and prepare you a paella. If not, walk into San Pedro and ask for Fernando's fish restaurant. You'll bless us for sending you there....

Rooms: 6 with bath & wc.
Price: S 10000 Pts; D/Tw 14000 Pts.
Breakfast: Included.
Meals: Dinner 2500 Pts (M). Snacks also available.
Closed: Never.

How to get there: From Málaga N340 towards Algecíras. Through San Pedro de Alcántara, under arch across road and exit shortly after for Benahavis. Back towards Málaga, under arch again and turn immediately right. House on right after approx. 200m.

Map No: 25

184

La Fonda
Calle Santo Domingo 7
29639
Benalmádena Pueblo
Málaga

Tel: (9)5 2568273
Fax: (9)5 2568273

Management: José Antonio
García

There ARE places on the Costa that have retained their identity and dignity through all these years of unbridled development. One of them is pretty, white-washed, geranium-clad Benalmádena Pueblo; don't confuse it with Benalmádena Playa, which is best avoided. In a quiet street just off the pretty main square, La Fonda is a perfect place for a first or last night in Spain — it is just a quarter of an hour from the airport. The Fonda was the creation of architect Cesar Manrique; he is known for his life-long battle to show that old and new buildings CAN look well together, providing the latter respect local custom. And this building is a hymn to the south; there are cool patios shaded by palms, potted aspidistras, geometric tiles, fountains, pebbled floors, all of it set off by glimpses of the glittering sea. Rooms are large, light, airy and marble-floored. Downstairs are wicker chairs and a shaded terrace. And the restaurant doubles as a Cookery School; treat yourself to a southern gourmet meal at half of what it would cost elsewhere. And do try to meet with the Fonda's manager José Antonio — his kindness makes the place even more special.

Rooms: 27 with bath & wc + 7 in adjacent building.
Price: S 5000-8000; D/Tw 7000-11000 Pts inc VAT.
Breakfast: Included.
Meals: Lunch/Dinner 3000 Pts (M); 3500-4500 Pts (C).
Closed: Never.

How to get there: From Málaga take N340 towards Algeciras. Exit 223 for Benalmádena/Arroyo de la Miel. Follow signs to Benalmádena Pueblo; signposted in village.

Map No: 26

Hotel Paraíso del Mar

Calle Prolongación de Carabeo 22
29780
Nerja
Málaga

Tel: (9)5 2521621
Fax: (9)5 2522309

Management: Enrique Caro Bernal

Nerja is one of the better-known resort towns of the Costa del Sol, hardly an auspicious beginning when searching for that 'special' hotel; but the Paraíso is just that. In a quiet corner of the town and well away from the main drag of bars and restaurants, it stands at the edge of a cliff looking out to sea. It has been thoroughly revamped thanks to the unflagging efforts of the hotel's most charming young manager. The main house was built some 40 years ago by an English doctor; the other part is more recent. There are mature terraced gardens dropping down towards the beach; jasmine, palms and bougainvillea give it all an utterly southern air. Many guestrooms have a view and some their own terrace. They are large with mostly modern furniture and all the trimmings; some have jacuzzi baths, all have bathrobes and good towels. Beneath the hotel are a sauna and a hot-tub, dug out of solid rock. The whole place is run on solar energy and it could be the place to recharge YOUR batteries and still survive on the 'Costa'.

Rooms: 12 with bath & wc.
Price: S 5500-8000 Pts, jacuzzi or sea view 7000-10000 Pts; D/Tw 6500-9500 Pts, jacuzzi or sea view 8500-12500 Pts, or with both 10000-13000 Pts; Ste 13000-17000 Pts.
Breakfast: Included.
Meals: None.
Closed: Never.

How to get there: From Málaga N340 towards Motril. Arriving in Nerja follow signs to Parador; the Paraíso del Mar is next door.

Map No: 26

186

Palacete de Cazulas

18698
Otívar
Granada

Tel: (9)58 644036
Fax: (9)58 644048

Management: Brenda Watkins and Richard Russell-Cowan

The oldest deeds of Cazulas date back to 1492 and are in Arabic! Even if the main building came much later, its debt to 'Alhambra' style, to things Moorish, is manifest. Wafer brick, terracotta, fountain, clipped hedge and palm combine exquisitely in this utterly southern, seductive summer palace. Incredible to think that the Costa is so close; tucked away at one end of a lush valley, the setting could not be more peaceful. It is like being in a 'time-warp'; the shepherd passing with his flock before him is the only traffic you'll see here. Rooms are plush, the furniture antique; there are sparkling new bathrooms, four-posters, views out across the estate. There is a columned and vaulted drawing room (see photo), and a memorable panelled dining room decorated with old pieces, where dinner could only be special. A private chapel is being restored as we write. A spring-fed swimming pool, walks along the valley floor, the proximity of Granada, and the owners' great enthusiasm for their newly-adopted home and hills are just a few of the many good reasons for coming.

Rooms: 9 with bath & wc.
Price: D/Tw 12000 Pts.
Breakfast: Included.
Meals: Dinner 3000 Pts (M); book ahead.
Closed: Never.

How to get there: From Almuñecar follow old road towards Granada via Jete to Otívar. Continue on for 5km then left at sign 'central Cazulas'. Continue for 1.5km until you see the twin-towered house.

Map No: 26

Hotel La Tartana

Carretera de Málaga Km 308
18697
La Herradura
Granada

Tel: (9)58 640535

Management: Begoña Guitián

Set slightly back from the busy coast road, La Tartana is the place to flee the commercialism of the rest of the Costa del Sol. This little B&B and restaurant is endearingly intimate. The house is only 30 years old but the use of materials from a former monastery has given an older mood to many corners. You enter through a plant-filled patio; this is where one is most aware that the house was modelled on the aristocratic mansions of Granada. We liked the bedrooms with their beams, beds and cut flowers; the bathrooms are somewhat darkened by their brown floor tiles. Room 103 is especially nice with antique furniture, old prints and a balcony. Magazines and books add a homely touch and there are fans for the summer heat. The lounge is an unusual mix of rustic and chintz but it works well. With its lovely mature garden, its enormous ficus housing hundreds of birds, its terraces and its cats, La Tartana should win you over.

Rooms: 6 with bath & wc.
Price: S 5000 Pts; D/Tw 6000 Pts; Tr 7000 Pts inc. VAT.
Breakfast: 500 Pts.
Meals: Dinner on request approx. 1200 Pts (M); 2000 Pts (C).
Closed: Never.

How to get there: From Motril N340 towards Málaga. Through Almuñecar and arriving at La Herradura keep on N340 and — don't miss it! — signposted off to right as you come round a bend.

Map No: 26

188

Palacio de Santa Inés

Cuesta de Santa Inés 9
18010
Granada

Tel: (9)58 222362
Fax: (9)58 222465

Management: Nicolás Garrido
Berastegui

Just yards from the Plaza Nueva, tucked away to the side of a quiet and leafy square at the heart of the Albaicín (the hill rising opposite the Alhambra was recently declared a World Heritage Site by Unesco), is this 16th-century palace. The building came to be known as 'The House of the Eternal Father' after the frescoes that surround the inner patio; perhaps the creation of a pupil of Raphael. Above them, two storeys of wooden galleries lead to bedroom or suite. These are the delight of owner Nicolás Garrido. His love of antiques, modern art and interior design has been given free rein; his creation is elegant, southern and unique. Each room is named after a famous figure of Granadan history; they are patrons of dark roof beams, split-levels, bright durries, wrought-iron beds and period lamps. Hang expense and book a suite with a small terrace looking straight out to the Alhambra. But come also to meet with delightful manageress, Mari-Luz; her warmth makes a stay at Inés a double treat. She serves you breakfast in a cosy room to one side of the main patio; there is also a large lounge with a mudéjar ceiling, a quiet retreat for musing over the wonders of the Alhambra.

Rooms: 6 with bath & wc + 5 suites with own kitchens.
Price: S 9500 Pts; D/Tw 12500-15000 Pts; Ste 18000 Pts; Ste with Alhambra view 20000 Pts.
Breakfast: 800 Pts.
Meals: None.
Closed: Never.

How to get there: Into centre to Plaza Nueva; then Carrera del Darro and, by FIRST BRIDGE, best to leave car, walk to hotel just up to left; someone from hotel can come to show you where to park. Or easier: any central public car park then taxi to hotel.

Map No: 26

Hotel Reina Cristina
Calle Tablas 4
18002
Granada

Tel: (9)58 253211
Fax: (9)58 255728

Management: Federico Jiménez
González

The Reina Cristina is a grand 19th-century townhouse, close to the cathedral and the lovely pedestrianised 'Bib-Rambla' square. Legend has it that Lorca spent his last night here, hidden by his friend Rosales who was living in this house. The hotel sits comfortably athwart time past and time present, quite able to please the most demanding of modern travellers. The (very dapper) rooms are set round an elegant lobby (it has a neo-mudéjar ceiling, a fountain, aspidistras and marble columns) all of it utterly in sympathy with tradition and climate. The downstairs dining room is perfect: not too big, with pretty rush-seated chairs, chequered table cloths, cut flowers and local ceramics . Make sure you eat at least once at the Cristina; the owner is very proud of the cuisine, which is a mix of local dishes and those 'we create ourselves'. There are also tapas in the café as well as home-made cakes... all mouth-watering. A favourite Granada address.

Rooms: 43 with bath & wc.
Price: S 6950 Pts; D/Tw 11250 Pts; Tr 13800 Pts; Ste 16550 Pts.
Breakfast: Included.
Meals: Lunch/Dinner 1400 Pts (M); 5000 Pts(C).
Closed: Never.

How to get there: From A92 exit for Mendez Nuñez then right onto Camino de Ronda. Just before bus station right into C/Emperatriz Eugenia then C/Gran Capitán. Right into Carril del Picón, left at end into Calle Tablas.

Map No: 26

190

Hostal Suecia

Calle Molinos (Huerta de los Angeles) 8
18009
Granada

Tel: (9)58 225044/227781
Fax: (9)58 225044

Management: Mari-Carmen Cerdan Mejías

Hostal Suecia is hidden away at the end of a quiet little street at the very foot of the Alhambra hill. It seems hard to believe that you're in the city and just a few hundred yards from one of Europe's architectural wonders. The Suecia is most seductive too, every inch a southern house with terracotta roof tiles, arched windows and an old sharon-fruit tree (that of the photo) in the front. But don't get the idea that the Suecia pretends to anything: within it feels like a family home. There is a pretty sitting room downstairs, a tiny breakfast room up above and bedrooms which vary in size and comfort, like those of your own house. The beds are comfortable, the rooms are spotless. Come for the most peaceful location in town, the roof-top terrace (no better spot to read 'Tales from the Alhambra') and leisurely breakfasts, not to mention the nearby 'Campo del Príncipe' where you can sit in a café and think of the generations who have fleeted across this lively square.

Rooms: 7 rooms with bath or shower & wc; 4 rooms sharing.
Price: S 3000-5000 Pts; D/Tw 6000 Pts; D/Tw sharing 4000 Pts;.
Breakfast: 450 Pts.
Meals: None.
Closed: Never.

How to get there: Entering Granada follow signs for Alhambra. Near Alhambra Palace hotel (by Alhambra) turn down Antequerela Baja which becomes Cuesta del Caidero. At bottom turn right into C/Molinos. After 30m right under arch to Suecia.

191

Map No: 26

Hotel La Fragua
San Antonio 4
18417
Trevélez
Granada

Tel: (9)58 858626/858573
Fax: (9)58 858614

Management: Antonio
Espinosa González

Just to the south of the towering peak of Mulhacén (at 3481 metres the highest peak in the Sierra Nevada), Trevélez is one of the prettiest villages of the Alpujarra. You climb steeply up to the heart of the village; La Fragua is shared between two old village houses next to the town hall. In one building there is the friendly little bar and above it a real eagle's nest of a pine-clad dining room with a panoramic view across the flat roof-tops. A wonderful place to sit and gaze between courses. The food is just like the place — simple and authentic. The locally-cured ham is utterly delicious and whatever you do leave some space for one of the home-made puddings. Just a few yards along the narrow street is the second house where you find your room; no fussy extras here, just terracotta floors, timbered ceilings and comfy beds. Up above is a roof terrace with tables and the same heavenly view. Your host, Antonio, knows walkers and their ways and will gladly help you plan your hikes. Visit the Alpujarra before it gets too well known.

Rooms: 14 with bath & wc.
Price: S 2800 Pts; D/Tw 4500 Pts; Tr 6000 Pts.
Breakfast: 250 Pts.
Meals: Lunch/Dinner 1500 Pts (M); 1500-2000 Pts (C).
Closed: 10 Jan-10 Feb.

How to get there: From Granada N323 towards Motril; C333 through Lanjarón; just before Orgiva take road to Trevélez. Climb up into village; La Fragua is in the 'barrio medio' next to town hall (ayuntamiento).

Map No: 26

192

Las Terrazas
Plaza del Sol 7
18412
Bubión
Granada

Tel: (9)58 763252/763034
Fax: (9)58 763034

Management: Francisco Puga
Salguero

You are high up in the Alpujarra, so high that on a clear day you can see down to the coast, across the Mediterranean and all the way to... Africa. Las Terrazas, as the name implies, stands on a terraced hillside on the southern edge of Bubión. You enter by a quiet bar; this is the only place in Spain apart from monasteries and churches where we have ever seen a 'Silence Please' sign on the wall. Breakfast is taken here. Unusually, it includes cheeses and cold sausage; no meals are served but there are many places to eat in the village. The rooms are just fine; nothing fancy, but with their terracotta floors, locally-woven blankets and framed photographs they have simple charm. Even if they are smallish those with their own terrace are remarkably inexpensive. (There are also self-catering apartments at Las Terrazas). Your hosts are the kindest of folk; they have 13 mountain bikes and happily help you plan your sorties on two wheels — or two feet.

Rooms: 17 with bath or shower & wc.
Price: S 2200 Pts; D/Tw 3400 Pts.
Breakfast: 225 Pts.
Meals: None.
Closed: Never.

How to get there: From Granada N323 towards Motril; C333 through Lanjarón; just before Orgiva take road to Pampaneira and very soon left to Bubión. In village on left.

193

Map No: 26

Villa Turística de Bubión

Barrio Alto s/n
18412
Bubión
Granada

Tel: (9)58 763112/763111
Fax: (9)58 763136

Management: Victor M. Fernández Garcés

A magic mountain hides under the Sierra Nevada; folded in upon itself, it protects soaring southern hills, plunging gorges where streams run through lines of leafy poplars to water the fertile fields and refresh the impeccably white villages that cling to the slopes. You too can belong to the Alpujarra for a spell, be dazzled by the contrasted 'alpine' snow and Mediterranean sun, discover the wild flowers and perhaps some of the indigenous wild animals. Simply take a house in this village (self-catering or hotel service) and live here. The village is a perfect replica of Alpujarran architecture, using the proper materials and colours with the right shapes, volumes and distribution; the houses are neat, functional, fully equipped; each has a terrace or garden with well-established plants and those heart-lifting views. Mottled light plays on the public spaces with their cool sitting areas and luxuriant plants; even the restaurant gets it just right. Odd to have a specially-created village in this book but it will work its magic on you too.

Rooms: 40 'casitas' with kitchen/lounge, bath & wc.
Price: Apt for 2-3 9500 Pts; Apt for 4-5 (1 bathroom)12000 Pts; Apt for 4-6 (2 bathrooms) 13100 Pts.
Breakfast: 800 Pts.
Meals: Lunch/Dinner 2000 Pts (M).
Closed: Never.

How to get there: From Granada N323 towards Motril; C333 through Lanjarón; just before Orgiva take road to Pampaneira. Just after left to Bubión. In village to top of village; signposted.

Map No: 26

194

Sierra y Mar
18416
Ferreirola
Granada

Tel: (9)58 766171
Fax: (9)58 857367

Management: Inge Norgaard and Giuseppe Heiss

Take the blue door for paradise; enter a sunny/shady, flowery/leafy walled garden, a magic world apart. For breakfast you will eat a minor feast under the spreading mulberry tree. This is a gorgeous place run by two northerners (Italian and Danish) who know and love their adopted country. They are relaxed, intelligent and 'green'. They have converted and extended an old Alpujarran house with utter respect for its origins; they like things simple, the emphasis being on the natural treasures that surround them not on modern gadgets or plastic paraphernalia. The house is furnished with old rural pieces, nice materials for curtains and bedcovers, all in good simple taste. Fear not, there are modern bathrooms and central heating. José and Inge run Spanish courses and organise walking tours. They delight in having guests, they rejoice each day in the exceptional gift to man that is the Alpujarra, they want to share all this with you. You can cook your own meals here or explore the nearby villages for restaurants.

Rooms: 8 with own bath & wc.
Price: S 4000 Pts; D/Tw 6000 Pts inc VAT. Min. stay 2 nights
Breakfast: Included.
Meals: None; kitchen for guests.
Closed: Occasionally in winter: check!

How to get there: From Granada N323, towards Motril; C333 through Lanjarón; just before Orgiva take road to Pampaneira.
Just before Pitres right towards Mecina; through village to Ferreirola.

Number Ten

Calle Mar 10
04288
Bédar
Almería

Tel: (9)50 398025
Fax: (9)50 398025

Management: Sheila and Peter Mills

Bédar stands at over a thousand feet, between the Cabrera and Filabres mountain ranges, with inspirational views out east across the Mediterranean. This part of Almería is blessed with year-round sunshine and abundant spring water; surprising when you stumble on such exuberant vegetation so close to those dry gulches and gulleys of 'spaghetti western' fame. Sheila and Peter know the land and its people, having restored a 400-year-old village house then thrown it open to all. Comfort was a first priority; marble floors and ceiling fans will keep you cool in summer, but when colder weather arrives the house is properly heated and a log fire will be burning in the large open-plan sitting-room. Bedrooms are beamed, decorated with traditional wooden furniture and all have views over the rooftops towards coast and Sierra. Best of all is the roof-top terrace; have an apéritif here before joining Peter and Sheila for dinner. "Just what the doctor ordered," wrote one guest in the visitors' book; "perfect house, perfect hosts," purred another.

Rooms: 2 with bath & wc.
Price: S 3400 Pts; D/Tw 4400 Pts inc VAT.
Breakfast: Included; cooked breakfast extra 500 Pts.
Meals: Dinner 1950 Pts (M), book ahead.
Closed: Never.

How to get there: From Alicante A7 south. Exit 525 for Los Gallardos. Onto N340 then right by cemetery following signs to Bédar. Under motorway; 4.6km from here you turn left; on up this road to Calle Mar and Number 10.

Map No: 27

196

Finca Listonero

Cortijo Grande   **Tel:** (9)50 479094
04639   **Fax:** (9)50 479094
Turre
Almería

Management: Graeme Gibson and David Rice

Lovers of desert landscapes, their barrenness, aridity, sense of eternity and proportion will be richly rewarded at the Finca Listonero with its wraparound views of the Sierra Cabrera. For the sybaritic, this sensitively-extended pink (original colour) farm-house has all the luxuries. David and Graeme, cultured and gourmet Anglo-Australians, have lavished much affection on this conversion. This and their attention to guests make it very special. The contrasts are a truly Spanish delight: bougainvillea defies the dry sierra with every flower; the delightful dining and drawing rooms, the fern-filled atrium, the antiques and 'objets' impose grandeur on the lowly origins. The guestrooms are all differently decorated and furnished. Breakfast is an easy-going occasion while dinner is definitely a serious matter with excellent regional and international dishes (ingredients from the garden) and good wines. Let yourself be pampered by the pool and guided towards the loveliest walks, villages or beaches in the area.

Rooms: 5 with bath or shower & wc.
Price: TW 10000-12000; S 7000-9000.
Breakfast: Included.
Meals: Dinner 3500 Pts (M).
Closed: Normally all Feb.

How to get there: From N340/E15 exit 520 towards Turre/Mojácar. 3km on, right through entrance to Cortijo Grande. Finca signposted on right after approx. 3.5km.

197   Map No: 27

Mamabel's

Calle Embajadores 3
Mojácar Pueblo
04638
Mojácar, Almería

Tel: (9)50 472448

Management: Isabel Aznar

Artists long ago discovered the charms of this pretty white village near the beach yet it is still a real clifftop village: slightly touristy but it has kept its identity. So has Isabel Aznar ('Mamabel') — a superb hostess; she greets you with the loveliest of smiles and treats you as her friend. Understandably well-known and loved in the village, she is proud of her land, her culture and the small guesthouse which she has gradually rebuilt and added to since first arriving in the mid-sixties. The rooms are prettily decorated; number 1 is the grandest with its canopied bed, antique table and many knick-knacks; not a hint of 'hotel' here. But all the rooms are charming and of course we'd all love one of those with a terrace looking down to the glittering sea. And where better to eat than in the little dining room where there are original paintings, brightly-painted chairs and food with an unmistakably Mediterranean flavour. A house that radiates warmth and welcome... one of our favourites.

Rooms: 6 with bath & wc.
Price: D/TW 5500-6500 Pts.
Breakfast: 650 Pts or English 1100 Pts.
Meals: Dinner 1750 Pts (M).
Closed: Never.

How to get there: From N340/E15 exit 520 then towards Turre/Mojácar. Up into village of Mojácar and signposted to right.

Hostal Family

Calle La Lomilla
(Apartado 2?)
04140
Carboneras, Almería

Tel: (9)50 138014
Fax: (9)50 138014

Management: René Salmeron

Gentle-mannered Frenchman René Salmeron came to Agua Amarga on holiday and like many of us who discover places as beautiful as this, he dreamed of coming to live and work here. And here he is, just behind one of southern Spain's most seductive beaches, running this simple whitewashed hostal and restaurant and making new friends. The building has just acquired a second floor and rooms at the front have sea views. Downstairs and upstairs rooms are simply furnished with all-wooden furniture and thick, Alpujarran blankets as bedspreads. In the rather kitsch courtyard restaurant (covered in winter) you can expect to eat well; René's food is 'Mediterranean with a French touch' — try his paté as a starter. There are decent breakfasts with home-made jams, yoghurt and fruit — or pancakes if you prefer. Thank heavens that there are still places on the Costa like this little fishing village worth visiting. Stay a couple of nights and explore the nearby Cabo de Gata National Park.

Rooms: 9 with bath & wc.
Price: D/TW 5000-7000; TR 9800; Q 11200 inc. breakfast and VAT.
Breakfast: Included.
Meals: Dinner 1800 Pts (M); Lunch w/e only.
Closed: Never.

How to get there: From N344 exit 494 for Venta del Pobre/Carboneras. Continue towards Carboneras then right towards Agua Amarga. Signposted to right in village.

199

Mikasa

Agua Amarga
04149
Nijar
Almería

Tel: (9)50 138073
Fax: (9)50 138073/138219

Management: Manuel Lezcano de Orleans

A modern building, an interior designer (Lidia's dried flowers and rustic tiles have been in 'Vogue Magazine') and much attention to detail. Mikasa is a luxurious mixture of the cleancut and the plush. Manuel and Lidia are much-travelled, cultivated, multi-lingual, enjoy all things cosmopolitan and know how to make guests feel cared for. A German newspaper will be provided if you are German (and so on for each nationality), beds are turned down every evening and adorned with a few chocolates, there are ceiling fans as well as air conditioning, good contemporary paintings on the walls and high-quality insulation. Some of the carefully-fitted bedrooms have king-size beds, some have terraces; they vary in size but all have excellent bathrooms. Breakfast is a huge spread that you can enjoy inside or out. There is a lovely park, the beach is very secluded (and quiet except in August) and one can swim here at least 10, sometimes 12 months a year. Worth the price for a supremely comfortable, quiet place to stay.

Rooms: 10 with bath & wc + 2 suites.
Price: D 10000-17000 Pts; Tw 10500-11500 Pts; Ste18000 Pts.
Breakfast: Buffet included.
Meals: Dinner 2000-3000 Pts (M). Book ahead.
Closed: Never.

How to get there: From N344 take exit 494 for Venta del Pobre/Carboneras. Continue towards Carboneras then right towards Agua Amarga. Signposted arriving in village.

PORTUGAL

"Sometimes a nation catches fire, and like a shooting star flames for a few generations across the dark sky of history. Then exhausted, it sinks again into the dreaming sleep of centuries... The people that once made the world's destiny had in the end to resign themselves to it."

JOHN TRAIN - *Wohl (Portugal)*

"Portugal's most remote province is composed of two distinct zones: the valleys and terraced, steep banks of the Douro river, the so-called terra guente *or warm region, where the grapes for Port wine are grown; and the* terrafria, *or cold region, of mountainous plateaux in the north - a luminous, dry landscape... an Iberian Attica with vestiges of the ancient economy based on rye, chestnuts and acorns, and poverty so great that... carts were pulled by men instead of animals... The head of the* minhoto *fishing family is the woman. It is she who runs the accounts minds the nets, sells the fish, and raises the children. She is invariably dressed in black, because she is almost always in mourning for her husbands and sons lost at sea."*

EÇA DE QUEIRO

Minho &
Trás-os-Montes

Casa do Poço

Travessa da Gaviarra 4
4930
Valença

Tel: (0)51 825235
Fax: (0)51 825469

Management: Leonardus C.
Visser

The fortress town of Valença stands on a hill dominating the Minho valley; three layers of fortifications reflect the strategic sensitivity of a border site where the river could be forded back in the 17th century. Venture up into this fascinating citadel and stay a while at Casa do Poço; the seductive cream façade raises expectations which are well met once inside. If you're struck by the thought that it feels like being in an antique shop...well, you are — all the furnishings are for sale! Poço's sitting-room and dining room are light, cheery rooms; the parquet floors, chandeliers and extensive use of glass are from a recent complete restoration. In good weather the roof terrace is wonderful at dusk. But most of all you'll remember Casa do Poço for its bedrooms, where silk-lined walls, antique lamps, parquet, original oils and carefully co-ordinated colours create an opulent mood. All earn a place in the 'special' category, but perhaps our favourite would be the 'Scotch' room because of its hand-painted bedsteads and stunning views. Leave exploring the old town to late evening; by then the day-trippers have left for home and Valença can once more work its magic.

Rooms: 7 with bath & wc.
Price: S 8000-11000 Esc; D/Tw 13000-15000 Esc.
Breakfast: Included.
Meals: None.
Closed: Never.

How to get there: Arriving in Valença follow signs to 'fortaleza'. Pass through three gates in town walls; follow one-way system round cobbled streets and you'll see cream façade of hotel.

Map No: 1

Quinta da Bouça

Pedreira
Cerdal
4930
Valença

Tel: (0)51 22646 / 824893
Fax: (0)51 23798

Management: Joaquim Veiga

Joaquim Veiga was determined to get things right when he set about renovating this old Minho farm-house; five careful years were spent on the project. The setting is ideal for a country B&B; the farm stands alone, surrounded by vines, and the old pilgrim's way to Santiago passes immediately in front — you can walk sections of it, north to Valença, or south to Ponte de Lima. Bouça is a working farm; children would love the myriad possibilities of old wine presses, carts, orchards and — of course — the animals. Joaquim's elderly aunt looks after Bouça and, though she speaks only Portuguese, you'll soon make yourselves understood. Renovation rather than restoration has created four spotlessly clean guest bedrooms; all furniture is chestnut and brand new and there are 'hydro-massage' baths, efficient heating, and firm mattresses. We particularly liked the upstairs rooms which have wooden floors (instead of the tiles down below) and exposed stone walling. The breakfast room is up on the first floor; it has a handsome pyramidal wood ceiling and sparkles like a new pin. Downstairs, the sitting room is used for wine tastings where you can get to grips with the estate's Vinho Verde.

Rooms: 4 with bath & wc.
Price: D/Tw 10000-15000 Esc.
Breakfast: Included.
Meals: None.
Closed: Never.

How to get there: From Valença N13 towards Viana. At km114.3 left towards Cerdal (careful: awkward turning). Continue for 600m then left; after another 600m right on track following signs for 'turismo de habitacão'.

Map No: 1

202

Casa da Anta

Lanhelas   **Tel:** (0)58 721595
4910   **Fax:** (0)58 721214
Caminha

Management: Germano Ramalhoso

If you're looking for local flavour stay with the Ramalhosa family at their old 17th-century house, tucked away in a narrow street next to the church. The Portuguese come from far and wide for the Minho folk dancing, organised by Germano on Saturday nights during the summer. They also come for the traditional Minho cooking which has earned its stripes over the past fifteen years; specialities are lamprey and pork, but you can expect whatever you choose to be good. There are superb home-made puds — the leite crema is a classic of the genre. In summer you dine out under the rambling vine on wooden tables and benches as staff bustle to and fro. During the colder months, huge braziers add warmth and atmosphere to the low-beamed restaurant. Rooms are less memorable but perfectly decent; we preferred those in the old house overlooking the central courtyard. They have planked floors and boarded ceilings; exposed granite adds a weightier note. Shower rooms are small. One of the six rooms on ground level is specially equipped for wheelchair users. The family also run a camping site just 2km away where guests at Anta can make use of pool and tennis court.

Rooms: 10 with bath & shower.
Price: D/Tw 8500-10000 Esc; S 7500-9000 Esc.
Breakfast: Included.
Meals: Lunch/Dinner approx 2000-3000 Esc (C).
Closed: Never.

How to get there: From Valença take N13 towards Porto/Viana. After approx 18km, left in village of Lanhelas at sign for Casa da Anta.

Quinta da Graça

Vilarelho
4910
Caminha

Tel: (0)58 921157 / (0)2
6090751

Management: Maria Helena Pacheco de Amorim

The pretty little town of Caminha hugs the southern bank of the Minho where it meets with the mighty Atlantic; the town's fortifications speak of an age when this was an important frontier post between Portugal and Spain. Close by are some of the country's loveliest beaches and, cradled on a hillside of the Coura Valley with heavenly views down to the sea, is the Quinta da Graça. This elegantly-mannered farm-house dates back to the 17th century; ivy, flowered borders and a statue of the Virgin grace the main façade. Guestrooms and apartments (in what were the servants' quarters) are delightful; most have period furnishings — some of it locally crafted, some of it more exotic Indo-Portuguese ware — and one bedroom has a complete set of Victorian furniture. We loved the old hand-painted tiles in the bathrooms (some with bath, others with shower). You breakfast at a heavy chestnut table in the charming old rustic kitchen. Once replete, wander through Graça's peaceful garden, take a pool-side seat overlooking river and valley, or settle down in the library with one of the hundreds of old tomes. Apartments have their own kitchenette and there are restaurants for all budgets close by.

Rooms: 7 with bath & wc + 1 suite + 3 apartments.
Price: S 10000; D/Tw 12500 Esc; Ste Ste/Apt 20000 Esc; extra bed 3000 Esc.
Breakfast: Included.
Meals: None.
Closed: Never.

How to get there: From Porto N13 to Viana do Castelo then towards Valença to Caminha. There to centre, right to main square with fountain. Then 2nd left up hill towards fortress. House just after sign 'Miradouro' close to block of flats.

Paço de Calheiros

Calheiros
4990
Ponte de Lima

Tel: (0)58 947164
Fax: (0)58 947294

Management: Francisco Conde de Calheiros

You feel you should be arriving by horse and carriage as you pass through the wrought-iron entrance gates, along the drive lined with plane trees and past vineyards and fountain. And there to greet you is the gracious twin-towered and ivy-clad main façade; a staircase leads up to the sculpted portal of the main entrance. The family has lived here for over six and a half centuries. The house was rebuilt in the 17th century, but the Calheiros have stayed resolutely at the helm; it was the charming Francisco, present Count of Calheiros, who threw the house open to all. Inside, things live up to expectations. There are several 'salons' brimming with antiques, all with big stone hearths and in one of the dining rooms there is a ten-metre-long table at which 30 can be seated! Choose between self-catering apartments or the grandest of doubles in the main building; many have their own hearths, all of them have period furnishing and they're large enough for a waltz. But leave time to wander the exquisite formal gardens, or saddle up a horse and ride the estate. The swimming pool has a glorious view and there's a tennis court too.

Rooms: 9 with bath & wc + 6 apartments.
Price: D/Tw 15500 Esc; Apt (for 2) 15500 Esc.
Breakfast: Included.
Meals: Occasionally available approx. 4500 Esc (M).
Closed: Never.

How to get there: From Braga N201 to Ponte de Lima. Arriving here cross river and after petrol station right towards Arcos de Valdevez/Valença. After 1km right towards A. de Valdevez then, after 4km, left towards Calheiros. On right after 2km.

Casa Santa Filomena

Estrada de Cabanas
Afife
4900
Viana do Castelo

Tel: (0)58 981619 /
(0)2 6174161/2
Fax: (0)2 6175936

Management: José Street Kendall

A grand entrance gate beckons you in to the Casa Santa Filomena, a solid, stone-walled building that dates back to the twenties. It is hidden away in a quiet corner of an already quiet village; your rest is assured. When we visited in early spring the old wisteria was a riot of tumbling lilac and mauve, as pretty a welcome as you might wish for. A high wall runs round the property; it girdles a small vineyard where Vinho Verde grapes are grown. Elsewhere the profusion of flowers is heady proof of the microclimate that this part of the Minho enjoys; it seems as if anything will grow here. The kindly, educated housekeeper, José, could not treat guests more kindly; his knowledge of the area and its history is reason enough for stopping by. Rooms are rather functional, but perfectly clean and comfortable. If staying here, do have dinner in; much of your meal will have been grown in Filomena's garden and this is the occasion to try the estate's wine. If there's anything that you'd especially like to eat — just tell José. The doves in the cot have good reason to coo over a home as peaceful as this.

Rooms: 3 with bath & wc + 1 suite.
Price: D 7500-8500 Esc; Ste 9500 Esc.
Breakfast: Included.
Meals: Lunch/Dinner 2500-3500 Esc (M).
Closed: Never.

How to get there: From Valença towards Viana/Porto on N13. Pass sign for Afife beach; 800m on, opp. bus stop on right, turn left, cross railway then straight on at crossroads; house on left after 700m.

Casa do Ameal

Meadela
4900
Viana do Castelo

Tel: (0)58 822403

Management: Maria Elisa de Magalhães Faria Araújo

Although this grand old Minho house has been absorbed into the fabric of the expanding town and is close to a large shopping centre, DO come and visit; once you pass into the entrance courtyard of Casa do Ameal, with its box hedges and gurgling fountain, you can leave the outside world behind. The Casa do Ameal was bought in 1669 by the de Faria Araújo family whose very numerous descendants still watch over the place; there are fourteen siblings in the present generation and five of the sisters still live at the house (most of the others arrive at the weekend!) These lovable elderly ladies welcome you with tea and a tour round the house; they will proudly show off the collection of handicrafts and the family costume 'museum' with such delights as their grandparents' christening robes. Accommodation is in two guestrooms and seven apartments, some sleeping two, others four; most have their own kitchenette. The rooms are furnished in simple 'rustic' style that goes well with the exposed stone walls The sisters speak English, French and Spanish and will gladly help you plan your excursions to Viana do Castelo, just two kilometres away.

Rooms: 2 doubles + 7 apartments (for 2 or 4 persons)
Price: D 11500 Esc; Apt (for 2) 11500 Esc, (for 4) 18200 Esc.
Breakfast: included
Meals: On request + self-catering.
Closed: Never.

How to get there: From Porto take the N13/IC1 dir. Viana do Castelo. Just before Viana enter Meadela village, pass main square, church and drive on until big supermaket 'Modelo'. Turn left as if to go to supermarket, but pass their car park, drive up the hill and turn left at gates to the house.

Map No: 9

Quinta de Malta

Lugar da Igreja
Durrães
4905
Barroselas

Tel: (0)58 773773

Management: Delfim & Alice Sobreiro

This handsome granite Minho manor house dates back more than three hundred years. Set in a beautiful mature garden — the hydrangeas are magnificent — and with vineyards producing the 'Loureiro' Vinho Verde, this is an interesting stop-over in northern Portugal. Delfim and Alice Sobreiro are young and enthusiastic hosts; their recent renovation of the quinta was a real labour of love. Their bedrooms — small suites really — are elegant, light and spacious. Delfim's flower arrangements, the views across the estate, canopied four-posters and small sitting room are all welcome extras — as is the efficient central heating if you come to stay during the winter months. Breakfast can be served in your room (a fire can be lit in the hearth), but the dining room is light and graceful. It would be a real treat to have dinner here; Delfim's mother's traditional Minho cooking is not to be missed and it is in keeping with the spirit of the house that your hosts are at table with you. Do try the estate's wine which is of considerable local repute. But first work up an appetite on the tennis court, or with a walk out from the quinta into the lovely Neiva river valley.

Rooms: 9 with bath & wc + 1 suite.
Price: D/Tw 10000-12000 Esc; Ste 12000 Esc.
Breakfast: Included.
Meals: On request. Dinner 2000-3000 Esc (M).
Closed: Never.

How to get there: From Braga to Barcelos on N103. Here take N204 towards Ponte de Lima; at village of Balugães, left onto N308 to Barrosellas. House near church.

Casa da Várzea

4990
Beiral do Lima
Ponte de Lima

Tel: (0)58 948603

Management: Sr Inácio Barreto Caldas da Costa

You'll spot Casa da Várzea from way off as you wind your way up from the valley below. It would be hard not to fall in love with the beauty of the place, cradled among terraced vineyards. Like so many of the grand old homes of Portugal it lay abandoned for many years. But Inácio Caldas da Costa, whose feelings ran deep for the house where he was born, took courage and after his retirement set about restoration of the family seat. Várzea now has six big, light and charmingly decorated rooms. Family antiques are here for you to enjoy; you may find yourself sleeping in grandmother's or great-uncle's bed. One room has a lovely old chest, typical of the Minho region, with a secret drawer for hiding away those gold sovereigns. Prints and framed embroidery, polished wooden floors and rugs are charmingly domestic. And in the public rooms wood-clad floors and ceilings lend warmth to grandeur. At breakfast there are long views from the airy dining room, not to mention home-made jams and fruit from the farm. There's a library, a pool with-a-view and the old wooden 'drying house' which now houses a second lounge-cum-playroom.

Rooms: 6 with bath & wc.
Price: D/Tw 11500 Esc.
Breakfast: Included.
Meals: On request. Approx. 2500 Esc (M).
Closed: Never.

How to get there: From Braga N201to Ponte de Lima. Here follow signs towards Ponte de Barca. After approx. 8km in S. Martinho da Gandra right to Beiral. Here just 100m past church at stone cross turn left. Along this lane to house.

Map No: 9

Casa do Monte

Lugar do Barreiro
Abade de Neiva
4750
Barcelos

Tel: (0)53 811519 /
(0)936 776125

Management: José de Sousa Coutinho

The house stands proud on a hillside in a tiny hamlet looking out across the green valley of Barcelos. The main drive cuts an arc upwards past carefully clipped hedges of box, enormous camellias, a statue and a ceramic plaque; it praises God for blessing the Minho with places as heavenly as this. Come if only to see these pampered gardens. The house is a well-mannered building which you might imagine to be older than its 60 years; light granite lintels, bright sky-blue windows and azulejos lend the façade a merry air. And the gaiety is mirrored inside the house; bright primary colours decorate panelling, skirting, chairs and tables in the unforgettable dining room. In the bedrooms the same idea adds cheer to radiators and window seats, beds and wardrobes. We marginally preferred those on the first floor but those giving out onto the lower terrace are special too — and all the rooms have views across the valley. In among the hedges are a pool and tennis court, but you might find the profusion of shrubs, trees and flowers of more interest; this is considered to be one of the loveliest gardens of northern Portugal. Try to catch the Thursday market in Barcelos.

Rooms: 6 with bath & wc.
Price: D/Tw 10000 Esc.
Breakfast: Included.
Meals: None.
Closed: Never.

How to get there: From Barcelos take road to Viana do Castelo. After 4km you arrive in hamlet of Abade de Neiva; Casa do Monte on right.

Quinta do Convento da Franqueira

Carvalhal c.c. N° 301 **Tel:** (0) 53 831606/
Franqueira (0) 53 831853
4750 **Fax:** (0)53 832231
Barcelos

Management: Piers and Kate Gallie

This gorgeous 16th-century monastery hides away among pine trees, cork oaks, eucalyptus and cypress — rich in history. The cloister is thought to have been built with stones taken from the ruins of the nearby castle of Faria; the Brothers came here for the splendid isolation and the abundant spring waters which now feed a swimming pool. The buildings have been gradually restored to former grace by the Gallie family; a labour of love and respect for 'how things were'. Rooms and suite are lovely indeed, of generous proportions, and furnished with fine antiques. There's a a four-poster in one room, old prints, pretty bedside lamps and tables and stuccoed ceilings. Colours are soothing and bathrooms have traditional hand-painted tiles. The house produces its own Vinho Verde from the six hectares of vineyards that lap right up to Franqueira's walls; Piers Gallie enjoys showing his guests round the winery and talking of wine. Children would be more interested in swings, gardens and the rocking horse in the play room. There is a huge tiled terrace overlooking lush and colourful gardens. Try to coincide with the wonderful Thursday market in nearby Barcelos.

Rooms: 4 with bath & wc + 1 suite.
Price: D/Tw 14000 Esc; Ste (for 2) 14000 Esc, (for 3) 17000 Esc, (for 4) 20000 Esc.
Breakfast: Included.
Meals: Occasionally available; approx. 4500 Esc (M).
Closed: End Oct-end Apr.

How to get there: From Braga N103 to Barcelos; at end of N103 right round ring road. Pass Renault garage then 2nd right towards Povoa de Varzim. Under bridge then left to Franqueira. Through village; take middle road of three up hill into woods to blue bar. Here right, pass church and left through gates.

Castelo do Bom Jesus

Bom Jesus
4700
Braga

Tel: (0)53 676566
Fax: (0)53 677691

Management: Dr. M. de Castro Meirelles

Castelo do Bom Jesus looks down over the city of Braga and all the way to the Atlantic coast. Enter beneath the grand portal sculpted with the family coat of arms; the blue-blooded Meirelles, part of the House of Bragança, have lived here since an ancestor built this grandest of homes in the 18th century. Foundations rest on those of a much older medieval fortress. Abandon yourself to an oasis of green and calm; palm fronds sway in the breeze, peacocks roam the gardens. The outside of the building was reformed in the Italian Romantic style; the present generation of Meirelles restored and renovated the interiors. Rooms are as sumptuous as you'd expect; the presidential suite is the grandest, with trompe l'oeil frescoes, period furniture and jacuzzi. You breakfast at a huge dining table in a light, graceful room beneath the family portraits; dress for dinner in the oval, chandeliered dining-room with its beautiful wrap-round fresco of fabulous gardens. In the lounge are grand piano and harp; a second salon is given over to the billiard table. And the gardens! — wind your way past exotic plants and trees via a grotto and on up to the belvedere. The estate has its own vineyards.

Rooms: 7 with bath & wc + 6 suites.
Price: Tw 13000-14000 Esc; Ste 16000-28000 Esc.
Breakfast: Included.
Meals: Lunch/Dinner from 2000 Esc (C).
Closed: Never.

How to get there: From Porto A3-IP then N14 to Braga. Here follow signs for Bom Jesus to top of the hill; right through gate just before Sanctuary car park.

Casa de Sezim

Apartado 410
Nespereira
4800
Guimarães, Nespereira

Tel: (0)53 523196
Fax: (0)53 523000

Management: Dr. António Pinto de Mesquita

The owners must be fond of Casa de Sezim — it has been in the family for more than 700 years. The first grapes were trod here in 1390! Today the estate's Vinho Verde is of prize-winning quality. As you pass under the elegant portal in Sezim's rich ochre façade (the present building is mostly 18th-century) the appetite is whetted; this grand old house — it bears the patina of long use — utterly seduced us with its understated elegance. You enter via an enormous, sober lounge with heavy old oak beams, granite floor and walls. The family coat of arms graces the hearth and blue-blooded forebears look down from their gilt frames. If only one could invite them down for a game of billiards ... The fun really begins upstairs in the bedrooms. Some have four-poster beds, others have tapestried headboards, perhaps a writing desk; all have some antique pieces and rich patterns on wallpaper, bedspreads and curtains. But the gaily decorated panelling is their joy. We'd probably sacrifice space and go for a tower room with a view. Most memorable are Sezim's panoramic paintings that date back to the early 19th century with their exotic scenes from the Old and the New Worlds.

Rooms: 8 with bath & wc + 1 suite.
Price: S 13000 Esc; D/Tw 16500 Esc; Ste 17500 Esc.
Breakfast: Included.
Meals: On request. Lunch/Dinner 3500 Esc.
Closed: Never.

How to get there: From Porto A3 towards Braga then A7 to Guimarães. There N105 towards Santo Tirso. Right in Covas (after passing petrol station and Ford garage); house 2.2km from here directly opp. 'Tecidos ASA'.

Quinta de Cima de Eiriz

4801
Encosta sul da Penha
Guimarães

Tel: (0)53 541750/ 514221
Fax: (0)53 514206

Management: João Gaspar and Maria Adelaide Gomes Alves

On a south-facing slope of the beautiful Penha mountain, this old Minho quinta has been completely restored. In the beamed and terracotta-tiled lounge, the old grape press has been transformed into an unusual raised bar. Marvel at the size of the granite lintels, flagstones and building blocks of the entrance hall. The post-box red of the doors and windows lends a lighter note. Bedrooms, in the old stable blocks, are 'mod-conned' with central heating and phone and have sparkling marbled and tiled bathrooms. Most memorable are their views out over the well-trimmed lawns and across the valley. Breakfast is a big meal; expect fresh orange juice, yoghurts, several types of bread and cake and Maria Adelaide's jams. Afterwards you could walk straight out to explore the Penha National Park; in the warmer months you can plunge into the pool on your return, and the balconied terrace is just the spot for a sun-downer; the views are long and rural. Just 10km away is Guimarães with narrow streets, castle and superb municipal museum, while closer still is the Santa Marinha da Costa Monastery, the best preserved medieval building of the region. Good value in a lovely area.

Rooms: 4 with bath & wc.
Price: D/Tw 9000 Esc.
Breakfast: Included.
Meals: None.
Closed: Never.

How to get there: From Braga N01 to Guimarães. There take road towards Fafe/Felgueiras. After 4 km right towards Felgueiras. After another 4km right at sign Penha/Lapinha (don't take first turn Penha/Calvos!). After 3km left at a stone cross; signposted.

Casa do Campo

4890
Molares
Celorico de Basto

Tel: (0)55 361231 /
(0)53 417832

Management: Maria Armanda Meireles

Casa do Campo is every inch the classic 'solar' or country manor. An enormous, ornately sculpted portal and a turreted outer wall protect the paved inner courtyard. The prize-winning gardens are a hymn to the camellia — the oldest one in the country is meant to be here and, thanks to careful topiary, they take on fabulous forms. The Meireles family has been here for centuries farming the surrounding estate and its vines. The art of receiving guests comes naturally to gracious Maria Armanda. The bedrooms are in a renovated wing and are of the sort that we love; no two are the same, they are decorated in classical style and have polished wooden floors, elegantly stuccoed ceilings, cut flowers, magazines and a feeling of space. Breakfast in the classically elegant dining room; or there is a smaller, less formal alternative. Settle in to the lounge with its old harpsichord or into the dream of a library with one of the many tomes on the gardens of Portugal — Casa do Campo features in them all, of course. The manor's splendid Renaissance chapel still has a weekly Mass.

Rooms: 7 with bath & wc + 1 suite.
Price: S 10000 Esc; D/Tw 12500 Esc; Ste 16000 Esc; extra bed (children to 12 yrs) 3000 Esc.
Breakfast: Included.
Meals: On request. Lunch/Dinner approx. 4000 Esc (M).
Closed: Christmas.

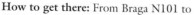

How to get there: From Braga N101 to Guimarães then N206 towards Fafe and Celorico de Basto/Mondim. At Gandarela right onto N304 to Fermil; here right onto N210 towards Celorico. House signposted after 1.5km.

215

Casa Agricola da Levada

Avenida de 1er Maio 70
5000
Timpeira
Vila Real

Tel: (0)59 322190
Fax: (0)59 346955

Management: Albano Paganini da Costa Lobo

When built in 1922 Casa Agricola da Levada stood alone, but the expansion of Vila Real has brought new neighbours. Nevertheless it has kept its charm and there are long walks out from the house, quiet spots galore in the grounds and fishing in the river Corgo that cuts across the estate. House and chapel were designed by the Portuguese architect Raul Lino; this graceful architectural style was the Portuguese answer to the French Art Deco. It is most attractive: granite off-set by white rendering and burgundy windows and doors. There are four stone-walled guest rooms whose comfortable beds and utter quiet guarantee a deep sleep. Young and friendly Inês and Albano live in with their baby; they always find time to share conversation, in the evening over a glass of wine or with a coffee at breakfast. And food is special at Levada; home-made breads and jams at breakfast (in the garden in summer) and dinners lovingly prepared by the farm's 72 year-old cook who has been at Levada for as long as anyone can remember. Nearly everything is home-grown, produced or baked. Try the estate-reared boar. There is a good house wine, or finer wines if you prefer. At nearby Casa de Mateus there are regular concerts during the summer months.

Rooms: 4 with bath & wc.
Price: D/Tw 10000-12000 Esc.
Breakfast: Included.
Meals: On request. 3500 Esc (M)
Closed: Never.

How to get there: From Porto IP4 towards Bragança. Exit for Vila Real Norte then follow signs for centre and then towards Sabrosa. At junction (Casa de Mateus to right) turn left, through Murça, over railway then river and house to right.

Map No: 10

216

Solar das Arcas

Arcas
5340
Macedo de Cavaleiros

Tel: (0)78 401135 /
(0)2 6100383
Fax: (0)78 401233

Management: Maria Francisca Pessanha

In this forgotten corner of Portugal this lovely mansion or, 'solar', has graced the centre of the village of Arcas for over 300 years. The owners are direct descendants of Manuel Pessanha of Genoa, who came to Portugal to teach the Portuguese the art of navigation. Nowadays the Pessanhas' extensive estates include fruit orchards and olive groves. The building is of lovely proportions; graciously carved mouldings surround windows and doors while the family coat of arms above the portal reminds you that this is a gentleman's residence — as does the imposing private chapel. 'Cosy privacy' is how the brochure (correctly) describes rooms and apartments. They have antique beds — the four-poster in one of them really caught our eye — and the apartments come with kitchenette and small lounge; one of them has its own bread oven. Food? Forgive us for quoting Arcas' brochure again: "You will feel that you belong to a real Portuguese family when you sit on a footstool savouring a glass of wine and nibbling at a piece of a smoked delicacy before the fireplace where iron vesssels boil and the revolving plate grills simple but first-rate meals".

Rooms: 1 with bath & wc + 7 apartments.
Price: D 15000 Esc; Apt (for 2) 12000 Esc, (for 4) 20000 Esc. Add 5% VAT.
Breakfast: Included.
Meals: On request or self-catering.
Closed: Never.

How to get there: From Bragança E82 towards Vila Real then just before Macedo de Cavaleiros right on 316 towards Zoio and after just 1km left via Ferreia to Arcas. House in village centre.

Map No: 10

"I awoke wrapped in a vast sweet silence. Along the river, where the slow and muddy water flowed past the rocks without breaking, a boat was descending slowly, with sail filled, and laden with barrels. On the far side, more terraces, pale green with olive trees, climbed to other crags, all bleached and exposed, drunk on the fine abundance of blue."

EÇA DE QUEIRO

Douro

Quinta da Granja

Rua Manuel Francisco de Aráujo 444
Aguas Santas
4470
Maia

Tel: (0)2 9710147 / 9720332

Management: António Nunes da Ponte

Porto may be just a few minutes drive away but Quinta da Granja's setting is utterly rural. This genteel 'solar' dates back to the 18th century, though parts of the estate predate the house. The beautiful gardens, with their ancient stands of camellias, azaleas and carefully trimmed box, were planted out some four hundred years ago! Both house and gardens have been sensitively restored by António Nunes da Ponte. Things are on a grand scale here, like the lounge which is more than one hundred feet long; it still feels most welcoming with its terracotta floor, rugs, period furnishing and family portraits in oil and photo. At one end it leads through into the solar's own Baroque chapel — nowadays only used for family weddings and other special occasions. The bedrooms are in the main building, the apartment in what was once the Priest's house. Here the mood is of simple elegance; there are handsome Dona Maria beds, carpeted floors and period bedside tables. Stay a couple of days here and find a favourite spot in the oasis of calm that is the garden; come late winter or early spring to see the camellias at their very best.

Rooms: 3 with bath & wc + 2 apartments.
Price: D/Tw/Apt (for 2) 16500 Esc.
Breakfast: Included.
Meals: None.
Closed: 1 Nov-1 May.

How to get there: From Porto towards Braga/Vila Real on ring road then A4 towards Vila Real. Take first exit for Ermesinde/Rio Tinto then left towards Alto da Maia. After 500m over bridge then immediately left and first right. Signposted.

Map No: 9

Albergaria Dona Margaritta

Rua Cândido dos Reis 53
4600
Amarante

Tel: (0)55 423110
Fax: (0)55 437977

Management: Maria Helena Silva

Beautiful Amarante spreads out along both banks of the Tâmega, as graceful and as peaceful a place as you could hope to find. And looking out across the willow-lined river, just yards from the S. Gonçalo bridge, Dona Margaritta is a delightful place to stay. Built as a private home in the early years of this century, it used to be called the Hotel Silva — the name it still goes by among local folk, should you get lost. Book one of the 'special' rooms; they have balconies that face the river, high ceilings, polished parquet floors and cheery floral curtains. And they are blissfully quiet. We thought that nos. 22 and 24 were among the nicest. Down a floor from reception there's a small dining room, but with luck it will be warm enough to eat out on the terrace beneath the enormous old wisteria; drinks are available here at other times of the day. Back inside, there's also a large lounge with rather '70s furnishing; rather soulless, we felt, but the owners and staff of Margaritta are exceptionally kind. They'll recommend a good restaurant close by. Make sure you don't miss the Amadeo de Souza Cardosa museum in the São Gonçalo convent.

Rooms: 22 with bath & wc.
Price: S 5000-6000 Esc; D/Tw standard 7000-9000 Esc; D/Tw special 8000-10000 Esc.
Breakfast: Included.
Meals: None.
Closed: Never.

How to get there: Take A4 from Porto towards Bragança/Spain. Exit for Amarante; into town centre, cross S. Gonçalo bridge then left up hill; hotel on left. N.B If lost ask for 'Hotel Silva'- Margaritta's previous name.

Casa de Aboadela

Aboadela
4600
Amarante

Tel: (0)55 441141/
    (0)2 9513055

Management: Jose Silva Rebelo
and family

You'll long remember arriving at this old granite farm-house; once you turn off the main road you twist and turn along the narrowest of lanes; and at the very end of a delightfully sleepy hamlet is this supremely peaceful spot. There is many a treat in the rambling gardens: an old granite maize store, a bubbling spring, gourds and pumpkins drying in the sun. Old millstones evoke the building's infancy. There are roses and oranges and vines and, in among them, secluded places for contemplation. Bedrooms and suite are in the main house, simply attired with the family furniture and lacking nothing; best of all are the views. (Just to one side in a converted outbuilding is the 'stone little house' (sic) which — like the rooms — is superb value). The lounge/dining room is similarly unpretentious: granite-walled with a tiled floor and potted plants. A French window gives onto a small balcony and lets in the morning light and the view. There are walks galore in this area, lovely rambles straight out from the house. The São Gonçalo monastery in Amarante is just a short drive away. A good base whence to explore the Douro, Minho and little-known Trás-Os-Montes areas.

Rooms: 3 with bath & wc + 1 independent house.
Price: D/Tw 6000 Esc; Ste 8000 Esc; Hse 7000 Esc.
Breakfast: Included.
Meals: None.
Closed: Never.

How to get there: From Amarante towards Vila Real on IP4. 9km from Amarante, left to Aboadela and follow signs for 'turismo rural', then 'tr' to the house.

220   Map No: 9

Pensão Estoril

Rua de Cedofeita 193
4050
Porto

Tel: (0)2 2002751/2005152
Fax: (0)2 2082468

Management: Benvinda Santos

We include this little family-run boarding house because it is central, clean and a good base if your purse doesn't stretch to the rather grander hotels of Porto. Rua de Cedofeita is one of the city's liveliest (pedestrianised) shopping streets. Half-way along, Pensão Estoril occupies three floors of a turn-of-the-century town house whose basement and ground floor are given over to a rather garish bar and restaurant. The pension — reached by the original bannistered staircase winding its elegant way up to the top floor — has been in the care of Benvinda and Manuel for twenty two years. Kinder folk you could not hope to meet. Bedrooms are very simple, some of them curiously shaped around the bath and shower rooms which were added piecemeal over the years. We'd prefer one of those looking out over the garden to the rear; a rare expanse of green in this part of the city. Most have small shower rooms, are carpeted and have phones — and the upstairs ones are surprisingly quiet. The terrace to the rear looks out across the garden — a place to unwind after a day of visits. A reliable and inexpensive alternative with plenty of good eating houses close by.

Rooms: 14 with bath & wc; 3 sharing.
Price: D/Tw 4500-5500 Esc; sharing 4000-5000 Esc.
Breakfast: 300 Esc (in downstairs bar).
Meals: In cafeteria; cheap!
Closed: Never.

How to get there: Arriving in Porto, follow signs into centre; head for Palacio de Cristal/Torre dos Clérigos, then to Praça Coronel Pacheco (ask). Leave car in Parking 'Praça Coronel Pacheco' in front of Police station. Estoril 100m.

Casa do Marechal

Avenida do Boavista 2652
4100
Porto

Tel: (0)2 6104702/03/04/05
Fax: (0)2 6103241

Management: Sarah Schneider

Elegant, cream and white, utterly-deco Casa do Marechal was built in 1940 and would sit as happily on the front in Miami as it does here in one of Porto's smarter residential areas. It looks like a wedding cake, with a rich layer of cream stucco running round at second floor level. Inside, things are just as flamboyant; the present owners have transformed an already grand house into a refined and luxurious guest house. There are just five bedrooms, decked out in pink, blue, green, beige and yellow. They are good-sized and carefully manicured; beds are five-star, each has a small writing table and all the usual modern extras, even hydromassage tubs with sparkling tiles all round. There is an orange-coloured lounge with a balcony, a roof terrace and garden with shady corners. At breakfast you can expect all the normal fare plus fresh fruit and even porridge if you're missing it. The restaurant serves dinners on weekdays; everything's bought fresh at the local market. The owners describe the food as 'a new gastronomic interpretation of French and Portuguese traditional cuisine'. (You may need the gym, sauna and Turkish bath in the basement!)

Rooms: 5 with bath & wc.
Price: S 21000 Esc; D/Tw 23000 Esc.
Breakfast: Included.
Meals: Lunch/Dinner approx. 3500 Esc (C).
Closed: Aug, Christmas and New Year.

How to get there: Arriving on motorway from Lisbon take exit AE-Sul. Turn left towards Castelo do Queijo onto Avenida da Boavista. Hotel is on the right opposite A.I.P. offices.

Map No: 9

Grande Hotel do Porto

Rua de Santa Catarina 197
4000
Porto

Tel: (0)2 2008176 / 2005741
Fax: (0)2 311061

Management: Antonio M. Alves

The Grande Hotel do Porto is one of the oldest hotels in Porto. It is invitingly central, close to the ever-colourful Bolhão market and on one of the city's oldest shopping streets. Its elderly grandeur is still very seductive. Settle down with newspaper amid marble columns and chandeliers in the grand salon. Wide corridors lead to the rooms where things are much less traditional; the hotel has been periodically refitted, the last time being in '93. The rooms are average sized and have all the equipment (the colour schemes and predominantly 60s furniture might not be our choice). Beds are comfortable and bathrooms are 'correct'. The restaurant serves a buffet breakfast; in the evening a pianist tinkles beneath the chandeliers while you eat. The underground (paying) car park is a big plus in the congested city centre. You won't need a car, being so plumb in the middle of things, and taxis are cheap. There are all the services you'd expect of an old-style hotel, like laundry, hairdresser and babysitter. It is larger than most of the places in this guide but we enthusiastically include the dignified old Grande. There is still something special about such places.

Rooms: 93 with bath & wc + 7 suites.
Price: S 11400-13400 Esc; D/Tw 12400-14400 Esc;
Ste 21000-24000 Esc.
Breakfast: Included.
Meals: Lunch/Dinner 2400 Esc (M).
Closed: Never.

How to get there: From Lisbon A1/E80 to Porto. Exit from ringroad towards V.N. de Gaia and then follow directions to centre. Cross Douro and continue towards centre. Just before Praça Dom João, Rua de Santa Catarina is on right. At entrance of this pedestrian street is a bell; ring and hotel staff will garage the car.

Quinta do Barreiro

Govinhes
5060
Sabrosa
Vila Real

Tel: (0)59 323121
Fax: (0)59 326553

Management: Inês
Albuquerque

If you want to spend time away from the rest of the world this could be just the place. This restored eighteenth-century farm-house sits on top of a hill at the heart of the Douro valley surrounded by 40 hectares of terraced vineyards where port grapes are grown. In spite of its isolation the house has every creature comfort: central heating, open hearths, an enormous lounge and a pool that overlooks the valley. Bedrooms are light, fresh and all have exceptional views. Your friendly young hosts, Inês and Albano, will be at Casa de Mateus to welcome you and will then escort you on the final leg to your hidden retreat. Here the housekeepers see to your every need; they'll even shop for you if you like. If renting the whole house (contact owners for terms) you can self-cater but meals can also be prepared. Do try and combine a visit here with the season of concerts of Baroque, classical and regional music that take place throughout the summer months at nearby Casa de Mateus — and perhaps the grape harvest, too. Vila Real is just twenty minutes away but you'll probably not even want to leave this place. A perfect place for meditation.

Rooms: 4 with bath & wc.
Price: D/Tw 8000 Esc or 5500 Esc for three or more nights.
Breakfast: 900 Esc.
Meals: On request. 1750-2500 Esc (M). S/c poss if renting whole house.
Closed: Never.

How to get there: From Porto IP4 towards Bragança. Exit for Vila Real Norte

then follow signs for centre. Here towards Sabrosa to the Casa de Mateus from where you will be brought or guided to the house.

224   Map No: 10

*"One of the most strangely and
profoundly indigenous parts of
Portugal - perhaps precisely
because it is, owing to its
remoteness, one of the least visited.
The northern part is hilly; in the
centre comes the lovely wide
orchard-strewn cup of the Cova da
Beira - where flourish the
tangerine-coloured lambs... It is
an awkward place to visit, but it
should be visited all the same."*

ANNE BRIDGE & SUSAN LOWNDES - *The
Selective Traveller in Portugal*

Beira

Estalagem Casa D'Azurara

Rua Nova 78
3530
Mangualde

Tel: (0)32 612010
Fax: (0)32 622575

Management: Isabel Raposo

In a quiet corner of a sleepy town, Casa D'Azurara is a place to unwind and be pampered. This manor house was built by the Counts of Mangualde in the 17th century, added to at the end of the 19th and renovated to create a small, luxurious hotel. There are two guest lounges downstairs; one has an enormous old granite hearth, the other high French windows with draped and flounced curtains. There are framed etchings, potted palms, books, cut flowers and a nice choice of fabric on chairs and sofas. Carpeted corridors (a lift if you need it) lead up to the rooms, where furnishing is either antique or repro; rich fabrics are used for bedspreads and curtains. Our first choice would be suite-like 206; it has a sloping ceiling, Dona Maria beds and double French windows. Breakfast is more interesting than some and includes a choice of breads, cheeses and cold meats. The dinner menu has a strong regional bias; there are interesting fish dishes and among the specialities is the duck — pato Conde Melo. Don't miss the gardens; magnolia, hydrangeas and camellia are all of amazing size. A hotel for both business people and travellers.

Rooms: 14 with bath & wc + 1 suite.
Price: S 13500-15500 Esc; D/Tw 14800-17000 Esc; Ste 19000 Esc.
Breakfast: Included.
Meals: Lunch/Dinner approx. 4000 Esc (C).
Closed: Never.

How to get there: From Viseu take IP5 towards Guarda. Exit for Mangualde; Estalagem in town centre, signposted. Careful not to confuse with 2nd modern Estalagem as you enter town.

225

Quinta da Ponte

Faia
6300
Guarda

Tel: (0)71 96126/
(0)1 3831508
Fax: (0)71 96126/
(0) 1 3831508

Management: M. Joaquina Aragão Sousa Alvim

Just a short drive from Guarda, at the edge of the Serra da Estrêla and beside an old Roman bridge that crosses the river Mondego, this elegant 17th-century manor house is as seductive as they come. The main façade is exceptionally beautiful; at one end is the Quinta's private chapel and next to it a granite portal leads through to the inner courtyard. In the main house is one of two guest lounges; it has an extraordinary stucco ceiling, family portraits and an abundance of dried flower displays. Next door is a billiards room looking out over the park; very handsome with estera matting and fine wooden ceiling. The dining room is in what was once the stable block; the granite feeding troughs have been preserved but your (generous) breakfast is nevertheless eaten from a plate! Choose between a room in the old house or a modern apartment looking across the pool to the park beyond. Rooms are light (French windows on two sides), decorated in greens and pinks, tiled throughout and each has a lounge with hearth; furniture is a mix of old and new. There is a second, larger guest lounge in a modern building next to the apartments. To top it all there is a beautiful garden, and walks along the river.

Rooms: 2 with bath & wc + 5 apartments.
Price: Tw 14000 Esc; Apt (for 2) 16000 Esc; Apt (for 4) 18000 Esc.
Breakfast: Included.
Meals: None.
Closed: Dec.

How to get there: From Guarda, take N16 towards Celorico da Beira. After approx. 12km, turn left at sign for Faia; follow 'turismo rural' signs to the house.

Map No: 10

226

Hotel Residencial Paloma Blanca

Rua Luís Gomes de Carvalho 23   **Tel:** (0)34 381992
3800   **Fax:** (0)34 381844
Aveiro

Management: Manuel Grosso Santos

The colourful azulejo-clad Aveiro is all too often passed by. But do make the diversion to this sleepy little town with its salt pans, lagoon and many waterways where gaily painted 'moliceiros'- the swan-necked boats used to collect seaweed — ply to and fro. Stay at the Paloma Blanca, a most seductive colonial-style building with exuberant gardens filled with palms, lilies and roses, wooden panels on walls and ceiling, antique rugs, lamps and other pieces. Long corridors brimming with plants, glass display cabinets, Art Nouveau pieces and a grandfather clock lead you to the bedrooms past a series of gaily painted local scenes. We'd choose one overlooking those lush gardens, but all are welcoming — some decked out in rustic-style furnishing, others with brightly painted Alentejo sets. Enjoy the   air-conditioning, writing set, minibars, phones in bathrooms — but you'll hardly need them with lovely Aveiro to explore. Our stay was made extra special by the kindness of Paloma Blanca's staff; they really seem to enjoy working here. In the warmer months you can breakfast amid the plants on the outside balcony.

Rooms: 49 rooms with bath & wc + 1 suite.
Price: S 5250-6750 Esc; D/Tw 10500-13500 Esc.
Breakfast: Included.
Meals: None.
Closed: Never.

How to get there: From Porto A1 towards Coimbra then IP5 to Aveiro. Here towards centre/rail station along Av.Lourenço Peixinho. At station make U-turn, turn first right and hotel is on left.

Casa da Quinta de São Lourenço

São Lourenço do Bairro
3780
Anadia

Tel: (0)31 528168
Fax: (0)31 528594

Management: Lígia Branca Mexia Leitão

This lovely 19th-century manor house stands quietly at the edge of a tiny hamlet surrounded by vineyards, olives, palms and pines. A carefully swept dragon-tooth inner courtyard, then a flight of stairs, lead you to the main entrance where you are greeted by the radiant smile of housekeeper Maria. She will usher you up to your room and will be at your beck and call throughout your stay. Once within, you soon become aware of owner Lígia's passion for interior decoration. Every corner of the house has been carefully considered; there are exuberant arrangements of dried flowers and fruit, carefully matched fabrics, hand-painted tiles. Flounces, canopies, sashed curtains and bows give it an unmistakable feminine feel; pinks, greens and creams are used with flair. Each room is different from the next, not a bit hotelly. We'd choose one on the first floor looking out across the vineyards — but all are splendid. Downstairs, lounge and dining room are as spruce as the rest of the house. At dinner — on the terrace in summer — the slant is distinctly regional, with sucking pig the speciality; the estate's Bairrada wine is the obvious first choice to accompany it.

Rooms: 7 with bath & wc + 1 apartment.
Price: S 10500-13000 Esc; D/Tw 12000-14500 Esc; Apt 17500 Esc exc. breakfast.
Breakfast: Included.
Meals: On request. Lunch/Dinner approx. 3000 Esc (M).
Closed: Never.

How to get there: From Lisbon, A1 towards Porto. Exit for Mealhade. Then follow N1 towards Porto. Pass Anadia, then left towards Vagos/Mogofores. After 1km, left again towards Mira. Through Mogoflores and after 3km, left at sign for house; careful not to miss it.

Map No: 9

228

Solar Abreu Madeira

Largo Abreu Madeira 7   **Tel:** (0)32 671183
3525
Canas de Senhorim

Management: António Alberto de Abreu Madeira

Abreu Madeira is like the Dão wines that are produced on its estates: rich, mellow and genteel. This lovely 18th-century manor house graces one side of the square opposite the parish church (it also has its own private chapel which pre-dates the main house) and the aristocratic lines of its façade suggest what lies beyond the grand main portal — a blue-blooded home where tradition and comfort go together. Public rooms on the ground floor are grand, yet still retain a 'homely' feel; there's a piano, the family porcelain and a wonderful old kitchen (its hearth alone could swallow up a Parisian 'studio'). The grandest of granite staircases sweeps up to the upper floor and the three guestrooms — and most lovely they are too. There are antique tables, Dona Maria and wrought-iron beds, old prints and attractive bathrooms with hand-painted tiles. As for breakfast — 'sumptuous' is the way the owners themselves describe it: home-made jams, cheeses, local honey, fruit, perhaps Senhora's gateau. It may keep you going until dinner when you can try the estate's Cachorrinho (Dão) wines and regional dishes. There is a terrace overlooking the vineyards and a special room for more serious wine-tastings.

Rooms: 3 with bath & wc.
Price: D/Tw 13000 Esc.
Breakfast: Included.
Meals: Dinner 3500 Esc (M).
Closed: Christmas Day.

How to get there: From Lisbon towards Porto and exit for Mealhada. Here, EN234 towards Mangualde/Nelas. Arriving in Canas de Senhorim, left following signs to centre, then 'Igreja Matriz' — house opposite church.

Casa da Azenha Velha

Caceira de Cima
3080
Figueira da Foz

Tel: (0)33 25041
Fax: (0)33 29704

Management: Maria de Lourdes Nogueira

This cherry-coloured house was once a flour mill (azenha) and has been carefully renovated; the decorative flourishes above doors and windows suggest a rather genteel history. Maria de Lourdes and her two dogs, a very sweet boxer and a husky, emerge to greet you. Bedrooms and the apartment are separate from the main house; surprisingly luxurious for their price, they've been decorated with great attention to detail and colour-coordination; even tiles match the fabrics, and bathrooms have deep, oval tubs. You breakfast in the kitchen of the main house; rail buffs will note that sleepers support the roof-bricks, an original and attractive feature. Here too is a snug living-room with leather sofas, a hearth and lots of knick-knacks. In the old stable block there's a self-service bar — jot down what you've had in a little notebook. Azenha is well geared towards family visits: there are plenty of board games, a snooker table and a pool; there's a tennis court and a chance to ride one of the six horses; cows graze nearby, unperturbed by it all. You're close to the busy little port of Figueira da Foz with restaurants and bars galore; or just north is Buarcos, much quieter and with a long sandy beach.

Rooms: 5 with bath & wc + 1 apartment for 4.
Price: D/Tw 11500 Esc.
Breakfast: Included.
Meals: Snacks normally available.
Closed: Never.

How to get there: From Coimbra N111 towards Figueira da Foz. Shortly before arriving there turn off towards Caceira and

then immediately left following signs 'Turismo rural'. After approx. 2km right and after 500m right again. House on left.

Map No: 9

230

Casa Pombal

Rua dos Flores 18   **Tel:** (0)39 35175
3300
Coimbra

Management: E. Denninghoff Stelling & L. Misker

Coimbra is a town to explore slowly; once capital of the (young) nation it is most famous for its VERY old University; try to visit in term-time when the students add so much life and colour to the town. At the heart of Coimbra, in a narrow street on a hill close to the famous seat of learning, Casa Pombal is a delectable place; friendly, utterly unpretentious, it will stir feelings of nostalgia for your student years and have you wondering about mature student grants. Four of the rooms have breathtaking views over the old city roofscape and down to the Mondego river. They are 'basic' but very clean and comfortable, sharing bathrooms and wc's on each floor. (There are 3 extra loos down in the hallway.) But sacrifice the en-suite for the much sweeter pleasures of those views and the relaxed atmosphere created by the friendly Dutch owners. Single folk would especially like this place where you're bound to meet up with fellow travellers. Breakfast comes with eggs, cereals, fresh juices and home-made jams and there are good (vegetarian if ordered) dinners served in the cosiest of dining-rooms. Pombal is the Portuguese for 'dovecote' and this old town house certainly got us cooing.

Rooms: 11 sharing bathrooms & wcs.
Price: S 3000 -3800 Esc; D/Tw 4800-6400 Esc.
Breakfast: Included.
Meals: On request. 2500 Esc (M).
Closed: Jan-March.

How to get there: In Coimbra follow signs 'Universidad' via Avenida Sá da Bandeira then towards Praça da Republica; last right just before the Praça (don't go as far as the University), right again on Rua Padre António Vieira. Park as close to end of street as possible.

231   Map No: 9

Quinta do Albergue do Bomjardim

Nesperal
Cernache do Bomjardim
6100
Sertã

Tel: (0)74 99647
Fax: (0)74 99647

Management: Hubertus Johannes Lenders

Eden-esque countryside laps ups to this elegant country house, approached along the narrowest of country lanes flanked by vineyards and groves of orange, olive and almond. If you enjoy wine you should book at least a night at Bomjardim; the Lenders have a well-stocked cellar and there is a cosy bar for tastings; the estate's wine is the obvious first choice — you could follow it with a glass of their own coñac. The four guest bedrooms are most delightful: big, light rooms with pine floors, high ceilings, antique beds and dressers and carefully chosen fabrics and colours. Two of them are in the main house and reached via a fine old granite staircase. The other two are in an outbuilding and, if booked together, can be joined to make one huge apartment for six; these have a south-facing verandah and are pleasantly furnished; there is a wood-burning stove and the same light and uncluttered feel of the main house. You can swim all year round here; the pool is indoors and there is a sauna and Turkish bath. There are also horses to ride, canoeing nearby and good walks galore; but find time to visit the winery with Hubertus — he will gladly reveal his oenological secrets.

Rooms: 4 with bath & wc.
Price: D/Tw 12000 Esc.
Breakfast: Included.
Meals: None.
Closed: Never.

How to get there: From Coimbra , IC8 towards Castelo Branco and exit to Sertã. There take N238 towards Tomar. At sign marking beg. of village of Cernache do Bomjardim, left at sign Nesperal-turismo rural. Follow signs (1.4km).

Casa do Capitão-Mor

Rua do Capitão-Mor 23
6110
Vila de Rei

Tel: (0)74 98213

Management: Maria Teresa Sanchez

We had the amazing fortune to happen upon the Casa do Capitão-Mor when driving north, getting lost... then following signs for 'turismo rural' into Vila de Rei. This is a sleepy old town of narrow cobbled streets; it was here that Viscount Beresford based his garrison when chasing the French into Spain. He certainly was at the centre of things; Maria Teresa and her husband will insist that you visit the obelisk on a hill-top just beyond the town, marking the exact centre of Portugal; they'll even issue you with an official diploma as proof to your friends! But — we digress. Beyond a rather sober façade is a spruce yet intimate home. There are sparkling parquet floors, rugs and silk tapestries, cabinets of china and porcelain and a collection of Minho pottery. There are aspidistras and ferns and standard lamps, books, magazines and card table, a huge open hearth and a small bar; it all feels cherished... and intimate. Breakfast was the best we had in Portugal; superb coffee, honey, home-made jams, cheese and bread fresh from the bakers, al fresco whenever possible. Your hosts are quiet, kind, educated folk. Make sure to get lost too — and visit them!

Rooms: 5 with bath & wc + 1 suite.
Price: S 6000-7000 Esc; Tw 7000-8000 Esc; Ste 9000-10000 Esc.
Breakfast: Included.
Meals: Lunch/Dinner on request well in advance approx. 3000 Esc.
Closed: For 2 weeks in Jan.

How to get there: From Lisbon take motorway towards Porto and exit for Abrantes (IP6). Arriving there, take EN2 to Vila de Rei. House signposted in village centre.

Map No: 16

"*The village of Sintra is... the most delightful in Europe: it contains beauties of every description natural and artificial. Places and gardens rising in the midst of roads, cataracts and precipices; convents on stupendous heights - a distant view of the sea and the Ragus... It unites in itself the wildness of the Western Highlands of Scotland with the verdure of the south of France.*"

LORD BYRON

Estremadura
&
Ribatejo

Casa do Outeiro

Largo Carvalho do Outeiro 4
2440
Batalha

Tel: (0)44 96806
Fax: (0)44 96806

Management: José Madeira and Odete Monteiro

The colossal Abbey of Batalha was built in thanks for Dom João's victory over the Castilian army in 1385; the independence of Portugal had been secured. From the outside it feels something of a Gothic white elephant but the innards are of exceptional beauty. Do stay at Outeiro should you come to visit. This small modern guest house is right in the centre of Batalha, its hillside perch ensuring that some bedrooms have a view across the town's rooftops to the great Abbey. José and Odete are the nicest of hosts; both manage to combine professional careers in the town with attending to their guests. Their bedrooms are roomy and functional; all have modern pine furniture but their private terraces and their size lift them into the 'special' league. And the extensive use of wood for floors and ceilings helps to add warmth to a modern building. Most of the area to the rear of the building is given over to the swimming pool. Your ever-helpful owners will advise you where to dine out and in the morning treat you to a generous breakfast that includes five or six home-made jams. Excellent value.

Rooms: 8 with bath & wc + 1 suite.
Price: D/Tw 6000-7000 Esc; Ste 10000 Esc.
Breakfast: Included.
Meals: None.
Closed: Never.

How to get there: On arriving in Batalha follow signs for centre. Casa do Outeiro is well signposted.

234

Map No: 16

Casa da Padeira

EN8 -S. Vicente
2460
Aljubarrota

Tel: (0)62 508272/
(0)931 321609
Fax: (0)62 508272

Management: Miguel Lacerda Ventura

Casa da Padeira takes its name from the baker's wife of Aljubarrota who, so legend has it, put paid single-handed to seven Spaniards; a ceramic plaque in the lounge fills you in on the details! Several centuries on, a much more gentle reception awaits you at this modern guest house. Miguel is an erudite host and his home is evidence of a broad interest in things 'cultural'; there are masses of books, many of them on the area, with wine particularly well represented. The library also has an enormous collection of classical music. Bedrooms are up on the first floor, some of them with ornate 'Bilros' beds, all with writing desks and nice lamps. We particularly liked the suite and the 'imperial' bedroom which has a balcony and a distant view of the National Park. You eat well at Padeira; breakfast is a banquet of cakes, cheeses, cold meats and different breads, while at dinner you can choose between six different set menus; fish is the speciality. And all those pottery figurines? — they're made by Miguel's father, a retired philosophy lecturer who has his workshop round the back. A modern home with a traditional welcome.

Rooms: 7 with bath & wc.
Price: S 8000-10000 Esc; D/Tw 10000-13000 Esc;
Ste 16000 Esc
Breakfast: Included.
Meals: Dinner 2400-3300 Esc (M).
Closed: Never.

How to get there: From Lisbon towards Porto on motorway and exit for Caldas da Reina. Continue on N1 past Rio Maior, then left to Alcobaça. Here towards Batalha on N8; house signposted on left after leaving Aljubarrota.

Map No: 16

235

Casa de S. Tiago do Castelo

Largo de S. Tiago
2510
Obidos

Tel: (0)62 959587
Fax: (0)62 959587

Management: Carlos Lopes

Don't miss Obidos. This prettiest of villages, cradled by its very old (14th-century) wall, is a beguiling maze of narrow cobbled streets softened by blue and ochre pastel washes and exuberant stands of bougainvillea and jasmine. There are cameo views at every turn. The 'house of St James' has been in the family for more than a century, though it was just recently that Carlos decided to throw it open to guests. A cheery French housekeeper welcomes you in; you'd never, from the outside, guess the extent of this old house. Decoration has been meticulously studied and carefully crafted. The bedrooms' most memorable features are massively thick walls (some windows are large enough for 'conversadeiros' — gossiping seats!) and dark wood ceilings. There are wrought-iron bedsteads, matching prints for curtains and bedspreads, swanky bathrooms and details that you'd only expect of a larger hotel, like logo-ed writing paper and envelopes. On one level is a small lounge with open hearth; down below is a bar (try a glass of the local cherry liqueur 'ginjinha'), a billiard room and, in the lee of the castle battlements, the most peaceful patio for sitting out.

Rooms: 7 with bath & wc.
Price: D/Tw 12500-15000 Esc.
Breakfast: Included.
Meals: None.
Closed: Never.

How to get there: On arrival in Obidos enter town through main gate. Continue to end of this street and house on right, just below castle.

236

Map No: 16

Quinta da Barbara

Av. Da N. Sra. Da Esperança 303/305
2710
Fontanelas

Tel: (0)1 9282678
Fax: (0)1 9282597

Management: Maria Briscot

Rather different from most places in this book, but Quinta da Barbara could be just the place if you want to stay in one spot for a longer period; the minimum stay here is 3 nights in low season, a week in high season. The houses are set among pine trees in a corner of the Sintra National Park — as peaceful and secluded a spot as you could hope to find. Each house — built to give the maximum privacy — has its own diner/open-plan kitchen/lounge with open fire place and three-piece — and a private terrace with barbecue. They are equipped with everything you may (or may not) need, even a dishwasher; maid service can be arranged if you would like, but towels and linen are regularly changed. You share the large (chlorine-free) swimming pool with other guests, as well as a clay tennis court. And the location is marvellous: the sea is just a kilometre away, Sintra a short drive and Lisbon a comfortable day-trip. If you are planning a longer stay in Expo year (or any time come to that), yet wanting to stay away from the noise and pollution of the big city, Barbara could be a near-perfect base.

Rooms: 5 houses.
Price: House (for 2) 8300-17000 Esc;
House (for 4) 12500 -24500 Esc; House
(for 6) 16000-31000 Esc. All inc VAT.
Summer minimum stay one week.
Breakfast: None; self-catering.
Meals: None.
Closed: 1 Nov-28 Feb.

How to get there: Lisbon to Sintra on
IC19. There take N247 towards Colares. Here right to Praia da Maças. On through village to north and1km after Azenhas do Mar Quinta signposted on right, before you reach Fontanelas.

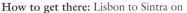

Map No: 16

237

Casa Miradouro

Rua Sotto Mayor 55
2710
Sintra-Vila

Tel: (0)1 9235900
Fax: (0)1 9241836

Management: Frederico Kneubühl

The gaily striped walls of Casa Miradouro make it an easy place to spot as you wind down from Sintra. The present owner left a successful career in Switzerland to launch himself into its restoration. This is a light, elegant and airy home with views out on all sides. Pass through a palm-graced porch and a handsome bannistered staircase leads you up to the bedrooms. Here antique beds and wardrobes rest on sisal floor matting; ceilings are high and have the original stucco mouldings. It all feels fresh and uncluttered — helped by the SIZE of the rooms — the two in the attic included. Views are to the sea or to the hills. The guest lounge has a similar unfussy feel; here the sisal matting balances less ethnic flounced curtains. There is an honesty bar with several different ports (etc) — and a hearth for sitting round in the colder months. Further downstairs is a modern breakfast room, simply decorated with four round tables and giving onto a large terrace. Classical music accompanies breakfast: cereals, cheeses, juices, yoghurts, whatever fruit happens to be in season and both savoury and sweet breads. Frederico is a gentle-mannered, attentive and truly charming host.

Rooms: 6 with bath & wc.
Price: S use 9500-15000 Esc; D/Tw 12000-18500 Esc.
Breakfast: Included.
Meals: None.
Closed: End Jan-end Feb.

How to get there: From Lisbon IC19 to Sintra. Here, follow signs for 'turismo'. At square by palace, right (in front of Hotel Central) and continue to Tivoli Hotel. There, down hill for 400m. House on left.

Map No: 16

Hotel Central

Largo Raínha D. Amélia
2710
Sintra

Tel: (0)1 9230963/4

Management: António Raio

The insatiable wanderlust of Byron inevitably took him to the village of Sintra, which he declared to be 'perhaps in every aspect the most delightful in Europe'. It remains a spell-binding place, a romantic cocktail of greenery, finery and — see the Pena palace — fantasy too. Right in the middle of what is now a small town is the Palácio Nacional, and plumb opposite is the Hotel Central. Our winter's photo of the façade doesn't quite do it justice; in summer this is a wonderful place to sit out and people-watch. In days gone by, the tea rooms were a place to be seen during the season. The whole hotel retains a distinctive turn-of-the-century feel; it can no longer be described as luxurious, with its darkening 40's tables and chairs and occasionally creaking floorboards, but the rooms are high-ceilinged, clean and fun. It's the sort of place where you sense the staff have been around for ever. We enjoyed our breakfast and lunch in the light, parquet-floored dining room — palms and Art Deco-type windows brought Graham Greene's novels to mind. If you want to stay right at the heart of things, the Central is a good bet. Try and book the suite; it costs the same.

Rooms: 10 with bath & wc + 1 suite.
Price: D/Tw 11000-16000 Esc; Ste 11000-16000 Esc.
Breakfast: Included.
Meals: Lunch/Dinner 3800 Esc (C).
Closed: Never.

How to get there: From Lisbon to Sintra on motorway/N249. There to centre and hotel is on main square by Palácio Nacional.

Pensão Residencial Sintra

Quinta Visconde de Tojal
Travessa dos Avelares 12
2710
Sintra (S.Pedro)

Tel: (0)1 9230738
Fax: (0)1 9230738

Management: Susana Rosner Fragosa

Although it is rather 'basic' we loved the air of faded grandeur enveloping this family-run guest house. It was built on a thickly-wooded hillside as a Viscount's summer residence in the days when fashionable Sintra was hill station to local and international gentry — and became a guest house just after the war. An original bannistered staircase winds up to the first- and second-floor bedrooms. These are enormous with high ceilings, wooden floors and endearingly dated furniture and fittings; it all has a distinctly timeless feel about it. (What matter the odd bit of peeling paint in bathrooms?) Ask for one of the two rooms with mountain views. Downstairs is an enormous dining room-cum-bar where snacks are normally available. But we'd all prefer to sit out on the terrace (with tea and cakes in the afternoon) with its beguiling views up to the fairy-tale Moorish Castle. And the garden is a delight: dripping with greenery, and with some old, old trees, a swimming pool and a small play area for children. Multilingual Susanna is a young, kindly and caring hostess. The village centre with its numerous restaurants is a short stroll away or, for the more energetic, paths lead steeply up for some fine walks.

Rooms: 9 with bath & wc.
Price: S 6500-11500 Esc; D 8000-12500 Esc; Tw 7000-11500 Esc .
Breakfast: Included.
Meals: Snacks only — available all day.
Closed: Never.

How to get there: As you arrive in Sintra follow signs for 'S. Pedro'. Hotel is to one side of road, signposted on left as you leave Sintra.

240

Map No: 16

Quinta das Sequoias (Casa da Tapada)

Estrada de Monserrate
2710
Sintra

Tel: (0)1 9243821
Fax: (0)1 9230342

Management: Maria Candida Gonzalez

There are few homes as lovely as this, few settings quite as majestic. High above Sintra with 40 hectares of private grounds to explore, this most beguiling of homes takes its name from the huge stand of redwoods that surrounds the house. The view is to-die-for; up to the Pena Palace, out to the forested mountainside and down to the distant coastline. The main building (standing atop enormous granite rocks) has a colonial air with its arches, eaves and balconies. Maria Candida's family rescued it from abandon and restored six first-floor guestrooms: beautiful old beds and dressers, hand-embroidered sheets and polished wooden floors and ceilings. One is a mezzanine with its own small lounge, two are tower rooms with windows on both sides. Public rooms are richly decorated with the family china, oils and pieces from the East; there are Indian figurines and salt boxes from Goa. The views from the lounge and high-ceilinged breakfast room lift them into another dimension; visit when the moon is full for a real spectacle. A terraced garden dripping with camellia leads down to the spring-fed pool and, just beneath, the sauna. Maria Candida is as gracious as her home.

Rooms: 6 with bath & wc.
Price: D/Tw 16000-22000 Esc.
Breakfast: Included.
Meals: Dinner 2800 Esc (M).
Closed: 24-25 Dec.

How to get there: From Sintra take Monserrate road. 1km after Hotel Setais turn left at sign to 'Quinta das Sequoias'. Continue 2km to house.

Casa da Pérgola

Avenida Valbom 13
2750
Cascais

Tel: (0)1 4840040
Fax: (0)1 4834791

Management: Patricia Gonçalves

Cascais remains a fishing village, although holidaymakers and a growing number of Lisbon commuters have added a veneer of sophistication. Duck into the narrow, cobbled sidestreets to find old Cascais. Casa da Pérgola remembers the days before the changes; the optimism of the belle époque is reflected in this grand villa's colourful façade with its red window surrounds, its purple tiles and a cloak of white, orange and mauve bougainvillea. Not a building that you'd miss as you wander by. Once inside, things take on a rather more subdued note: pastel colours, marble and antiques. In the upstairs sitting-room there are old paintings, pillars, elegant occasional tables and a grandfather clock whose gentle tock-tocking (paradoxically) makes it feel slightly beyond time; there is a faint whiff of a British sea-side hotel. Bedrooms are all named after flowers, apart from one known as 'angels'. Those at the front are larger; some have balconies, some period beds, nearly all have fancy stucco cornicing and all a comfy chair. Throughout there are old prints (some of the Saints) and the overall feel is more home than hotel. Particularly good value in the low season.

Rooms: 11 with bath & wc.
Price: D/Tw11500-15500 Esc; D/Tw with balcony 13500-17500 Esc.
Breakfast: Included.
Meals: None.
Closed: Mid Nov-end Mar.

How to get there: From Lisbon A5 towards Cascais/Estoril. Exit for Abuxarda. Go to bottom of hill, turn right then straight over at roundabout. Pérgola in first street to left.

Map No: 16

As Janelas Verdes
Rua das Janelas Verdes 47
1200
Lisboa

Tel: (0)1 3968143
Fax: (0)1 3968144

Management: Manuel Duarte
Fernandes

Tucked away in the old city just yards from the Museum of Ancient Art, this old aristocratic town house (the writer Eça de Queirós lived here) is one of our most special places in Portugal. From the moment you are greeted by the ever-smiling Palmira you feel like an honoured guest at As Janelas. Off to one side of reception is the lounge, graced by marble-topped tables (you breakfast here in winter), a handsome fireplace, piano and comfy chairs. Good weather means you can breakfast out on the patio (or have a candle-lit apéritif); enormous ficus and bougainvillea run riot, a fountain gurgles and wrought-iron tables stand on dragon-tooth cobbling. A grand old spiral staircase leads you up to the rooms. Six of them have views down to the river (book early if you want one); they are furnished with repro beds, flounced curtains and delicate pastel colours. Dressing gowns, towels, even the bag for the spare loo roll, are embroidered with the JV logo. And instead of a 'do not disturb' sign you're provided with a hand-embroidered little pillow that says 'shhh!'. A delectable small hotel.

Rooms: 17 with bath & wc.
Price: D/Tw 'Standard' 18500-26000 Esc; D/Tw 'Superior' 21500-29800 Esc; Tr 'Standard' 23400-33700 Esc; Tr 'Superior' 26500-38000 Esc. (S use: deduct approx. 10% from Tw). Children under 12 free if sharing parent's room.
Breakfast: Included.
Meals: None.
Closed: Never.

How to get there: E90 motorway across River Tejo then exit for Alcantara. Straight on at roundabout. Follow tram route for approx. 500m. Hotel close to Museo de Arte Antiga on right.

Map No: 16

243

Hotel Britânia

Rua Rodrigues Sampaio 17
1100
Lisboa

Tel: (0)1 3155016
Fax: (0)1 3155021

Management: Manuel Duarte Fernandes

This gem of a hotel, just a step back from Av. da Liberdade, was designed by Cassiano Branco — it is a true museum-piece of '40s architecture and now ranks among Lisbon's listed buildings. The fun begins in the reception area which is flanked by twin ranks of marble columns; port-hole-windowed doors lead through to the bar, just the place for a gin sling. During recent renovation, paint was stripped away here to reveal what appears to be a sea-monster from Camoes' 'Lusiades' (or there again, it may be Neptune); and there's more to be discovered. A stunning wood and chrome staircase leads up to the bedrooms (there's a lift too); these are generous, with their own private entrance halls; beds, stools, chairs and writing tables are all 'period', even if the fabrics look more modern and rather in the Laura Ashley vein. Bathrooms are also original, with huge sinks, tubs and marble walls. There's all the gadgetry that you'd expect of a 3-star hotel (you may manage to bath without recourse to your tub-side phone). And if beds are period, mattresses are new. Only breakfast is served at the Britânia; it's an enormous buffet and would probably keep you going all day.

Rooms: 30 with bath & wc.
Price: D/Tw 'Standard' 16500-20250 Esc; D/Tw 'Superior' 19800-23500 Esc; Tr 'Standard' 20800-25400 Esc; Tr 'Superior' 25000-30500 Esc. (S use deduct approx. 10% from D/Tw). Children under 12 free if sharing parent's room.
Breakfast: Included.
Meals: None.
Closed: Never.

How to get there: Follow signs to centre and Pr. Marquês de Pombal then towards Praça dos Restauradores. Left just before Metro 'Avenida'. Rodrigues Sampaio is 2 streets east of Av. de Liberdade.

Map No: 16

Pensão Ninho das Aguias

Costa do Castelo 74
1100
Lisboa

Tel: (0)1 8867008 /9

Management: Filomena Miranda

The name ('eagle's nest) couldn't be more fitting; from the Pensão's perch on a steep hillside beside the Castelo de S.Jorge you look out across the Baixa district to the Bairro Alto beyond. There can be few better places to watch the sunset in this wonderful city or to see in the dawn. The adventure begins at the street entrance; pass through and a creaking spiral staircase leads you up to emerge onto the main terrace of the pensão. In the small reception area a stuffed eagle hovers precariously above a door, utterly in keeping with the quirky eccentricity of the place. The best rooms, of course, are those with the views out front; the furnishing is a mish-mash of old and new, the colour schemes in places 'surprising', but rooms are clean and mostly big and airy. Within the house climb another spiral staircase and you emerge into a tiny tower room — you'll forgive the shabby furnishings for the octagonal feast for the eyes. Although no meals are on offer there is a cheerful little café just next door, and Alfama is within easy walking distance. If you're travelling by car it is best to cage the beast in city-centre parking and let a taxi negotiate the tortuous streets up to the pension.

Rooms: 6 with own bath & wc; 10 sharing.
Price: D/Tw 6000-7000 Esc; D/Tw sharing 5000 Esc.
Breakfast: None; café next door.
Meals: None.
Closed: Never.

How to get there: Into centre of Lisbon to Praça do Comércio. Here take Rua da Alfândega. 2nd left onto Rua da Madalena, then 3rd right up to Alfama. Here take Rua da São Tome, then left onto Rua da Costa do Castelo. Pensão next to Castelo.

Residencial Florescente

Rua Portas de Santo Antão 99
1150
Lisboa

Tel: (0)1 3463517/3426609
Fax: (0)1 3427733

Management: Jacinta Antunes

Another of the bright and cheerful family-run pensions that we are happy to include alongside some rather grander neighbours. Over many years, Florescente has built up a reputation as a friendly, clean and fun stop-over right at the heart of Pombaline Lisbon. You are brilliantly central, yet spared the rumble of traffic; Santo Antão is a pedestrianised thoroughfare and a great place to sit out in a café or restaurant and watch the world go by. You dip in off the street into the small tiled reception area; a small fountain gurgles in the corner and the young staff are immediately attentive. The original bannistered and tiled staircase, more than a century old, leads up and up ... and up. Narrowish corridors lead along to the bedrooms which are mostly small to medium in size and simply decorated with a very southern choice of print on the walls. There are high-ceilings with stucco mouldings — a reminder of a more illustrious past. We loved the rather smaller attic rooms with their stand-up balconies, well worth the haul up to the fifth and top floor. No meals are on offer, but just step outside and choose your café, restaurant or fruit shop. Ask for an air-conditioned room in the summer.

Rooms: 52 with bath & wc; 20 sharing.
Price: S 6000 Esc; D/Tw 6000-7000Esc; D/Tw sharing 5000-6000 Esc.
Breakfast: None available.
Meals: None.
Closed: Never.

How to get there: Arriving in Lisbon, follow signs into centre; down Avenida da Liberdade and park near Rossio in Restauradores car park. Residencial Florescente in pedestrian street parallel to Liberdade, approx 100m to north of Rossio.

Map No: 16

Quinta de Santo Amaro

Aldeia da Piedade
2925
Azeitão

Tel: (0)1 2189230
Fax: (0)1 2189390

Management: Maria da Pureza de Mello

Looking out to the Arrábida mountains this genteel residence was where the de Mello family would pass the summer months; first would come the harvesting of the grapes and then the wine-making. Maria's feelings for this heavenly place ran deep; she decided to make it her first home and to bring new life to it all by opening her doors to paying guests. The bedrooms and apartments are the stuff our B&B dreams are made of. There are planked floors and ceilings, wrought-iron bedsteads, oil paintings and hearths; there are window seats and old tiles, period bathrooms and pianos. No room or apartment is alike; when you arrive in winter it is to a log fire and, throughout the year, to a bottle of wine. One of the apartments would be a wonderful base for several nights; Lisbon is an easy drive, as are the beaches of the Setúbal peninsula. But what makes it all so very special is Maria herself, a lady with boundless enthusiasm and energy; meet with her at breakfast (a feast of home-made breads, jams, cheeses, ham and freshly squeezed orange juice from Amaro's groves) and heed her advice on where to eat and what to visit. Grand Cru Portugal … unforgettable.

Rooms: 2 with bath & wc + 2 apartments.
Price: D/Tw/Apt (for two) 13000 Esc.
Apt (sleeps 6) 195000 Esc weekly.
Breakfast: Included.
Meals: None.
Closed: Never.

How to get there: From Lisbon, motorway towards Setúbal; exit for Vila Nova de Azeitão. Here towards Sesimbra and, after 3.5km, pass garish blue and white gate on left; take next turn on left, 'Estrada dos Arcos', and S. Amaro at end.

Map No: 16

247

Quinta do Casal do Bispo

Estrada dos Romanos 13
Aldeia da Piedade
2925
Azeitão

Tel: (0)1 2191812/2180042

Management: Pedro M. de Macedo Santos Bastos

Within easy driving distance of Lisbon, close to good beaches yet in an utterly bucolic setting, Casal do Bispo is perfect for a longer stay. The house stands in 60 hectares of National park — you wind up through the estate via a long snaking drive and there among the trees is the beguiling tile-clad façade of the main house; the corner-tiles' upward tilt gives it a rather oriental air. Within, the lounge is an enormous room with French windows to three sides. There are rugs, deep sofas, corner lamps, a handsome wood ceiling; this is a house that has reached its middle years in fine condition. The breakfast room is rather smaller, uncannily quiet; even the grandfather clock is hushed. Iñes is young and most sympathetic and it is good to talk with her at breakfast; a cut above most, it includes cold meats, cheeses, eggs and cereals as well as the usual 'continental' stuff. The most handsome of the guest rooms is on the ground floor; it has its own hearth, beautiful old floor tiles and antique furniture. The upstairs rooms, some with sloping attic roofs, are smaller and more simply furnished. Find time to do a walk or two from the house, perhaps back down to the chapel for a picnic.

Rooms: 6 with bath & wc.
Price: D/Tw 12000-14000 Esc.
Breakfast: Included.
Meals: None.
Closed: Never.

How to get there: From Setúbal take N10 to Vila Nogueira de Azeitão. Here take N379 towards Sesimbra for 2.2km, then left onto Estrada dos Romanos. Left at chapel and follow track to house.

248

Quinta da Alcaidaria — Mór

2490
Ourém

Tel: (0)49 42231
Fax: (0)49 42231

Management: Maria Teresa Vasconcelos Alvaiazere

This lovely wisteria-clad manor has been the family seat for more than 300 years and is every inch the grand country house: stately cedar-lined main drive, box-hedged gardens and its own private chapel. The main house is a cool, gracious building; light streams in to the high-ceilinged rooms while marble floors, arches and delicate plasterwork remind you that you are in the south. Don't miss the chance to dine (remarkably inexpensively) around the enormous 'pau santo' dining table. The chandeliers and the collection of old china may inspire you to dress for dinner. Guest apartments are in a converted outbuilding; doubles are in the main house and most pukka they are too. There are old dressers, Dona Maria beds, comfortable chairs, perhaps a grand old tub with feet; all rooms have beautiful moulded pine ceilings and big bathrooms ... generously tiled and marbled. Each room is different from the next; all are first-class. Add to this the natural kindness of your English-speaking hosts (they often invite guests to join them for a glass of port) and you begin to get the measure of this altogether charming guest house.

Rooms: 6 with bath & wc + 1 suite.
Price: D/Tw 16000-19000; Ste 16000-19000 Esc.
Breakfast: Included.
Meals: Light snacks and occasionally dinner with family — 2500 Esc (M).
Closed: Never.

How to get there: From Ourém take Tomar road. After just 2km at fork turn left towards Seica and then IMMEDIATELY turn left into cedar-lined avenue leading to house.

Casa da Avó Genoveva

Rua 25 de Abril 16
Curvaceiras
2300
Tomar

Tel: (0)49 92219
Fax: (0)49 92219

Management: José and Manuela Gomes da Costa

This is close to beautiful Tomar, but what first impresses you on arrival at Avó Genoveva is the QUIET of the place. And the huge old palm trees and pots of geraniums gracing the dragon-tooth courtyard, the soft-salmon and white of the buildings give it a truly southern charm. Inside, public rooms are plush but homely; in the lounge there are family photos, woodburner, piano and card table while in the dining room there are antique dressers, a terrracotta floor and a collection of old crockery. You're spoiled for choice when it comes to the public rooms: in the music room feel free to put on a record (classical and 'fado' in abundance), the snooker room doubles up as a library and there is a small bar, well-stocked with Portuguese wines. And what bedrooms! Dark pine ceilings, family antiques, old paintings; doubles are up an old stone staircase in the main house, while the apartments are across the way in the old granary. A respectable distance from the house are tennis court, swings and pool — and there are bikes, too. Your hosts are kindly, educated people who delight in sharing their wonderful home.

Rooms: 3 with bath & wc + 2 apartments.
Price: D 11000 Esc; 1 bed Apt 13500; 2 bed Apt 18000 Esc.
Breakfast: Included.
Meals: None.
Closed: Never.

How to get there: From Tomar take road towards Lisbon. After approx. 9km in Guerreira turn right to Curvaceiras. After 4km house signposted on left.

250

Map No: 16

Pensão Residencial União

Rua Serpa Pinto 94
2300
Tomar

Tel: (0)49 323161
Fax: (0)49 321299

Management: Joaquim Farinha Rodrigues

Plumb on the main artery through the old town this family-run pension has a long track record; it was the town's very first hotel and just last year celebrated its 100th birthday. The gala dinners (see the scrap book in reception) may no longer take place but the União remains the right choice in Tomar. A pretty tiled entrance beckons you in and up to the first floor reception and bar. Rooms are reached along corridors that twist and turn; easy to see why it took the painters six months to get round when last redecorating. The dining room is where you are most in touch with the past of the building; tables and chairs are distinctly forties whilst the door mouldings have an Art Deco air. High windows give onto the inner patio, a quiet spot to sit out when its warm enough. União's room are very simple: forgive the rather kitsch prints and random mix of styles for they are roomy with high ceilings, have very comfy beds and there is plenty of hot water. 102 and 103 were the nicest that we saw, with their old Italian lamps. No meals are on offer so head out into the backstreets of this lovely old town where there are restaurants galore. Book ahead in summer.

Rooms: 28 with bath & wc.
Price: S 4500 Esc; D/Tw 6000-6500 Esc; Tr 7500 Esc.
Breakfast: Included.
Meals: None.
Closed:

How to get there: On right hand side of main street of 'centro histórico'.

Quinta da Cortiçada

Outeiro da Cortiçada
2040
Rio Maior

Tel: (0)43 478182
Fax: (0)43 478772

Management: Teresa Nobre

Few settings are as utterly peaceful as that of Quinta da Cortiçada; this soft-salmon building, reached by a long poplar-lined avenue, nestles in the greenest of valleys. As we arrived a heron rose from the lake and flapped slowly away, a sweet welcome — as was the gentle smile of the housekeeper who was waiting at the main entrance. Inside the building the silence feels almost monastic — birdsong instead of vespers. You have the choice of two lounges; one has a games table, high French windows on two sides and is dignified by the family 'oratorio' (altarpiece). The other leads out to a covered verandah with wicker tables and chairs. Where Cortiçada feels most homely is in the dining room where you rub shoulders with your fellow guests round the lovely old oval dining table should you dine in. Along the marble-paved corridor the rooms have old Dona Maria beds, antique dressers, thick rugs on the pine floors — and all of it wonderfully clean. Bathrooms are 4-star plush, while sensitive lighting and carefully chosen fabrics help to make it all extra-special. And, like that heron, you're welcome to fish in the lake.

Rooms: 6 with bath & wc + 2 suites.
Price: D/Tw 15000-16000 Esc; Ste 18000-19000 Esc.
Breakfast: Included.
Meals: On request. Lunch/Dinner 3800 Esc (M).
Closed: Christmas Day.

How to get there: From Rio Maior follow signs towards Outeiro/Correias. Through Arruda dos Pisões and on to Outeiro; Quinta on left.

Map No: 16

Quinta da Ferraria

Ribeira de S. João
2040
Rio Maior

Tel: (0)43 95001
Fax: (0)43 95696

Management: Teresa Nobre

Quinta da Ferraria stands amid vineyards and olive groves; a channel cut from the nearby river powered the mill and a ran a turbine powerful enough to light up the whole farm long before electricity arrived in Rio Maior. Recently the farm was totally renovated to create a handsome, small country hotel; although this has been set up for both business and pleasure, the exceptionally green and peaceful setting and the abundance of WATER make it special enough to please both types of guest. Guestrooms have pine floors and ceilings, soft Alcobaça fabrics and head-to-toe tiling in bathrooms. Pine is also the main feature of the sitting-room; sisal matting, rugs and an open hearth add warmth to a very large space. The dining room, by contrast, felt rather soulless due to its wedding-banquet dimensions. But this is a good stop-over, especially for a family; there are riding stables, plenty of sheep and a farm museum. Next to the dining room you can still see the original olive-milling machinery. And, as the brochure points out, here are 'blue-distanced horizons and clear, sparkling air to invigorate, stimulate and enhance life and living'.

Rooms: 12 with bath & wc, 1 suite + 2 apartments.
Price: S 10000-11700 Esc; D/Tw 11800-14000 Esc; Ste 13600-15700 Esc, inc. breakfast. Apt 16400-18700 Esc excl. breakfast.
Breakfast: 850 Esc if not included.
Meals: On request. Lunch/Dinner 3800 Esc (M).
Closed: Christmas Day.

How to get there: From Rio Maior N114 towards Santarem. The Quinta is signposted on right 8km from Rio Maior.

253

"To enter Portugal from Spain is to come from a baked, dusty, tattered, plain into a well-kept garden, 'like flying from the Middle Ages into the Present' wrote Hans Christian Andersen. 'All around I saw whitewashed, friendly houses, hedged woods, cultivated fields...'"

Alentejo

Herdade da Sanguinheira

Longomel
7400
Ponte de Sôr

Tel: (0)931 269401
Fax: (0)42 26697

Management: Anette and Nuno Vaz Pinto

Hidden away in the lovely northern Alentejo, among stands of cork oak, mimosa, eucalyptus and pine, this lovely old 'monte' (Alentejan farmstead) couldn't fail to cheer the most world-weary. Four kilometres of (smooth) dirt track separate the farm from tarmac and traffic; you round a final bend and are greeted by a long, low building with the distinctive chimney stacks of the region, ochre edgings to doors and windows — and a front garden brimming with oleander, wisteria, palm and bougainvillea. Guests sleep in their own houses; three of them sleep four, one of them six; all have their own kitchens and sitting rooms with open hearths. Furnishing is 'smart rustic' — so too is the dining room where meals are served, if you prefer to let someone else do the cooking. There's lots to do at the 'monte': at the equestrian centre lessons and treks (up to a week!) on Lusitanian thoroughbreds, mountain bikes and even a ski-boat for hire. And any number of lovely walks out into the forest. Add to this a games room, reading room and play room — and Sanguinheira becomes a wonderful place for a full and active family holiday, or just for writing those memoirs …

Rooms: 3 houses with 2 twins + 1 house with 3 twins.
Price: House (for 4) 22000 Esc; house (for 6) 33000 Esc. Minimium stay 2 nights.
Breakfast: Included (self-service).
Meals: Self-catering or Lunch/Dinner 3000 Esc (M). Children under 12 2000 Esc (M).
Closed: Never.

How to get there: From Ponte do Sôr take road towards Gavião. After approx 6km, pass by sign to Longomel. Pass sign at entrance to village of Escusa. 50 yards on, left onto track (past maguey cacti) and follow for just over 4km to farm.

El Rei Don Miguel

Rua Bartolomeu Alvares da Santa 45
7320
Castelo de Vide

Tel: (0)45 919191/90
Fax: (0)45 91592

Management: Maria Victoria Ribeiro Chamiço Heitor

Castelo de Vide is one of the Alentejo's most memorable hilltop villages; within the town walls built by Dom Afonso in the thirteenth century, the old Jewish quarter (you can visit the synagogue) climbs anarchically up towards the castle. Just to one side of the lower town's main square, this fine old town house has just recently become a most special little B&B. A granite staircase leads up to the first floor and the living quarters. Perhaps the house's most salient feature is its polished wooden flooring in guest and public rooms. The many antiques in lounge and corridors are eloquent evidence of Dona Maria's passion for period furniture. We particularly liked the quiet drawing room with its many old pieces and open hearth (there is always a fire in the colder months). Bedrooms are rather more modern; all of their wooden beds, writing and bedside tables are brand new — as are curtains and bedspreads in matching (local) fabric. Special wall insulation and double glazing guarantee a warm, peaceful night and the whole of the house is as clean as can be. Marvellous value at any time of the year.

Rooms: 7 with bath & wc.
Price: Tw 7000-10000 Esc.
Breakfast: Included.
Meals: None.
Closed: Never.

How to get there: From Portalege towards Marvão on E802, then left on 246 to Castelo de Vide. At main square of town, turn left onto main street; hotel on left.

Map No: 17

Casa do Parque

Avenida da Aramenha 37
7320
Castelo de Vide

Tel: (0)45 91250
Fax: (0)45 91228

Management: Victor Manuel Pereira Guimarães

In a beautiful backwater of the Alentejo, surrounded by stands of chestnut and acacia, the hilltop village of Castelo de Vide is girt around with its 13th-century town wall. Steep cobblestone alleys run up the hill through the old Jewish 'call' to the Castle; make sure to visit the spring whose waters are said to cure everything from diabetes to dermatitis. The nerve centre of the lower town is the leafy Praça Dom Pedro V and tucked away at one end of it you'll find the gaily canopied Casa do Parque. The family are proud of the 'hospitalidade portuguesa' to which guests are treated; the feeling of homeliness spills over into the prettily-furnished guest rooms. They are surprisingly well 'appointed' (even though bathrooms are smallish) considering the price, and are spotlessly clean; they have attractive wooden furniture and the mattresses lead you gently into the arms of Morpheus. In the colder months, hot-air heating warms the room in minutes. And full marks to the Casa do Parque for its home-cooking. Don't miss dinner and a chance to try the 'migas alentejanas', or one of the roast dishes; the dining room is a large, functional affair where you'll probably be the only foreigner among many local enthusiasts.

Rooms: 26 with bath & wc.
Price: S 4000; D/Tw 6500 Esc.
Breakfast: Included.
Meals: Lunch/Dinner 1950 Esc (M), approx 4500 Esc (C).
Closed: Never.

How to get there: From Portalege towards Marvão on E802, then left on 246 to Castelo de Vide. Here into centre then right along the top of the park; hotel at end on left.

Quinta das Varandas

Serra de São Mamede
7300
Portalegre

Tel: (0)45 28883

Management: João Malato Correia

A number of grand old mansions and exuberantly decorated churches bear witness to the time when Portalegre grew rich from its silk-weaving and woollen industries. Just a short drive from the town, Quinta das Varandas is a romantic stop-over, tucked away on a wooded hillside of the Serra de São Mamede national park. The abundant bird-life of the park means that nightingales will sing you to sleep in the warmer months, while breakfast is, in the owners' words, 'a real symphony'. The Quinta's rooms are light and uncluttered, decked with antiques and with beautifully moulded ceilings; we were particularly taken by the room in what was once the kitchen, with views out across the surrounding forest. Bathrooms use local stone to fine effect. The public areas have the same ample, light feel to them as do the bedrooms; the lounge has wickedly comfortable sofas. But the Italianate garden remains clearest in our memory — a beautiful place for a pre-dinner stroll, with fountains, hedges, and pathways, all lit up at night. Dinner here won't break the bank and the wine list is impressive.

Rooms: 5 with bath & wc + 1 suite.
Price: D/Tw 10000 Esc; Ste 15000 Esc.
Breakfast: Included.
Meals: On request. Lunch/Dinner 2500-3500 Esc.
Closed: Never.

How to get there: From Lisbon take A6 to Estremoz and from there follow signs to Portalegre. Follow signs for centre of Portalegre then right at signs for 'Serra'. Continue 5.5km and Quinta is on left.

Map No: 17

257

Monte dos Pensamentos

Estrada da Estação do Ameixial   **Tel:** (0)68 333166
7100   **Fax:** (0)68 332409
Estremoz

Management: Cristóvão Bach Andresen Leitão

The young owners of Monte dos Pensamentos, Cristovão and Teresa, are giving new life to this country house that looks up to the old town walls of Estremoz. The house has been owned by Cristovão's family for nearly 200 years and successive generations have added and embellished. The towers and arches added by one forebear give it a distinctly oriental air. The style inside is more traditional: vaulted ceilings, a mix of terracotta and parquet floors, loads of family antiques and a huge collection of old hand-painted plates that spills out along the corridor. We liked the bedrooms. They are decorated with old dressers and beds, some have screens, some original fireplaces; parquet floors add cosiness as do comfy chairs, books, magazines and dried flowers. The owners, relaxed and utterly charming, have a young family but still find time to offer guests lunch or dinner — just discuss the sort of food you'd like with Teresa the morning before. Riding can be arranged with an English neighbour and nearby Estremoz is not to be missed.

Rooms: 4 with bath & wc.
Price: D/Tw 11000 Esc.
Breakfast: Included.
Meals: Lunch/Dinner 2500 Esc (M).
Closed: Never

How to get there: From Estremoz take Lisbon road. After 2km at sign for 'turismo rural' turn right and house is 200m along on right.

Herdade da Barbosa

E.M. 504, Estremoz-Sotileira
S. Bento do Cortiço
7100
Estremoz

Tel: (0)68 24510
Fax: (0)68 3336375

Management: Maria Rita Reynolds de Souza

A short drive from the old walled market town of Estremoz, this classic old Alentejo farmstead is an isolated and peaceful place, however troubled its recent history. Collectivised after the Revolution, it was then abandoned until Rita's family managed to buy it back and restore it. Inside there are intriguing triple niches in two of the rooms, now graced by the naïve Estremoz figurines that Rita collects. She also collects HATS — there are more than 150, many in the unusual circular entrance hall. In sitting and dining rooms there are splendid vaulted ceilings — Alentejo builders are masters of the art of wafer-bricking — and these are nicely counterbalanced by handsome, grey schist floors. Bedrooms are mostly traditionally furnished; some have wrought-iron bedsteads, others the bright hand-painted Alentejo beds; nearly all have views. Best of all is the utter TRANQUILLITY of Barbosa; you hear nightingales and owls at night, and during the daytime little but distant sheep bells. The farm has its own reservoir where you can fish or, in season, watch the passage of the wild geese and water fowl.

Rooms: 4 with bath & wc + 2 apartments.
Price: S 7500 Esc; D/Tw 9500 Esc; Ste 9500 Esc; 1 bed Apt 12500 Esc; 2 bed Apt 18000 Esc.
Breakfast: Included.
Meals: None.
Closed: Never.

How to get there: From Estremoz towards Portalegre. At outskirts of Estremoz left at sign 'Agroturismo 6km'. Follow signs to Herdade da Barbosa.

Casa da Borba

Rua da Cruz 5
7150
Borba

Tel: (0)68 94528/
(0)1 8483161
Fax: (0)68 841448

Management: Maria José Tavares Lobo de Vasconcelos.

This gem of a house was built by Maria Jose's forebears at the end of the 17th century; the surrounding estate is given over to olives, vineyards and livestock. The house earns a mention in the 'inventario artistico de Portugal'; once you pass through the main entrance, an extraordinary neo-classical staircase leads you up to the first-floor living quarters. And what bedrooms await you here! They have high, delicately moulded ceilings and parquet floors softened by Arraiolos rugs and are crammed with the family antiques. The 'Bishop's room' (where the Archbishop of Évora stayed) has an 18th-century canopied bed; 'Grandmother's room' has an unusual lift-up sink; there are baths with feet, old prints, and long curtains in front of the windows looking over a delectable garden. The sitting room and breakfast room are similarly elegant; breakfast arrives via the 'dumb waiter'. Your hosts are quiet, refined folk and they skimp on nothing to help you; at night, hot water is delivered to your room together with cake and a selection of teas. During the day choose between the long covered gallery, a corner of the garden, or the billiards room.

Rooms: 5 with bath & wc.
Price: D/Tw 14000 Esc.
Breakfast: Included.
Meals: Lunch/Dinner 3500-4000 Esc (M).
Closed: Never.

How to get there: From Estremoz N4 to Borba. Casa da Borba in town centre close to Correios.

Map No: 17

Casa de Peixinhos

7160
Vila Viçosa

Tel: (0)68 98472/98859
Fax: (0)68 881348

Management: José Dionísio Melo e Faro Passanha

Casa de Peixinhos is, like vintage port, a rich, mellow experience, the fruit of time and patience. Once you pass under the main portal and into the cobbled courtyard, the main façade has a distinctly exotic feel; its arches and triple turrets are softened by whitewashed walls with broad bands of ochre. Inside the main building the mood is more classical; this is a superbly maintained aristocratic house and, though much of the décor and furnishing is 'period', everything sparkles freshly. The sitting room is a handsome introduction to the house, with mouldings, a leather three-piece and the family coat of arms above the hearth. Leading off it is the dining room; here the mouldings are enhanced with gold drapes, chandeliers and beautifully arranged flowers. This is the sort of place where you might dress for the traditional Alentejo cuisine on offer. Rooms are among the loveliest we have come across in Portugal, some decorated predominantly in blues, others in sang de boeuf, each one different. One has Dona Maria beds, another canopied twins; all of them have gorgeous bathrooms with locally quarried marble. The whole house is most regal.

Rooms: 7 with bath & wc + 1 suite.
Price: S 13500 Esc; D/Tw 16000 Esc; Ste 21000 Esc.
Breakfast: Included.
Meals: On request. Lunch/Dinner 3000 Esc.
Closed: Never.

How to get there: From Évora to Vila Viçosa. Here follow signs towards Borba into Vila V. town centre. Just past Mercado Municipal, turn right and follow signs.

Hotel Convento de São Paulo

Aldeia da Serra
7170
Redondo

Tel: (0)66 999100
Fax: (0)66 999104

Management: José Almeida

Superlatives do the setting no justice, so go and see. Monks of the Paulist Order came here at the end of the 14th century and for 500 years (until Pombal embarked on Disestablishment) embellished and beautified their place of work and worship. A mantle of quiet wraps the building; as you pass through the enormous old door your voice instinctively drops. Visit if only to see the hand-painted tiles that decorate chapel, corridors and gardens; the largest collection in Europe. A red carpet softens the roller-coaster terracotta floor and sweeps you along to the rooms. Each one occupies two of the former cells, their uncluttered feel entirely in keeping with São Paulo's past. But there are some lovely 'pieces', many of them heirlooms of the Leotte family (owners for the last 150 years). In bathrooms there are brass taps and white marble while public rooms, too, live up to expectations. The dining room feels cosy, the sitting room has gracefully vaulted ceilings and well-dressed sofas; eclectic modern art lends a more frivolous note. Outside is a beautiful tiled patio depicting the four seasons and there are any number of walks out through the thickly wooded slopes of this 600 hectare estate. The spirit soars.

Rooms: 17 with bath & wc.
Price: D/Tw 18000-30750 Esc; S use 13750-26500 Esc; Extra bed 6500 Esc.
Breakfast: Included.
Meals: Lunch/Dinner approx. 4500 Esc.
Closed: Never.

How to get there: From Évora to Redondo. There, as you leave town on Vila Viçosa road, turn left past Intermarché supermarket then follow signs to Aldeia da Serra. Monastery 2km beyond village.

Map No: 17

Quinta da Espada

Apartado 68
Estrada de Arraiolos Km 4
7001
Évora

Tel: (0)66 734549/93130
Fax: (0)66 735264

Management: Isabel de Mello Cabral

Quinta da Espada ('of the sword'; the one hidden here by no less a man than Geraldo Geraldes, he who snatched Évora back from the Moors), surrounded by groves of olives and cork oaks and with views down to Évora, is a low, whitewashed, mimosa-graced building with ochre window surrounds and a perfectly authentic atmosphere. Guest rooms vary in size and colour scheme, with hand-painted Alentejo furniture everywhere; terracotta tiles, estera matting and dark beams creating further rustic warmth. Little touches, like towels with a hand-embroidered 'Quinta da Espada' motif, add a touch of gentility to it all. Slate, used in place of tiles, makes the bathrooms memorable. The Green room occupies what was once the (small) family chapel. We particularly liked the smaller salon where you breakfast and dine in front of the hearth during the colder months. You may well be tempted by the Alentejo cooking on offer, but if not you can make use of a well-equipped guest kitchen. Do stay two nights and walk into Évora along tracks that lead out from the Quinta, or head out to explore the 20 hectare estate.

Rooms: 4 with bath & wc + 1 suite.
Price: S use 9000 Esc; Tw 12000 Esc; Ste 14000 Esc.
Breakfast: Included.
Meals: On request. Lunch/Dinner (M) 4000 Esc.
Closed: Never.

How to get there: From Évora take the road towards Arraiolos and after 4km Quinta is signposted to right.

Casa de Sam Pedro

Quinta de Sam Pedro
7000
Évora

Tel: (0)66 27731
Fax: (0)66 22126

Management: Antonio Pestana de Vasconcelos

Another delectable address, close to wonderful Évora and utterly bucolic. As you turn in off the narrow country road and follow a winding track through old olive groves, a sense of well-being takes hold. The house offers a benevolent greeting; acacias throw shade cross its uncluttered façade and the air is filled with birdsong. Inside, the decoration is gentle, unshowy: a grandfather clock, parquet floors set against old azulejos, gilt mirrors and the family china. The dining room is elegant but cosy and the kitchen as lovely as a kitchen might be; we could imagine snuggling down with a good book on one of the sofas in front of the white-tiled hearth, beneath the collection of old plates and copper saucepans. (We'd also choose to breakfast here — tell your host if you feel the same ...) The peace of the place makes you more aware of those gently creaking floorboards as you climb to your room. Here the decoration is again subdued and utterly 'family'; perhaps a Mater Dolorosa above a bed, a lovely old antique wardrobe, or a fine old dressing table. Wholly authentic — this is the type of rural tourism we admire.

Rooms: 3 with bath & wc.
Price: D 11500 Esc; Tw 11500 Esc.
Breakfast: Included.
Meals: None.
Closed: 15-30 Aug and 15-30 Dec.

How to get there: From Évora take Estremoz road, but immediately left at roundabout towards Igrejinha. Continue, then left at fork towards Sr. dos Aflitos. After approx. 2.5km, entrance on left to Sam Pedro. Keep left on track.

Map No: 17

Quinta da Nora

Estrada dos Canaviais
7000
Évora

Tel: (0)66 32868
Fax: (0)66 33781

Management: Manuel Fialho

Although it is just 30 years old, once inside you might well imagine that Quinta da Nora is much older; many recycled materials were used during its construction, such as the hand-painted tiles that came from a Lisbon palace. On the (winter's) day that we passed the welcome blaze in the hearth made us want to snuggle down and read up on nearby Évora. We were won over by the rooms; they are medium/large and have the gay hand-painted furniture of the Alentejo — from tables to wardrobes, to chairs, to candelabras, to mirrors. Parquet floors and dark roof beams add further cosiness. Breakfast is a sociable affair taken round the huge oak dining table; 'almost a lunch' is how the owners described it. The house is surrounded by seven hectares of vineyards and you should sample a few bottles of this VERY drinkable tinto. The Quinta's young owners are most charming and will happily help you plan your sorties, both gastronomic and cultural. Honest prices, particularly so with the irresistible Évora nearby.

Rooms: 3 with bath & wc; 2 sharing bath & wc.
Price: D 7000-9000 Esc; D/Tw sharing 6500 Esc.
Breakfast: Included.
Meals: None.
Closed: 15 Dec-15 Jan.

How to get there: From Lisbon to Évora. There, around ring road, under aqueduct, and left at roundabout towards Estremoz. After 100m, left towards Igrejinha. After approx. 400m right towards Bairro do Bacelo. Da Nora signposted on right.

Pensão Policarpo

Rua Freiria de Baixo 16
7000
Évora

Tel: (0)66 22424
Fax: (0)66 22424

Management: Michèle
Policarpo

This grand town mansion was built by the Counts of Lousã in the 16th century, only to be lost to the State during the purges of Pombal. It was abandoned, but then rescued some 60 years ago by the Policarpo family. They carefully set about restoration and created the intimate guest house that the city had lacked and still have buckets of enthusiasm for their work. The breakfast room is a delight; it has a high, vaulted ceiling and the three enormous windows capture the morning sunlight. Fado at breakfast takes your meal into another dimension; outside is a terrace where you can eat al fresco on warmer days. There is a cosy sitting-room (in what once was the kitchen) with hand-painted tiles and a part of the old town wall was swallowed up within the house as Évora grew outwards. Bedrooms are reached via the original granite staircase. Some have vaulted ceilings, many have pretty hand-painted Alentejo furniture and a number have antique bits and bobs. Our favourite was 101, with its original tiles and inspirational view. A private car park is a big plus in a town of narrow streets and zealous traffic wardens.

Rooms: 12 with bath or shower & wc; 8 sharing bath & wc.
Price: D/Tw bath & wc 7500-9500 Esc; D/Tw shower & wc 6500-7500 Esc; D/Tw sharing 5500-6500 Esc.
Breakfast: Included.
Meals: None.
Closed: Never.

How to get there: Arriving in Évora from Lisbon, follow ring road round city until you see signs for Policarpo (close to Misericórdia church). Hotel has car park under archway.

Monte da Serralheira

Monte da Serralheira
7000
Évora

Tel: (0)66 741286/743957
Fax: (0)66 741286

Management: George and Lucia van der Feltz

George and Lucia discovered the wide, open space of the Alentejo some twenty years ago and here they are now, farming the land just outside Évora and well integrated into the local community. And they appear just as enthralled by this wonderful land as they were in their pioneering days. The generosity of your hosts is reflected in the dimensions and fitting out of guest apartments that occupy what once were the workers' quarters. They have their own terraces, four of them have wood-burning stoves and all are high-ceilinged. They have all you need for self-catering. This could be the place for a longer (family) stay; leave guide books behind and instead let yourself be guided by Lucia or her recommendations; she is a professional guide and has a number of well-documented 'circuits' out from Serralheira. And if BIRDS are your thing, stay here; George is an expert. You'll listen to the nightingales if you are here of a spring night. This isolated 200-year-old farm-house, with exuberant bougainvillea and wisteria, whitewashed walls offset by blue trimmings and splendidly isolated setting is a most 'special' place.

Rooms: 1, 2 and 3 bed apartments sleeping 2-6 with bath & wc.
Price: Apt (for 2) 7000-8500 Esc; Apt (for 4) 12000-12500 Esc; Apt (for 6) 14000-14500 Esc. Extra bed 1500 Esc.
Breakfast: 750 Esc if not self-catering.
Meals: None.
Closed: Never.

How to get there: From Lisbon to Évora. There, right onto ringroad. First right after Hotel Don Fernando. Pass station and dog-legover railway towards 'parque industrial'. Follow this road to very end to the farm.

Casa de Terena

Rua Direita 45
Terena
7250
Alandroal

Tel: (0)68 45132
Fax: (0)68 45155

Management: Susana Jones Bianchi

Terena is a peaceful hilltop village with tumble-down castle and church bells, and not a bit touristy. It is far enough off the beaten track to ensure that tourists will be a long time in coming. Groups of village ladies were sunning themselves, bent over their lace, the day that we visited and we could see why quiet-mannered Susana was inspired to move here from Lisbon. It was a labour of love to nurse this grand old village house back to life. From the inner dragon-tooth patio a grand marble staircase sweeps you up to the bedrooms. Here the ingredients include old dressers, wrought-iron bedsteads (but new mattresses), Alentejo rugs, terracotta tiles, dried flowers and views out to the reservoir beyond — and all sparkling like the newest pin. Ceiling fans cool things down when the heat sets in while the suite has its own wood-burning stove for the colder months. The downstairs sitting room has wafer-bricked, vaulted ceilings and a collection of old cross-stitch (some by those village ladies?) gracing the walls. The tranquillity and beauty of Terena, and Susana's enthusiasm, make the journey — or slight diversion if you are en route to, or from Spain — worthwhile. Abundant birdlife if ornithology is your thing.

Rooms: 6 with bath & wc + 1suite.
Price: D/Tw 10000 Esc; Ste 15500 Esc.
Breakfast: Included.
Meals: None.
Closed: For 10 days at Christmas.

How to get there: From Évora towards Beja and then left towards Requengos. There, left to Terena. House next to castle in village.

Horta da Moura

Apartado 64
7200
Reguengos de Monsaraz

Tel: (0)66 550100
Fax: (0)66 550108/55241

Management: Ludovina Calado

This is luxury 'à la campagne'. The setting is splendid: a gentle slope among groves of holm oaks and olives with the perfect hill town of Monsaraz rising up to the east a short walk away. Facilities here are far from 'rustic'; there is a bar plus restaurant, tennis court, swimming pool, snooker and even a horse-drawn carriage for forays out from the farm. But in its architecture the building stays faithful to local tradition: stone floors, wafer-brick vaulted ceilings and the whitewash off-set by broad bands of blue and ochre wash. The rooms we saw have details like fruit bowls and embroidered towels and were huge; they have their own hearths, sofas, big beds, barrel-vaulted ceilings and several have views out over the estate. Bathrooms, too, are 4-star-plush and the air-conditioning/hot-air heating is a big plus in this land of extreme winter and summer temperatures. The cosy dining room offers traditional Alentejo pork dishes, game when in season and an honestly priced wine list (though the Alentejo reserves might tempt you to excess). More 'hotelly' than some places in this book, but it has a big heart.

Rooms: 19 with bath & wc, 6 suites + 2 apartments.
Price: Standard D/Tw 13000-14000 Esc; 'Superior' D/Tw 15000-16500 Esc; Ste 20000-22000 Esc; Apt (for 4) 28000-30000 Esc; Apt (for 6) 42000-46000 Esc.
Breakfast: Included.
Meals: Lunch/Dinner 3000 Esc (M).
Closed: Never.

How to get there: From Évora towards Beja then left towards Reguengos. Here left towards Monsaraz and shortly before village hotel is well signposted.

Casa Dom Nuno

Rua do Castelo 6
Monsaraz
7200
Reguengos de Monsaraz

Tel: (0)66 55146
Fax: (0)66 55400

Management: Isidro Lopes Pinto

Don't miss Monsaraz. This remarkably well-preserved medieval village looks sternly out from behind its battlements across the plain beneath. Arrive by night and you'll see it from ten miles away, hovering ethereally in the night sky. Within the walls the silence, narrow streets and herring-bone cobbling are bewitching indeed. Isidro opened this old, old village house some 12 years ago (his neighbours thought he'd lost his wits — Monsaraz was still 'undiscovered'). The house is deliciously labyrinthine; there are several different levels, staircases lead up and down, corridors twist and turn. And the rooms are of the sort we love: varying in size and floor plan according to the dictates of the old house, they have comfy beds, pretty Alentejo furniture, beamed ceilings and decent bathrooms. Some have views, some have lovely moulded recesses — no two are alike. The guest sitting-room, too, has interesting arches, angles and a fine inglenook at one end. Isidro has time to chat and advise you on which of the four village restaurants you might choose for dinner. Stay two or three nights and use this as a base from which to explore this most beautiful corner of the Alentejo.

Rooms: 8 with bath & wc.
Price: D/Tw 8000 Esc; S use 7500 Esc.
Breakfast: Included.
Meals: None.
Closed: Never.

How to get there: From Évora first towards Beja and then branch left towards Reguengos. There follow signs to Monsaraz. House within battlements close to church and castle.

Monte do Sobral

Estrada Alcaçovas-Viana
7090
Alcaçovas

Tel: (0)66 94101/94717
Fax: (0)66 94105

Management: Maria da Encarnação Fernandes

Splendidly isolated and surrounded by its 300 hectare estate, Monte do Sobral is every inch the classic Alentejo farmstead: blue and white, Roman-tiled, long, low and broad-chimneyed. Most of the apartments occupy the old stable block; each is different from the next, all have old floor tiles, a hearth, low-beamed ceilings and a small lounge. A couple of them have a wooden mezzanine — children would love them. A flock of bird prints, antlers above the hearths and animal skins on the floor reflect the owner's love of the hunt. Each of the smallish apartments has a small fridge — a useful extra in the fierce summer months. Across the way in the main farm-house there is an unusual guest lounge; this too is a mezzanine affair with a small bar in one corner. Do dine in at least once on traditional country fare prepared by Sobral's cheery housekeeper; it is remarkably good value. Otherwise, Alcaçovas is just a short drive away. If you tire of the pool and its long views out across the beautiful open countryside, there are horses to ride — even a cart that can be harnessed up — mountain biking and walks across the estate. Particularly good for family holidays.

Rooms: 6 apartments.
Price: Apt 4000 Esc p.p.
Breakfast: Included.
Meals: On request. Dinner 2000 Esc (M).
Closed: Never.

How to get there: From Montemor towards Évora then right towards Viana. Monte do Sobral signposted to right.

Casa Santos Murteira
Rua de S. Pedro 68/70/72
7090
Alcaçovas

Tel: (0)66 94744/(0)66 94571
Fax: (0)66 94105

Management: Maria da
Encarnação Fernandes

This old village house was just too good not to share. The main façade captures the eye with its exquisite wrought-iron balconies and Baroque flourish above the cornicing; at its midst a guardian angel stands sentinel. The style within could be described as 'homely elegance'; the lounge is a gem with its polished parquet floor, comfy chairs, chandelier and collection of books and oils. The Virgin and Christ child look on from above the hearth. The cream-and-mustard dining room is just as special; light floods in from shuttered windows to two sides and there is a beautiful Arraiolos rug beneath a Queen Anne-ish dining table. Just outside is a terrace for al fresco meals when it's warm. The rear of the house has a more alentejano feel with its terracotta tiles, wafer bricking and bands of blue highlighting windows and doors. A spring-fed pool sits prettily in an orange grove. There are just six bedrooms and they are among the very nicest we know; fine old beds, marble-topped bedside tables, planked and rugged floors, and splendidly moulded and corniced ceilings. Housekeeper Josefina does her best to make your stay a special one.

Rooms: 6 with bath & wc.
Price: D/Tw 11500-12500 Esc.
Breakfast: Included.
Meals: Dinner occasionally on request.
Closed: Never.

How to get there: From Évora take ring-road round town until Alcaçovas signposted. There, Rua de S. Pedro runs parallel to main street; house half-way up on left.

Map No: 16

Castelo de Milfontes

7645
Vila Nova de Milfontes

Tel: (0)83 96108
Fax: (0)83 997122

Management: Ema M. da Câmara Machado

Carthaginians, Romans, Moors and even Algerian pirates have all coveted the remarkable strategic site now occupied by the Castelo de Milfontes; you see why when looking out across the river estuary to the Atlantic breakers beyond. The present fort dates from the 16th century and was rescued from abandon by the family some fifty years ago. This is no ordinary 'hotel'; the spirit of (genteel) welcome is captured in the plaque above the hearth which reads 'viver sim amigos não é viver' (living without friends is not living). Full board is de rigueur at Milfontes and dinner is the occasion to get to know your fellow guests and to meet Ema, who graciously officiates at table. It is an occasion to dress for; at 8 o'clock a maid announces that it is time to pass through to the dining room — silver service and traditional Portuguese cuisine awaits you. The rooms have views that defy description; we think 'tower room 1' is one of the loveliest we have seen anywhere. The furniture matches the Castle; perhaps an old writing desk, a baldequin bed, original oils — and all poised between vaulted ceilings and parquet floors. The Castelo's fame has spread far and wide and guests return year after year.

Rooms: 7 with bath & wc.
Price: Tw 26000-28000 Esc (Full board for two).
Breakfast: Included.
Meals: Lunch and Dinner included.
Closed: Beg. Nov 97-end Apr 98 for renovation.

How to get there: From Lisbon, A2 to Setúbal, then N10 towards Évora and branch right on N5/N20 toward Grandola. Left on N120 to Santiago and on to Cercal. Here, N390 to V.N. de Milfontes. Castle at edge of estuary by beach.

Map No: 23

Verdemar

Casas Novas
7555
Cercal do Alentejo

Tel: (0)69 94544

Management: Nuno Vilas-Boas and Christine Nijhoff

Although only a short drive from the mighty Atlantic and some wonderful beaches, Verdemar's setting is bucolic. Hidden away among stands of old cork oaks beyond the blue and white main gate is a most special country retreat. Guest rooms are spread around the out-buildings but the focus of life here is the main farm house and dining room (see photo). The atmosphere is easy and cosy; a beam and bamboo ceiling, an open kitchen/bar, wooden stools and chairs. You'll share fun and good food around one big table — al fresco , of course, in summer. Nuno, a professional chef for 20 years in Amsterdam, loves to have your company as he prepares dinner and likes to exchange a recipe or two. Leading off the kitchen, the lounge is equally cosy — guitar, paintings, an old lamp; a cool place to escape the heat of the summer. Christine writes that Verdemar is 'the perfect place for people with little children'. They'll meet ducks, chickens, donkeys, cows and sheep. And a special children's dinner is prepared early evening. Bedrooms, too, are just right; no hotelly extras but nothing lacking. A favourite address, our type of idyll — with the true spirit of honest hostelry.

Rooms: 5 with bath & wc + 1 apartment.
Price: D 5500-8500 Esc; Tw 5000-7000 Esc; Apt 6000-9000 Esc.
Breakfast: Included.
Meals: Dinner 3000 Esc (M).
Closed: Never.

How to get there: From Cercal (do Alentejo), take N262 towards Alvalade. Verdemar signposted on left after 7km.

Algarve

Inn Albergeria Bica-Boa

Estrada de Lisboa 266
8550
Monchique

Tel: (0)82 92271
Fax: (0)82 92360

Management: Susan Clare Cassidy

Bica-Boa's name was inspired by the many springs that well up on this thickly wooded mountainside up above Monchique; winding your way up from the western Algarve the exuberant vegetation of the place takes you by surprise. There are stunning walks galore and, if you venture up here, do stay at Bica Boa. The hotel stands just to the side of the road but there is little traffic and the four guest rooms are tucked away to the rear of the building. They are fresh, light and simply decorated with wooden floors and ceilings — and all have views out across the valley. There is a quiet little sitting room with the same view; a corner chimney, azulejo-clad walls and a chess table give a homely feel. Bica Boa's restaurant is popular with locals and ex-pats up from the coast; fish is the speciality, from sole to stuffed squid to lobster (order ahead). There are terraces for al fresco dining when the weather is right and a terraced garden with quiet corners for sitting out. Susie has lived here for many years and has a deep attachment to the area and its people; she will help organise walks for you, can sometimes even accompany you herself and is as kind a hostess as you could hope to meet.

Rooms: 4 with bath & wc.
Price: TW 9500-11500 Esc.
Breakfast: Included.
Meals: Lunch/Dinner 4500-5000 (C).
Closed: Never.

How to get there: From Faro take motorway N125 west towards Lagos. Exit for Portimão/Monchique. Climb up to Monchique, then follow signs to Lisbon through town. Bica-Boa is approx. 300 yards after leaving town on right; well signposted.

Map No: 23

Pensão Residência Dom Henrique

Sítio da Mareta
8650
Sagres

Tel: (0)82 620000/3
Fax: (0)82 620001

Management: Andreas Bergmann

Sagres' big claim to fame is that it was here that Henry the Navigator ('Dom Henrique') set up his school of navigation. Plumb in the centre of town, Dom Henrique is a small, modern hotel where sea-facing rooms have views and terraces that lift this little hotel into the 'special' league. They are average sized, irreproachably spick and span and have small bathrooms; they come with nice wooden furniture and good mattresses and bedding. It was wonderful to awake to a blushing dawn, to hear the crash of the waves and to look out to the Atlantic sandwiched between headlands to the east and west. Dom Henrique's lounge and dining room are light and simply furnished with wicker furniture and potted plants. (The yellow and turquoise decoration could be a mite garish for some.) The dining room gives onto a sea-facing terrace where a bar serves sun-downers in the warmer months. The beach is just a couple of hundred yards away and so too are exhilarating walks along the cliff's edge. This quiet little hotel is marvellous value out of season.

Rooms: 18 with bath & wc.
Price: D/Tw low season 4000-6000 Esc; D/Tw high season 13500-15000 Esc.
Breakfast: Included.
Meals: Lunch/Dinner 2250 (M), 3000 (C).
Closed: Never.

How to get there: As you enter Sagres, at roundabout turn left. On arriving at small square with café on corner, turn right. Hotel at end on left.

276

Quinta das Achadas

Estrada da Barragem
8600
Odiáxere
Lagos

Tel: (0)82 798425
Fax: (0)82 799162

Management: Beatrice and
Willy Hagmann

It took seven long months of work from dawn until dusk for Willy and Beatrice to redecorate/convert the Quinta das Achadas. Hats off to this quiet-mannered Swiss couple for creating one of the very best B&Bs of the Algarve. The approach is a delight: a winding drive through groves of olive, almond and orange trees which then give way to a sub-tropical garden where maguey and palm, geranium and bougainvillea, pine and jasmine jostle for position. The guest bedrooms, each with its own small terrace, look out across the gardens and are in the converted barn and stables; some have modern furniture, others antiques (our favourite is 'Hibiscus') and the innumerable South American bits and bobs are mementos from Willy's work in those parts. In colder weather you breakfast in a cosy dining room (it doubles as a bar — just help yourself) but most of the year it's mild enough to sit out on the terrace; try the 'gourmet' breakfast' and you'll be hooked. If you're in the apartments you can prepare your own food; 'Bougain-Villa' (sic) was our favourite, but they are all special.

Rooms: 3 with bath & wc + 3 apartments.
Price: D/Tw approx. 10300-16000 Esc inc. breakast; Apt approx. 14500-21500 Esc.
Breakfast: Included. Approx 1500 Esc extra if in Apt.
Meals: None.
Closed: Never.

How to get there: From Portimão, N125 towards Lagos. In village of Odiáxere, right at sign for Barragem. House signposted on right after 1.2km.

Map No: 23

Quinta da Alfarrobeira

Estrada de Palmares
8600
Odiáxere
Lagos

Tel: (0)82 798424
Fax: (0)82 799630

Management: Nanette Kant

Quinta da Alfarrobeira stands on a hill just inland from the Algarve coast and is surrounded by six hectares of old fruit groves. Nanette and Theo, a young couple from Holland, fell in love with the place and moved down from Amsterdam to set up their dream home. You'll most probably want to do the same as you sit beneath the enormous alfarrobeira (carob) and gaze out across the old olive and almond trees, or watch Tjacco, the couple's young son, playing happily with his adopted pets on a sunny flower-filled patio. Choose between a room in the main house or one of two new apartments built in traditional Algarve style where terracotta, beam and bamboo are the essential ingredients. We loved their light, airy feel and the antique furnishings that have been collected piecemeal from all over Europe. There are biggish bathrooms, private terraces and big views — and kitchenettes in the apartments if you plan to cook for yourself. Add to this the lovely walks out from the Quinta (just 1.5km down to the sea), exceptionally kind hosts and you begin to get the measure of this altogether most special place.

Rooms: 1 with bath & wc + 2 apartments.
Price: D 12000 Esc; 'Stable' Apt 8000-13000 Esc; 'Farmhouse' Apt 10000-15000 Esc.
Breakfast: Included.
Meals: None; self-catering.
Closed: Never.

How to get there: From Faro motorway (E1) then N125 to Portimão and on towards Lagos. In village of Odiáxere left at square towards Meia praia/Palmares. After approx. 1.3 km (cow sign on right) turn left onto dirt track, house on right.

Map No: 23

278

Casa Três Palmeiras

Apartado 84
8501
Portimão

Tel: (0)82 401275
Fax: (0)82 401029

Management: Dolly Schlingensiepen

The setting is a dream; from Casa Três Palmeiras' perch right at the cliff's edge the view is incomparable, a symphony of sea, sky, and rock — ever-changing according to the day's mood and ever-beautiful. The house was built in the sixties, but the 'Zen' design is still modern as we head for the next century. The house is given a distinctly exotic feel by three enormous palm trees and the simple arches that soften the façade and give welcome shade to the guest rooms once the temperature starts creeping up. Rooms have everything you might expect for the price. There are marble floors, double sinks and big fitted wardrobes, yet they remain uncluttered. Best of all, they lead straight out onto the terrace whence those heavenly views (and a sea-water pool). There are always freshly cut flowers and a bowl of fruit awaiting guests and it is obvious that Brazilian Dolly is happy in her role as hostess; after years in the Diplomatic service, entertaining comes naturally. A path leads from the house straight down to the beach; get up early and even in mid-summer you may find you have it to yourself. Book well ahead if you plan to stay in summer.

Rooms: 5 with bath & wc.
Price: S use of Tw 17650-23800 Esc; Tw 20500-26600 Esc.
Breakfast: Included.
Meals: Snacks available throughout day.
Closed: Dec-Jan.

How to get there: From Portimão dual carriageway towards Praia da Rocha. Right at last roundabout and at next roundabout

double back and turn up track on right after 50m. Right along track at first villa.

The Garden Cottages
8100
Loulé

Tel: UK agent: 0181 3668944

The Vale Judeu, or 'Valley of the Jews', is a lush valley in the Algarve hinterland; mild winters, long hours of sunshine and rich soil allow nearly everything to grow in profusion. The English owner found this old wine farm in ruins in the early '70s and has put in years of patient restoration and planting. This is a place of peace and privacy; behind the whitewashed outer wall the cottages stand apart from one another facing the gardens and — tucked away beyond — an enormous round pool. Each cottage has a sun and a shade terrace, a prettily tiled kitchen, sitting room and bedroom and is large enough for four — though only let to two. Dried flowers, eucalyptus beams and terracotta give a 'country' feel, while mementoes from Africa and Turkey add an exotic note. There are magazines and a carefully compiled file with details of restaurants, shops and visits; you'll feel instantly at home. What we remember most are the gardens: olive, pomegranate, almonds and lemon and, beneath them, a profusion of flowers of every hue. The benign climate means that visiting out of season is just as special.

Rooms: 5 cottages with bath & wc + lounge/kitchen.
Price: Weekly approx 57200-85800 Esc. per cottage depending on season. Details on request.
Breakfast: Self-catering.
Meals: Self-catering.
Closed: Never.

How to get there: Information will be sent by UK agent (see above) or direct from owner (phone/fax (0)89 328637.)

La Reserve
Santa Bárbara de Nexe
8000
Faro

Tel: (0)89 90474 / 90234
Fax: (0)89 90402

Management: Victor and Katia Fuchs

La Reserve is tucked away in the gentle hills that lead down to the Atlantic coast. You'll mention the gardens in your postcards home; nearly everything grows in this land of year-round sunshine and mild winters — and the hotel's gardens are a celebration of southern flora. There are bananas, palm trees, cacti and geraniums; bougainvillea, carob, oleander and cypress; orange and lemon and olive and almond. The already organic lines of the building, pool and terracing are further softened by this profusion of flora. Lounge, reception and bar are all open-plan, light and with marble used to cooling effect. All suites face south and each has a sitting room with a corner hearth, first-class beds, a small kitchenette and bar and a large terrace; from those on the first floor you can see the Atlantic sparkling in the distance. Double sinks, a second bathroom in the duplex apartments, freshly cut flowers and bath robes are just a few of the many 'extras'. And the Victor Fuch's restaurant is reputed to be one of the finest on the Algarve; you may even eat quail with truffles.

Rooms: 20 suites.
Price: Ste 28000-40000 Esc.
Breakfast: Included.
Meals: Lunch/Dinner approx. 10000 Esc (C).
Closed: Never.

How to get there: Coming from Spain, leave motorway at exit 4 for Loulé Sul. Take first right towards Sta Bárbara de Nexe. There, right by church and after approx. 100m, right again. Hotel along this road on left.

Monte do Casal

Cerro do Lobo
Estoi
8000
Faro

Tel: (0)89 91503
Fax: (0)89 91341

Management: Bill Hawkins

After more than a dozen years at the helm, Bill Hawkins has firmly established Monte do Casal's credentials as one of the Algarve's most special small hotels. This former farm-house is tucked away in the gentle hills of the Algarve hinterland, a low, white building surrounded by exuberant stands of bougainvillea, mature palms, olives and almonds. Inside, the eucalyptus and cane roofing and the terracotta floor tiles create an unmistakably Mediterranean atmosphere. Food is a cornerstone of the hotel's fame; Bill trained in the kitchens of Claridges and the Savoy and his French-based cuisine ("I enjoy sauces") and well-stocked wine cellar are a formidable partnership. But if you do fancy a change, ask for his 'cryptic-map-guide to the Algarve'; it will lead you towards treasures you would otherwise miss and picnic hampers can be provided for your forays. The guest bedrooms have fine old brass cornered 'travel' furniture and decent bathrooms; nearly all have private terraces overlooking pool and gardens. But do book early, especially if planning a visit in season. Children over 16 welcome.

Rooms: 8 with bath & wc + 5 suites.
Price: Tw 6300-13900 Esc; Deluxe 7350-15250 Esc; Ste 8600-18600 Esc. Minimum stay 2 nights.
Breakfast: Included.
Meals: Lunch/Dinner 5100 Esc (M), from 5000 Esc (C).
Closed: Never.

How to get there: From Faro take N2 north towards São Bras. Exit for Estoi. Here at square take road towards Moncarapacho; hotel is approx 2.5km along this road signposted to left.

Convento do Santo António

Atalaia 56
8800
Tavira

Tel: (0)81 325632
Fax: (0)81 325632

Management: Isabel Maria Castanho Paes

Monks of the Capuchin order built the church of Santo António and its diminutive cloister; they chose a wind-swept place of rare beauty. Isabel is almost apologetic that "the home has only been in the family for four generations". A portrait of great-grandmother officiates over one of the vaulted corridors that runs the length of the cloister (Santo Antonio looks benignly on from his chapel at the end of the other) and it was grandfather, much travelled, who planted the exotic garden. Here are rooms to remember; varying in size (and price) they have great charm; here a vaulted ceiling, there a fine dresser; here a seaward view, there a hand-knotted rug. It is a Lusitanian feast of hand-crafted terracotta and ceramic tiles, of rich alcobaça fabrics and carefully chosen (often naïve) paintings. We loved the Chapel room (one of two 'specials') with its high ceilings and bathroom sitting snugly inside what once was a chimney breast! Lounge and bar are just as special and it would be heavenly to breakfast in summer with Gregorian chant to accompany your feast. Hardly surprising that the glossies run features on Isabel's creation. And what a PEACEFUL spot.

Rooms: 6 with bath & wc + 1 suite.
Price: D/Tw 15600-18000 Esc;'Special' D/Tw 18000-21600 Esc; Ste 24000-28000 Esc. (Min. stay Oct-Mar 3 nights; April-Sept 4 nights).
Breakfast: Buffet, included.
Meals: On request. Dinner 3500 Esc; Lunch occasionally for families.
Closed: Dec-Jan.

How to get there: From Faro, N125 then M/way IP 1 towards Espanha. Exit 7 to Tavira. Here, under archway to r/bout and straight on towards 'Centro Saude'. On, over T junction and once past church right towards 'Centro Saude'. Bear right past army barracks, then first left, then after 200m fork right to Convento. Or ask a local!!

Useful Vocabulary – Spanish

We hope that the following words and phrases may be of use.

Before Arriving (therefore over the telephone).

Do you have a room for the night?	¿Tiene una habitación para esta noche?
How much does it cost?	¿Cuánto cuesta?
We'll be arriving at around 7p.m.	Estaremos llegando sobre las siete.
We're lost!	Estámos perdidos.
We'll be arriving late.	Vamos a llegar tarde.
I'm in the phone box at.....	Estoy en la cabina en...
I'm in the 'La Giralda' bar in.....	Estoy en el bar 'La Giralda' en...
Do you have any animals? I'm allergic to cats.	Tienen animales? Tengo alergia a los gatos.
We would like to have dinner.	Quisieramos cenar.

On arrival.

Hello! I'm Mr/Mrs X.	¡Hóla! Soy Señor/Señora X.
We found your name in this book.	Encontramos su nombre en esta guía.
Where can we leave the car?	¿Dónde podemos dejar el coche?
Could you help us with our bags?	¿Podría ayudarnos con las maletas?
Could I leave this picnic food/bottles in your fridge?	¿Podríamos dejar esta comida/estas botellas en la nevera?
Could I heat up the baby's feeding bottle?	¿Podríamos calentar este biberón?
Can the children sleep in sleeping bags on the floor?	¿Podrían dormir los niños en sacos de dormir en el suelo?
How much will you charge for that?	¿Cuánto nos cobrará para éso?

Things you need/that go wrong.

Do you have an extra pillow/blanket?	¿Podría dejarnos otra almohada/manta?
A light bulb needs replacing.	Es necesario cambiar una bombilla.
The heating isn't on.	No está encendida la calefacción.
How does the air conditioning work?	¿Cómo funciona la climatización?
We've a problem with the plumbing.	Tenemos un problema de fontanería.
The room smells!	¡La habitación huele mal!
Do you have a quieter room?	¿Tiene una habitación menos ruidosa?
How does the cooker work?	¿Cómo funciona el horno?
Please ask the man in the room next door to stop singing/dancing.	Dígale al hombre de al lado que deje de cantar/bailar.
Where can I hang these wet clothes?	¿Dónde podemos colgar esta ropa?
Could we have some soap?	¿Hay jabón por favor?
Could you give us some hot water to make tea - we have our own teabags!	¿Podría dejarnos agua caliente para hacer un té? ¡El té ya tenemos!
Would you possibly have an aspirin?	¿Tendría una aspirina por favor?
Could you turn the volume down?	¿Podría bajar un poco el volumen?

How the house/hotel works.

When do you begin serving breakfast?	¿A qué hora empiezan a dar el desayuno?
We'd like to order some drinks.	Queremos tomar algo, por favor.
Can the children play in the garden?	¿Pueden visitar la finca los niños?
Is there any danger?	¿Es peligroso?
Can we leave the children with you?	¿Podemos dejar los niños con vosotros?
Can we eat breakfast in our room?	¿Podemos desayunar en la habitación?

Local information.

Where can we buy petrol?	¿Dónde hay una gasolinera?
Where can we find a garage to repair our car?	¿Dónde hay un taller de coches?
How far is the nearest shop?	¿Dónde está la tienda más cerca?
We need a doctor.	Nos hace falta un médico.
Where is there a chemist's?	¿Dónde hay una farmacía?
Where is the police station?	¿Dónde está la comisaría?
Where's a good place to eat?	¿Dónde come uno bien por aquí?
Where can we find a cash-dispenser?	¿Dónde hay un cajero automático?
Could you recommend a good walk?	¿Podría recomendar algun paseo bonito?
Do you know of any local festivities?	¿Hay alguna fiesta local en estos dias?

On leaving.

What time must we leave?	¿A qué hora tenemos que dejar libre la habitación?
We'd like to pay the bill.	Nuestra cuenta, por favor.
How much do I owe you?	¿Cuánto debemos?
We hope to be back.	Esperamos volver.
We've had a very pleasant stay.	Nos ha gustado mucho estar aquí.
This is a beautiful spot.	Este es un lugar divino.
Thank you so much.	Muchas gracias.

Eating out (or in).

Where's there a good tapas bar?	¿Dónde hay buenas tapas por aquí?
Could we eat outside, please?	¿Es posible comer fuera?
What's today's set menu?	¿Qué tienen hoy de menú?
What do you recommend?	¿Qué es lo que Usted recomienda?
What's that man over there eating?	¿Qué está comiendo aquel hombre?
We'd like a dish with no meat in it.	Queremos algo que no tenga carne.
What vegetarian dishes do you have?	¿Qué platos vegetarianos tienen?
Do you have a wine list?	¿Hay una lista de vinos?
This food is cold!	¡Esta comida está fría!
Do you have some pepper/salt please?	¿Hay pimienta/sal por favor?
What tapas do you have?	¿Qué tapas tienen? *see introduction!
We'd like half a plateful of that one.	Una media ración de aquella por favor.
A plate of this one.	Una ración de esta.
Please keep the change.	La vuelta es para usted.
Where are the toilets?	¿Dónde están los servicios?
The toilet is locked!	¡El servicio está cerrado con llave!
It was a delicious meal.	¡Estaba muy rica la comida!
I'd like a white/black coffee/	Un café con leche/un café solo.
/weaker coffee.	/un café menos cargado.
Coffee with just a little milk.	Un café cortado.
Tea/camomile tea	Un té/una manzanilla

**remember, the safest way to order tea with milk is to ask for 'un té, y un poco de leche, pero aparte'. It's tempting to ask for 'té con leche' - but you may well end up with a glass of hot milk with a teabag plonked in the top! Milk is nearly always UHT so if you really need your tea we recommend drinking it with a slice of lemon 'té con limón'. Or take your own along and just ask for 'un vaso de agua caliente' in the bar. Your request will rarely be refused.

Useful Vocabulary – Portuguese

Before Arriving (therefore over the telephone).

Do you have a room for the night?	Tem um quarto para esta noite?
How much does it cost?	Quanto custa?
We'll be arriving at about 7pm.	Nós chegaremos por volta das sete da tarde.
We're lost!	Estamos perdidos!
We'll be arriving late.	Vamos chegar tarde.
I'm in the phone box at…	Estou na cabine telefónica em…
I'm in the 'La Giralda' bar in…	Estou no bar 'La Giralda' em…
Do you have any animals? I'm allergic to cats.	Você tem algum animal? Sou alérgico a gatos.
We would like to have dinner.	Queríamos jantar.

On arrival.

Hello! I'm Mr/Mrs X.	Olá! Eu sou o Senhor/ Senhora X.
We found your name in this book.	Encontramos o seu nome neste livro.
Where can we leave the car?	Onde podemos deixar o carro?
Could you help us with our bags?	Podia ajudar-nos com as nossas malas?
Could I leave this picnic food/bottles in your fridge?	Podia deixar esta comida/garrafas para picnic no seu frigorífico?
Could I heat up the baby's feeding bottle?	Podia aquecer o biberon?
Can the children sleep in sleeping bags on the floor?	As crianças podem dormir no chão em sacos camas?
How much will you charge for that?	Quanto é que você cobrará por isto?

Things you need/that go wrong.

Do you have an extra pillow/blanket?	Você tem uma outra almofada/um outro cobertor?
A light bulb needs replacing.	É preciso mudar uma lampada.
The heating isn't on.	O aquecedor não está ligado.
How does the air conditioning work?	Como funciona o ar condicionado?
We've a problem with the plumbing.	Temos um problema com a canalização.
The rooms smells!	O quarto cheira mal!
Do you have a quieter room?	Tem um quarto menos barulhento?
How does the cooker work?	Como funciona o fogão?
Please ask the man in the room next door to stop singing/dancing.	Por favor, peça ao homem do quarto ao lado para parar de cantar/dançar.
Where can I hang these wet clothes?	Onde posso secar estas roupas?
Could we have some soap?	Queríamos sabonete por favor?
Could you give us some hot water to make tea—we have our own tea bags!	Podia-nos dar água quente para o nosso to chá—nós temos as nossas próprias saquetas de chá.
Would you possibly have some aspirin?	Tem aspirina, por favor?
Could you turn the volume down?	Pode baixar o volume?

How the house/hotel works.

When do you begin serving breakfast?	A que horas começa a servir o pequeno-almoço?
We'd like to order some drinks.	Queríamos tomar algumas bebidas, por favor?
Can the children play in the garden?	As crianças podem brincar no jardim?
Is there any danger?	É perigoso?
Can we leave the children with you?	Podemos deixar as crianças convosco?
Can we eat breakfast in our room?	Podemos tomar o pequeno-almoço no quarto?

Local Information.

Where can we buy petrol?
Onde fica a próxima estação de serviço?

Where can we find a garage to repair our car?
Onde há uma oficina para repararmos o nosso carro?

How far is the nearest shop?
Fica muito longe a próxima loja?

We need a doctor.
Precisamos de um médico.

Where is there a chemist's?
Onde há uma farmácia?

Where is the police station?
Onde fica o posto de policia?

Where's a good place to eat?
Onde há um sítio onde se coma bem?

Where can we find a cash-dispenser?
Onde há uma caixa automática?

Could you recommend a good walk?
Era capaz de recomendar um bom passeio?

Do you know of any local festivities?
Sabe de algumas festividades locais?

On leaving.

What time must we leave?
A que horas temos de libertar/deixar o quarto?

We'd like to pay the bill.
Queríamos pagar a conta.

How much do I owe you?
Quanto devo?

We hope to be back.
Esperamos regressar.

We've had a very pleasant stay.
Tivemos uma estadia muito agradável.

This is a beautiful spot.
Este é um lugar muito bonito.

Thank you so much.
Muito obrigado.

Eating out (or in).

Where's there a good tapas bar?
Onde há um bar com bons aperitivos?

Could we eat outside, please?
Podemos comer lá fora?

What's today's set menu?
Qual é o menu para hoje?

What do you recommend?
O que nos recomenda?

What's the man over there eating?
O que é que aquele senhor está a comer?

We'd like a dish with no meat in it.
Gostaríamos de um prato que não seja de carne.

What vegetarian dishes do you have?
Que pratos vegetarianos tem?

Do you have a wine list?
Tem uma lista de vinhos?

This food is cold!
Esta comida está fria.

Do you have some pepper/salt please?
Tem pimenta/sal por favor?

What tapas do you have?
Que aperitivos tem?

We'd like half a plateful of that one.
Gostaríamos de meia dose daquele por favor.

A plate of this one.
Uma dose deste.

Please keep the change.
Guarde o troco.

Where are the toilets?
Onde ficam as casas de banho?

The toilet is locked.
As casas de banho estão fechadas.

It was a delicious meal.
Foi uma óptima refeição.

I'd like a white/black coffee/ weaker coffee
Queria um café com leite/café simples/ café fraco

Coffee with just a little milk.
Café com um pouco de leite.

Tea**/camomile tea.
Chá/Chá de camomila

**remember, the safest way to order tea with milk is to ask for 'um chá e um pouco de leite, mas aparte'. It's tempting to ask for 'chá com leite'—but you may well end up with a glass of hot milk with a teabag plonked in the top! Milk is nearly always UHT so if you really need your tea we recommend drinking it with a slice of lemon 'chá com limão'. Or take your own along and just ask for 'jarro com água quente' in the bar. Your request will rarely be refused.

Special Places to Stay
BRITAIN

Second (1998) edition

If you, too, wince at the sight of another lovely old
17th-century room vandalised to make way for a
bathroom... then this book (ALL our books) is for you.

Britain is over-run by chain hotels, bad taste and
commercial 'establishments'. Even private homes that do
B&B are squeezed mercilessly to fit into the mould. So we
have searched the country for what WE consider to be the
nicest, the most friendly, and genuinely attractive houses,
hotels and inns. (Most are very comfortable too.)

Our standards are high: places HAVE to be special.
Then we accept them, and let them do their own thing.
With over 500 special places to stay throughout the British
Isles this book is a MUST for the sensitive traveller.
Price: £10.95

Alastair Sawday's
French Bed & Breakfast

Alastair Sawday's

**French
Bed &
Breakfast**
1997/8

Edited by
Ann Cooke-Yarborough

The much loved guide to the best and most attractive
B&Bs throughout France. Now with over 600 houses.

The third (1997-1998) edition of this immensely popular
guide for the open-minded visitor to France, a mouth-watering
menu of homes to choose from wherever you are in France.
You can stay, often at ridiculously low cost, in châteaux,
manors, cottages, town-houses, and even B&Bs in Paris.
The average per person price for B&B is £15!

So you can do better than your friends who sleep in those
soulless hotels along the autoroutes, or trawl hopefully through
the directories of B&Bs. Choose a B&B we have selected for you,
take off into the by-roads and make friends, perhaps in a
beautiful old house. If it is in this book you can hardly go wrong.
Price: £12.95

Alastair Sawday's Special Places to Stay in Ireland

All the magic of Ireland in our choice of lovely places to stay.

Ireland - one of the last havens in Western Europe still unspoilt by mass tourism - is the perfect setting for the fifth Sawday guide. Our inspectors have collected a series of gems that nestle in this wide and wild land where taking in weary travellers is part of the Celtic tradition. The Irish of today are definitely worthy descendents of their ancestors on this score.

Each of the 200-odd B&Bs, farmhouses, mansions and family-run hotels boasts something that makes it truly special - usually a welcome stemming not from the contents of your wallet but from your hosts' genuine enjoyment in meeting people.

We have weeded out any hint of over-commercialism, pretension or half-heartedness in the owners' approach and brought you the loveliest, gentlest, most seductive places to stay in this green and misty country.

Full colour photography, masses of detail, reliable practical information. Available for £10.95.

Alastair Sawday's Guide to
Special Paris Hotels

A night in Paris is far too precious to be spent in the wrong hotel.

You are off to Paris, full of hope, but there is a nagging doubt: where to stay? So you ask friends who went last year, or before... and cross your fingers. The risk of ending up in a touristy monster, or recently-spoiled favourite, is ever-present.

This book is like an up-to-date and ultra-reliable friend who knows *all* the Paris hotels and makes choices for you... whether you are rich or poor, artistic or not.

Written with wit and style by an Englishwoman living in Paris, this highly personal selection of 70 of Paris's nicest, most attractive and welcoming hotels is all you need to make your visit a complete success. You can easily save the cost in just one night's sleep in the right hotel.

Colour photographs and lots of detail. A delightful book and the only one of its kind. Price: £8.95

ORDER FORM for the UK. See over for USA.

All these books are available in the major bookshops but we can send them to you quickly and without effort on your part. Post and packaging is FREE if you order 2 or more books.

	No. of copies	Price each	Total value
French Bed & Breakfast – 3rd Edition		£12.95	
Special Paris Hotels		£8.95	
Special Places to Stay in Spain & Portugal		£10.95	
Special Places to Stay in Britain		£10.95	
Special Places to Stay in Ireland		£10.95	

Add Post & Packaging: £1 for Paris book, £2 for any other, **FREE** if ordering 2 or more books.

TOTAL ORDER VALUE
Please make cheques payable to Alastair Sawday Publishing

We are moving towards a system of annual publishing, whereby we get new books out before Christmas and publish the next edition automatically one year later.

All orders to: Alastair Sawday Publishing, 44 Ambra Vale East, Bristol BS8 4RE Tel: 0117 9299921. (Sorry, no credit card payments).

Name _____

Address _____

_____

_____ Postcode _____

Tel _____ Fax _____

ORDER FORM for USA.

These books are available at your local bookstore, or you may order direct. Allow two to three weeks for delivery.

	No. of copies	Price each	Total value
French Bed & Breakfast		$19.95	
Special Paris Hotels		$14.95	
Special Places to Stay in Spain & Portugal		$19.95	
Special Places to Stay in Britain		$19.95	
Special Places to Stay in Ireland		$19.95	
Add Post & Packaging: $4 for Paris book, $4.50 for any other.			
TOTAL ORDER VALUE *Please make cheques payable to Publishers Book & Audio*			

All orders to: Publishers Book & Audio, P.O. Box 070059, 5446 Arthur Kill Road, Staten Island, NY 10307, phone (800) 288-2131. For information on bulk orders, address Special Markets, St. Martin's Press, 175 Fifth Avenue, Suite 500, New York, NY 10010, phone (212) 674-5151, ext. 724, 693, or 628.

Name _____

Address _____

_____

_____ Zip code _____

Tel _____ Fax _____

REPORT FORM

Comments on existing entries and new discoveries.

If you have any comments on existing entries –
anything from details on prices to the reception you
got, the atmosphere, the hosts, the house –
then please let us have them.

If you have a favourite spot which you are willing to
share with us, so we may feature it in our next edition,
let us know.

Please fill in the following information:

Report on:
Entry no. _____   Date _____

Names of owners _____

Name of house _____

Address _____

_____

_____ Tel. No.: _____

Please tick the appropriate box:

☐ Should continue as a main entry

☐ Should not be continued

☐ Should be considered for inclusion as a main entry

My reasons are _____

_____

_____

_____

_____

_____

_____

_____

_____

_____

Any of the following additional information will be appreciated.
(Please tick)

 I enclose a photograph of the property
(We cannot return material sent to us)

 I am happy for you to use an edited version of
my description

I am happy for my name to appear
in the book

Name _____

Address _____

_____

Tel. No.: (only if you don't mind) _____

I am not connected in any way with the owners of this property

Signed _____

Please send the completed form to:
Alastair Sawday Publishing, 44 Ambra Vale East,
Bristol BS8 4RE, UK.

THANK YOU SO MUCH FOR YOUR HELP!

HOJA DE RESERVA
Spanish Reservation Form

ATENCION DE:
To
DE PARTE DE:
From

NOMBRE DE ESTABLECIMIENTO:
Name of hotel, inn, B&B etc

Estimado Señor/Estimada Señora,
Dear Sir/Madam

Le(s) rogamos de hacernos una reserva en nombre de: _____
Please could you make us a reservation in the name of

Para _____ noche(s)
For   *nights(s)*

Llegando   día _____ (mes) _____ (año) _____
Arriving   *day*   *month*   *year*

Saliendo   día _____ (mes) _____ (año) _____
Departing   *day*   *month*   *year*

Necesitamos _____ habitacíon(es)
We require   *room(s) i.e. how many rooms*
                                  you require

* Tick type   Doble   *(double)*   _____
   required   Individual   *(single)*   _____
                   Triple   *(triple)*   _____
                   Quadruple   *(quadruple)*   _____
                   Tipo Suite   *(suite)*   _____

Apartamento *(apartment)*_____

Requeriremos también la cena: Si _____ No _____ Para _____ persona(s)
We will also be requiring dinner   *yes*   *no*   *for*   *person(s)*

Les rogamos de enviarnos la confirmación de esta reserva a la siguiente dirección:
Please could you send us confirmation of our reservation to the address below
(ésta misma hoja o una fotocopia de la misma con su firma nos valdrá)
(this form or a photocopy of it with your signature could be used)

Nombre:
Name
Dirección:
Address

O pasárnosla por fax en este número:
Or fax it to us at this number

                                          * quitando el primer 0 del prefijo

Muchas Gracias - *Thank you*

(Special Places to Stay in Spain and Portugal)

FORMULÁRIO DE RESERVA
Portuguese Reservation Form

Á ATENÇÃO DE:
To
DE PARTIE DE:
From

NOME DO HOTEL, ESTALAGEM, PENSÃO, etc.
Name of hotel, inn, B&B etc

Estimado Senhor Estimada Senhora,
Dear Sir/Madam

Agradeciamos que efectuassem uma reserva em nome de:
Please could you make us a reservation in the name of

	Para _____ noites				
	For *nights*				
Chegada a	dia _____ mês _____ ano _____				
Arriving	*day* *month* *year*				
Partida a	dia _____ mês _____ ano _____				
Departing	*day* *month* *year*				
Desejamos	quarto				
We require	*rooms(s) ie how many rooms you require*				

* Tick type required

Duplo *(double)* _____
Individual *(single)* _____
Triplo *(triple)* _____
Quádruplo *(quadruple)* _____
Suite *(suite)* _____

Apartamento *(apartment)* _____

Também desejamos jantar: sim _____ não _____ para _____ pessoas
We shall also be requring dinner   *yes*   *no*   *for*   *person(s)*

Agradeciamos que nos enviassem confirmação desta reserva para o endereço acima mencionado
Please could you send us confirmation of our resevation to the address below
Pode utilizar este formulário ou uma fotocópia do mesmo com a sua assinatura
(this form or a photocopy of it with your signature could be used)

Nome *(name)*
Endereço *(address)*

Ou enviar-nos um fax para o seguinte número
Or fax it to us at this number
                    * ignorando o primeiro 0 do prefixo
Muito obrigado *(Thank you)*

(Special Places to Stay in Spain and Portugal)

INDEX OF NAMES

INDEX OF PLACES

Sanlúcar de Barrameda	Posada de Palacio	152
Sant Ferriol	Rectoria de la Miana	74
Sant Jaume de Llierca	Can Jou	73
Santa Eulalia de Oscos	Hotel Rural Casa Pedro	15
Santa María de Mave	El Convento	118
Santander	Hostal Mexicana	37
Santander	Hotel Central	36
Santiago de Compostela	Hostal Hogar San Francisco	3
Santiago de Compostela	Casa Grande de Cornide	4
Santiago Millas	Guts Muths	113
Santo Domingo de Silos	Hostal Santo Domingo de Silos	123
Santo Domingo de Silos	Hotel Tres Coronas de Silos	122
Sarvise	Casa Frauca	52
Segovia	Hotel Infanta Isabel	130
Segovia	Casón de la Pinilla	127
Sertã	Quinta do Albergue do Bomjardim	232
Sevilla	Hotel Simón	156
Sevilla	Hostería del Laurel	157
Sevilla	Patio de La Cartuja	158
Sigueruelo	La Posada de Sigueruelo	128
Sintra	Quinta das Sequoias (Casa da Tapada)	241
Sintra	Hotel Central	239
Sintra	Casa Miradouro	238
Sintra	Pensão Residencial Sintra	240
Sitges	Hotel La Santa María	88
Sobrado	Hotel San Marcus	6
Somiedo	Hotel Valle del Lago	32
Somiedo	Hotel El Coronel	31
Somiedo	La Corte	17
Tarifa	Hurricane Hotel	175
Tarifa	100% Fun	176
Tarifa	Hotel Restaurante Antonio	174
Tavérnoles	Mas Banús - Casa Rural	77
Tavertet	El Jufré	78
Tavira	Convento do Santo António	283
Toledo	Hostal del Cardenal	134
Toledo	Hostal Descalzos	135
Toledo	Hotel Pintor El Greco	136
Tomar	Casa da Avó Genoveva	250
Tomar	Pensão Residencial União	251
Torrecabelleros	Molino del Rio Viejo	124
Tossa de Mar	Hotel Diana	83
Tremp	Casa Guilla	59
Tremp	Casa Mauri	60
Trevélez	Hotel La Fragua	192
Trujillo	Mesón La Cadena	103
Trujillo	Finca Santa Marta	104
Turre	Finca Listonero	197
Ubeda	Palacio de la Rambla	148
Udabe	Venta Udabe	49
Valderrobres	La Torre del Visco	93
Valderrobres	Mas del Pi	92
Valdeverdeja	Casa Bermeja	141